From God - Through my *Life* to Yours

A Ladies One-Year Devotional

Decatur Baptist Church
Decatur, Alabama

FROM GOD — THROUGH MY LIFE TO YOURS

ISBN: 0-935515-51-8

Published by:
DECATUR BAPTIST CHURCH
2527 Danville Road
Decatur, AL 35603

Produced by:
EVANGEL PUBLICATIONS
Huntsville, Alabama

Scripture quotations are from the King James Version of the Bible.
Printed in the United States of America.

Contents

Chapter *Page*

Dedication IV
Preface V
January 7
February 39
March 69
April 103
May 135
June 167
July 203
August 237
September 271
October 305
November 339
December 375
Index 409

Dedication

In May 2002, when I felt impressed by God for us to write our own devotional book, I never dreamed what a wonderful gift He had in store for us. God has brought a great writing, proofing, and typing team together, and I would like to thank our Pastoral Staff — Bro. Rex Terry, Bro. Danny Holmes, Bro. Will Sims, Bro. Charlie Butts, Bro. Jeff Gilliam, Bro. Joe McKaig — and my precious husband, Doug Ripley, for helping me with scriptural content and clarity. Thank you, Bruce Pieper, Denise Phillips, Anita Williams, and Suzanne Spiers for using your God-given abilities for grammar and sentence structure. Thank you, Pam Bolasevich, for your creativity for our book cover that illustrates this project as a gift from God, through us and to others. And the utmost thanks to Dawn Kent for sharing this vision and dream with me and bringing this book to a reality.

All of the ladies that left their comfort zones and opened themselves up for God to produce a heart-inspiring lesson of what they had learned from Him and Him alone are the true jewels in this project. I realize many times these lessons and experiences were during low times in their lives and yet, as they allowed God to have rule and reign in their lives, He taught them things that they could have learned no other way than through this experience.

Thank you, ladies, for your involvement. Thank you for allowing this project to become a reality in all of our lives. My prayer is that each and every day God will not only reveal His goodness to you but that you also will have the opportunity to climb into the life of another sister in Christ. Please enjoy *From God — Through My Life To Yours*.

Katy Ripley

Preface

This devotional book began many years ago when Decatur Baptist Church caught the vision of discipleship. Watching the ladies of our church read and teach the Word of God with confidence has been a wonderful journey. I continue to be amazed at the insight into the Scriptures that they have been given. Once they caught the vision of John 6 that the Holy Spirit will teach the Bible to those who desire to know it, our ladies have never been the same. This devotional book, *FROM GOD — THROUGH MY LIFE TO YOURS*, allows all of us who read it to walk alongside them and observe their intimate relationships with God. Most of those whose names you read will never be famous nor have national recognition. They are just ordinary people who have an extraordinary walk with God and have allowed Him to speak to their hearts. By sharing what God has taught them, their experiences can be a blessing and encouragement to other sisters in Christ.

I want to personally thank all of the wives of our missionaries and the wives of preachers and pastors who have ministered to our church down through the years. Their contributions add a very special touch to this book. Thank you to all of our ladies who through their devotionals have allowed us to understand and appreciate them even more as we learn through their experiences. Thank you to Dawn Kent, who has given countless hours of her time overseeing this book, and thank you to my wife, Katy, who had the vision and confidence that all of this could be done.

Our publisher has told me that to his knowledge, no church has ever attempted and completed such a project. I commend all of you because you are truly special people. This book, *FROM GOD — THROUGH MY LIFE TO YOURS*, truly lives up to its title.

Dr. G. Douglas Ripley
Pastor Decatur Baptist Church

A Mother's Love

There he is on his coffin in the cart,
And there in the crowd of creepingers,
And yet a crowd of weepingers,
Is a woman,
And the law is the breaking of her heart,

There he stands on the scaffold,
See, he speaks,
There is a woman holding her hands,
They'll soon be folding,
And the tears are raining down her cheeks.

That's him there in his coffin lying low,
And a woman,
The first to love him and the last to
Bend above him,
Is his mother, but I guess you would know.

Frank Stanton,
Former Editor, *Atlanta Constitution*

1 A Fresh, New Start

"It is of the Lord's mercies that we are not consumed, because his compassions fail not. They are new every morning: great is thy faithfulness" (Lamentations 3:22-23).

God encourages us in Ephesians by saying "let not the sun go down upon your wrath." He is trying to explain to us the opportunity we have of beginning each day, new and fresh. We cannot go back and live yesterday again, but we are wise to let go of the anger as we end the day. If we go to bed with the anger, we many times will wake up with that anger. God's design is for us to enjoy His faithfulness and the compassion He has toward us. We will not acknowledge the blessing of rising to each new day if we allow our wrath to be carried over to the next day.

As we begin this new year, may we enjoy God's faithfulness with all that He enabled us to accomplish this past year and bury the disappointments and disasters. As we see the failure of carrying over our anger from one day to the next, let's realize the same kind of hindrance of bringing last year's troubles into our new year. May we awake each day of this new year with thanksgiving to God for His mercies. The best prescription for a good morning is to not let the sun go down on your wrath. And the best advice for this new year is to rejoice that we have a new start, a brand new beginning of exciting things we can do for God.

Dear God, thank You for Your mercies that are new to me each day. May I give this day to You and live it as You would have me to.

Katy Ripley

2 God Has A Purpose In It All

"And we know that all things work together for good to them that love God, to them who are the called according to his purpose" (Romans 8:28).

I think we all wonder sometimes why God allows us to go through such difficult times in our lives. Many of you might be like I was as a new Christian — I really expected life to simply be a bed of roses once I got saved. But it's not like that at all. Life is full of its problems for the saved, as well as the unsaved. What we don't usually realize, though, is that it's actually those trials and tribulations that God brings into our lives that grow us into the person He wants us to be. Knowing and accepting that is how we can trust that all things, even the bad things, are truly working together for our good.

Recently I ran across a story that really spoke to me. It was about a young boy who found a cocoon and brought it into his house to watch the butterfly break free. As he watched and saw that it was having a hard time, he reached down and widened the opening to make it easier. In doing that, he crippled the butterfly. The struggling to get free is what actually strengthens and forms the wings that it would need to fly and function in life. Without the struggles, the butterfly's wings were limp and useless, and it would soon die.

You see, many times in our lives we are actually crippled, spiritually speaking, if we look for the easy way out, or if someone bails us out. The struggles, trials, and tribulations that we face each day are ordered by God to strengthen us. So instead of looking for an escape, we should submit our will to His perfect will. He wants to make us into something very beautiful if we will just let Him accomplish His purpose in us.

Tammy Allred
Missionary to Mexico

3 WHO'S THE BOSS?

"Thine, O Lord, is the greatness, and the power, and the glory, and the victory, and the majesty: for all that is in the heaven and in the earth is thine; thine is the kingdom, O Lord, and thou art exalted as head above all" (I Chronicles 29:11).

The sovereignty of God is such a difficult concept to grasp, but my son, Tyler, taught me exactly what that meant one day when he was five years old. Tyler was at a time in his life when he was really trying to understand the concept of "Who's the boss?" He would ask this question in every place and situation we encountered. It seemed every day, several times a day, we would be asked questions like: "Who is the boss of our house?", "Who is the boss at McDonald's?", "Who is the boss at my school?", "Who is the boss at Wal-Mart?", "Who is the boss at Daddy's office?"

These questions were a constant in our home for what seemed to be a very long time. One day, we were driving down the road when from the back seat Tyler announced, "Mommy, I know who is the boss of the whole world!" Imagine my surprise to hear a declaration rather than a question. "Who?" I asked. To which Tyler replied, "God! He made it all, so He is the Boss of it all!" What a simple truth expressed through the words of a small child! It is also a truth that most adults fail to grasp. How much we can learn from little children if we only take the time to listen!

Dear Lord, You are the Lord of all. Help me to never lose sight of the fact that You are the Creator of everything. For that very reason alone, I want to recognize Who You are and bow my knee to worship You. Help me to always see You through the eyes of a child and love You with the heart of a child.

Susan Harney

4 WE CAN ALWAYS TRUST HIM

"Now unto him that is able to do exceeding abundantly above all that we ask or think..." (Ephesians 3:20).

Living in a foreign country as a missionary can be quite a challenging, yet exciting, experience. New situations arise daily which require wisdom from God, yet out of it all, He receives much glory.

For instance, Nelly, a young lady from a village, was responsible for the daily cleaning of our Teacher Training Institute building. Usually she was cheerful and full of praises to her heavenly Father. One day, however, Nelly arrived in tears. When asked why she was crying, she said, "Our family cow broke its leg and must be killed. The cow is expecting a calf in two days." Then she added, "Please pray about this problem. Our family of 12 is very dependent on the milk, cheese, and butter for our food. We also sell these milk product, so that we have some cash available."

Having never prayed about a cow before, I silently asked God to help me. We prayed, and Nelly settled down in peace and contentment, assured that somehow God would be able to fix the problem. The cow was killed, and its calf survived only two days after being delivered by the veterinarian. Everything seemed to be getting worse.

A lady who heard about the situation sent us some money to buy another cow, and Nelly's father found one for the exact amount, which was about half the price of good, healthy cows. While the former cow had produced four liters of milk a day, the new cow produced 16 liters of milk a day! God answered prayer in a remarkable way! He took away the lesser to substitute the much. How He delights in proving Himself faithful!

What about your situation? Are you trusting Him as He

removes something you deem so necessary in your life? Is He preparing to replace it with something of greater worth? Let us be found faithful as we allow Him to arrange our unique circumstances in such a way that He can receive much honor and glory.

Loreen Ittermann
Missionary to Moldova

5 HUGS AND I LOVE YOU'S

"The Lord hath appeared of old unto me, saying, Yea, I have loved thee with an everlasting love: therefore with lovingkindness have I drawn thee" (Jeremiah 31:3).

The Bible tells us in Jeremiah 31:3 that Christ loves us with an everlasting love. Letting my children know that I love them has always been very important to me, because I grew up in a home where I did not remember hearing "I love you" until I was 27 years old. As for hugs, what in the world were they? This made a big impact on my life, because I had always heard in Sunday School that Jesus loved me. There I was, a little girl who felt so worthless and unloved, but Jesus loved me.

From the time I found out I was pregnant with my children, I told them that I loved them every day. From the minute they were born, I showered them with hugs and "I love you's." They have always known that Mom was never too busy that I could not stop for hugs. I now have a beautiful God-fearing daughter-in-law who I can share my love with, as well as those hugs. Hugs and "I love you's" are two of God's special ways of soothing a weary heart or overflowing it with joy. Let us not forget those hugs and "I love you's."

Lord, thank You that You were there from the beginning and loved me so much, even when I felt unloved. Thank You for all the love You have given to me, so I in turn can give it to others. Thank You for Your arms that are always around me in that special hug.

Vickie Copeland

6 WHAT IS THE LEAST YOU CAN DO FOR HIM?

"Not forsaking the assembling of ourselves together, as the manner of some is; but exhorting one another: and so much the more, as ye see the day approaching" (Hebrews 10:25).

Stop just a moment and think about all that God has done for you. How long would it take you to write a list of everything He has done for you and blessed you with? Once I begin to think about who I am, where I have been and what I have become, my list could go on and on! Do you ever just ponder on who you would be, where you would be, and what you would be doing if you never met the Lord? So often I take for granted my circumstances, situation, family, and friends. It makes me wonder why God is still working on me, and He is faithful to me through it all.

Through His faithfulness and grace, He has taught me not only to be grateful for what He has done and is doing in my life, but also to reciprocate His faithfulness to me. After all He has done for you, think about this — What is the least thing you can do for Him? My answer is to be faithful, especially to church. How much time a week do you devote to your husband, children, job, etc.? Now, how often do you attend church? This has always been a pet peeve of mine. I have always felt that the least we can do for Christ is assemble with fellow believers once a week. Assembling as believers not only pleases Him, but it also makes you feel a part of the body of Christ.

You have so many distractions during the week in your daily life. Sunday should be a time for refreshment and renewal. How awesome it is to put behind everything that has happened during the week and focus on the Lord! Don't we all need that? I am not implying that this should replace our personal relationship with God, but it should be a priority after that.

So I encourage you to examine your life. Are you giving Him the first day of the week? Have you ever wondered why we worship on the first day of the week? Do you think it might be to give Him first place?

Ginger Richey

7 Sometimes "Doing" Means Waiting

"I can do all things through Christ which strengtheneth me" (Philippians 4:13).

I first claimed this verse in the fall of 1978 when I was asked to take the teacher position in a four-year-old kindergarten class at the Christian school where we attended church. I had been saved only a year and felt totally inadequate and highly doubtful of my abilities to do this task.

I learned through this experience that God does not call us to a task without enabling us to perform it. He wants us to be successful. I claimed that Scripture many times over the next 16 years when called to a task that took me out of my comfort zone concerning my abilities. I always associated that verse with a call to a task or ministry — something that involved activity or "doing."

Then nine years ago, some heart breaking situations came into my life that really rocked my world. Suddenly, I was faced with situations where I was not called to "do" something. It was quite the opposite; in fact, there was nothing I could "do." I had to now claim this verse for strength to simply wait and let God "do." Waiting on God is still one of the hardest things that God asks of me, but I have learned through Christ I can still "do" all things — even when the "doing" is waiting.

Sharon Collier

8 The End Of The Earth

"Hear my cry, O God; attend unto my prayer. From the end of the earth will I cry unto thee, when my heart is overwhelmed: lead me to the rock that is higher than I. For thou hast been a shelter for me, and a strong tower from the enemy" (Psalm 61:1-3).

We have all been to the "end of the earth," that place where life just got too hard, burdens became too difficult, or the cross was too heavy to carry any further. Sometimes the storm rages so hard or so long that we wonder what will be left of our heart when it is over. Maybe the storm we are facing is a sick or injured child, financial difficulties, or a stressful relationship. Whatever the case, we are overwhelmed and find ourselves on the edge and facing a decision. What do we do now? Do we jump off or hide in some hole of self-pity and depression? Do we blame others or cry out against God?

In Psalm 61, David did cry out, but it was a plea for God to hear him and help him in his desperate situation. David knew that there was a place to hide when life's circumstances became unbearable. It was not in self-pity or in bitterness but in the Rock.

God is the Rock that shelters us in the time of storm. He is the Strong Tower that protects us from our enemies, even the unseen enemies of discouragement, depression, and bitterness. The winds are going to blow. The hard times are going to come, but God is always there for us. When we find ourselves at "the end of the earth," we must realize that this is not the end, but the place to reach out to the Rock and let Him hold us. It is the place to grow, learn, become stronger, and cling to our precious Lord more than ever before.

Karen Woodward
Missionary to Romania

9 SOMEBODY IS WATCHING

"Let no man despise thy youth; but be thou an example of the believers, in word, in conversation, in charity, in spirit, in faith, in purity" (I Timothy 4:12).

Sometimes we get so involved in our daily lives and routines that we have to be reminded to take the time to "smell the roses" and "enjoy the journey." It is so easy to get caught up into what is happening in our lives. We begin doing things and saying things that either just make us feel better, or we try to guarantee the outcome of a situation to be in our favor. Many times, we do not stop to realize whom we affect by our actions and our words.

I grew up in a Christian home with my older brother and sister. The way I saw my parents act behind closed doors at home is the same way everyone else saw them act in public. They never asked us to do something or not to do something that they were not already trying to put into practice and live themselves. The words spoken and the actions taken by my parents instilled in each of us that the most important thing that you did was for Christ. How you lived affected those things around you and revealed the goals you truly desired for yourself and your family.

While I watched my dad go through a huge trial in his life, he never once asked God: "Why me?", "What for?", "How come?" He always knew God had something better for Him. He did. My father went home to be with the Lord in October of 1995. Even while he was in the emergency room in excruciating pain, my dad looked at us and said, "It's so comforting to know the Lord."

We all need to recognize that each word we speak is being heard, and each action we take is being watched more than we realize. Somebody is watching and waiting to see how we react to a situation, or how we respond to a tragedy, or just what kind of faith we really have while going through trials. Our lives preach a message, and we are either an encouragement or a discouragement to someone. What we say and what we do each day is partly responsible for how others deal with situations that are brought into their everyday lives. We as Christians have a huge responsibility to live as Christ.

Lisa White

10 DAVID'S BLESSING

"...Who am I, O Lord God? and what is my house, that thou hast brought me hitherto?" (II Samuel 7:18).

David has finally become king over Israel. It has been many years since Samuel anointed David to be the king. Saul is now dead, and David is on his rightful throne. It is amazing that this shepherd boy has made it to the top. His enemies are now being defeated at every turn since God's hand of blessing is with David. Then the prophet Nathan is sent to give a message to the king.

Nathan comes to David with an encouraging word from the Lord. "...Thus saith the Lord of hosts, I took thee from the sheepcote, from following the sheep, to be ruler over my people, over Israel. And I was with thee whithersoever thou wentest, and have cut off all thine enemies out of thy sight, and have made thee a great name, like unto the name of the great men that are in the earth. And thine house and thy kingdom shall be established for ever before thee: thy throne shall be established for ever..." (II Samuel 7:8-9, 16). What a great blessing God has given this humble shepherd boy! Not only has God taken David from nothing to everything, but He also promises to keep blessing David's lineage. David responds to Nathan's message with sufficient awe and understanding of what God is doing in his life. "...Who am I, O Lord God? and what is my house, that thou hast brought me hitherto?" (II Samuel 7:18). His worship is heartfelt as David praises God for His mercy and love being poured into his life. God has taken each one of us from nothing and made us His child. He did not just save us from damnation, He also sent His Spirit to dwell within us as our Guide and Comforter. God has chosen to bless us, not because we are worthy and have great things to offer Him, but because of His great love poured out on us in Christ Jesus.

As you read these verses in II Samuel 7, remind yourself from where God drew you to a place of His cherished child. Take time to remember God's blessings in your life. Praise Him for His abounding love and mercy in your life.

Kathy Schaaf
Missionary to Jordan

11 GOD, WOULD YOU LEND ME YOUR EYES?

"Look not every man on his own things, but every man also on the things of others" (Philippians 2:4).

One morning while I was driving to work at the salon where I am a stylist, it seemed that everywhere I went someone was doing less than the speed limit, cutting me off, or just sightseeing. Can you relate? It seemed that I was the only one who had an agenda that must be completed. When I arrived at the salon, almost every client was late or had an excuse for why they could not keep their appointment. This was very frustrating!

I had not verbalized this frustration, but God knew what was in my heart. Later in the break room, some of the other stylists were talking. As I walked in, the only part of the conversation I heard was: "Oh well, the world does not revolve around me anyway." God used that to prick my heart. You know, sometimes we get so focused on ourselves that we don't see what other people are experiencing. It is easy to get caught up with responsibilities of life and forget that we are to care for and serve others.

Since that time, my prayer to God has been to let me see others as He sees them. We must be sensitive to the needs of those we come in contact with. Perhaps one day someone will be sent your way so you can meet their need of encouragement or lead them to Christ. God may even send someone your way that you don't like! Wow! Wouldn't that be a lot to ask of us?

We need to have the mind of God and be ready to do what He asks us to do. When we begin to see people as God sees them, we will have love, compassion, and patience. We will not see them as a burden, but as a soul that God loves and Jesus died to save. When this becomes our attitude God can use us for His glory.

Jo Clifton

12 HE CARES FOR ME

"How excellent is thy lovingkindness, O God! therefore the children of men put their trust under the shadow of thy wings" (Psalm 36:7).

One night while I was sitting in my living room, I told God that He did not get much when He got me, but He got all of me. I asked Him to use me wherever He wanted, even if He just needed a warm body somewhere. He took me at my word.

A few days later, Debbie McKaig, our church preschool director at the time, called and asked if I would be the director over the infant nursery. Without a thought I said yes. Debbie said she was glad. She had called others before me, and they all told her they needed to pray about it. For once in my life, I was all "prayed up." I knew God was working.

If you have never been in the infant nursery, let me tell you what goes on in there. You are just a warm body – someone to hold those little babies, hug them, comfort them, feed them, and then clean them up. When you think you are done with the messy clean-up part, you just start all over again.

I spent one year in that nursery every Sunday, loving those babies. Meanwhile, God spent that year showing me how much He loved me. When I was scared, He held me. When I was good, He hugged me. When I was sad, He comforted me. He fed me and clothed me. Whenever I was messed up, He cleaned me up. Whenever God would clean me up, we would just start over again.

Just like I never tired of taking care of those babies, God never tired of taking care of me.

Melissa Herring

13

A Portrait Of Jesus

(Based on the Book of John)

Thou, Lord, art the Word,
The Lamb of God, John proclaimed.
Son of God, Creator, Temple,
In Thee do we abide.
God Incarnate, Son of Man.
Light of the World, walk by my side.
Bridegroom, Messiah, You give Living Water.
Christ, my Savior, One with the Father.
Bread of Life, You sustain me,
Giver of the Spirit, the Great I Am.
The True and Good Shepherd, You order my steps.
The Resurrection and the Life, I am in Your debt.
The King of Israel, of David's line,
Through Thee, eternal life is mine.
You have been a Servant to me
Let me now be a servant to Thee.
The Way, the Truth, the Life art Thou,
The True Vine, bearing the fruit of my soul.
The High Priest who ministers to me,
King of the Jews who crucified Thee.
Fulfiller of Scripture, You have called me by name.
Here am I, worthless and small,
Made radiant and perfect by calling You "Lord."
Take my hand and make me whole.
Thank You, Precious Keeper of my soul.

Ruth Shelton

14 Recognize The Blessings

"Blessed be the Lord, who daily loadeth us with benefits..." (Psalm 68:19).

God has done many marvelous works in my life, and I have always thought that I was properly grateful to Him. When our family moved to Zambia, Africa, to begin missionary work some years ago, I became aware of the real magnitude of God's blessings upon my life.

I realized the great privilege I'd had of being born in America. While our nation has slipped far from its original Christian heritage, we still experience great blessings from God in so many ways. I have a new appreciation for my heritage and a new awareness of the Lord's hand upon my life.

In this African country that has many traditional practices which are evil and harmful, there is much fear and superstition among the people. Eighty percent of the population lives in poverty, and very few jobs are available in urban centers. The great AIDS crisis is touching almost every family here, which adds to the miserable plight of these people. Recent drought has caused hunger and starvation. Hopelessness abounds.

When I see all these effects of sin before my eyes, it is clear to me the benefits that I have enjoyed before turning to Christ in my youth. I thank God for His protection and providence. I was not born into a Christian home, but my parents never dreamed of marrying me off at age 12 for the bride payment's sake, a common practice in Africa. I never trembled in the dark upon hearing noises outside, thinking it was my ancestor coming to trouble me. When times were tough, I was never pulled out of school to roam the streets begging for food or money upon my father's insistence.

You see, God has loaded me with benefits! I now recognize just how abundantly He has blessed me. This awareness fuels my desire to spread the Word to the people around me, so that they can break the cycle of misery and begin a new life with the God of all blessings. Let's open our eyes and see anew the wonders of His grace in all of our lives!

Jody Hayton
Missionary to Zambia

15 THE GIFT OF GIVING

"Bring ye all the tithes into the storehouse, that there may be meat in mine house, and prove me now herewith, saith the Lord of hosts, if I will not open you the windows of heaven, and pour you out a blessing, that there shall not be room enough to receive it" (Malachi 3:10).

My mother had tremendous faith and believed strongly that you cannot out give God. She paid tithes on every dollar she received, not just what she earned. I saw the provision of God manifested in her life in so many ways.

Mother had four children, and she took us to church at every opportunity. My dad died at an early age from complications related to alcoholism, so Mother raised us virtually by herself. Many times we did not know where our next meal would come from, but Mother always paid her tithes. Mysteriously, a box of food would appear at our back door, or someone would make an extra casserole and bring it over. We did not have to beg, and no one ever knew the extent of our need.

For years, I have paid tithes just like Mother did. God has always blessed me, and I am so grateful to God for all He has given me. Each year, our pastor preaches sermons on giving during the entire month of January. During one of his sermons on giving, the pastor asked those who needed a financial blessing to stand up. I was embarrassed to stand, but wanted God's blessing so bad, I stood along with several others. The entire congregation prayed for us.

About a week later, a couple of friends from Florida called me, and they wanted to help with my financial situation. They asked for my bank information and said they would wire $1,000. They are Christians who have been very blessed financially, and we pray for one another like family. Reluctantly, I gave them the information they requested, but only after they told me God had impressed them to help me. A few days later, I received a bank statement. To my amazement, they had sent $2,000!

Financial blessing is only one of the many ways God has blessed me. One of my greatest gifts comes from the knowledge that you cannot out give God. Thanks to Mother and to God, I am able to give with a thankful heart.

Dianne Stewart

16 YES, I'M LOOKING YOUNGER

"Who satisfieth thy mouth with good things; so that thy youth is renewed like the eagle's" (Psalm 103:5).

Ever since I hit 40, I have noticed many changes in my body. Almost every day I find new wrinkles. I have not only seen a change in my skin, but I have also seen a change in my energy level. Emotionally, I could also feel old as I go through the struggles of life. David felt this way in Psalm 102.

In the following verses in Psalm 103, I discovered what keeps me going, God's Rejuvenating Treatment. Let me share these exceptional products with you. It will not cost a penny. Truly, I can save you a great deal of time and money spent in therapy sessions or treatments.

Steps 1 and 2 of God's Rejuvenating Treatment are to bless the Lord (Psalm 103:1-2). Step 3 is to not forget His benefits (Psalm 103:2). What benefits? He forgives me, He heals me, He redeemed me, He crowns me with mercy, and He fills me with good things (Psalm 103:3-5). As a result, my youth is made new like the eagle's. God is saying that if I concentrate on the good that He gives me, I will not feel over 40. Like the strongest and most majestic bird, I can fly through a storm.

This is all the treatment I really need to feel younger. Do I still use my cleanser, toner, moisturizer, and some extras? Yes, of course I do, every morning and night. But nothing makes me feel younger than worshipping God and remembering His benefits every morning and night.

Next time you see me, you might wonder: Where does a missionary wife get enough money for plastic surgery?

Annita Hoagland
Missionary to Mexico

17 CAPTIVITY TURNS INTO A BLESSING

"Thou wilt shew me the path of life: in thy presence is fulness of joy; at thy right hand there are pleasures for evermore" (Psalm 16:11).

It was November 1996, and I was going through a tough time in my life. To get away from it all, I decided to drive to Johnson City, Tennessee for a weekend to see my son play junior football.

I had only traveled ten miles out of town when my check engine light came on. This never happens, so why now? I stopped at a Shell station, bought a quart of oil, and was about to be on my way when a man came out of the station and said, "Ma'am, you have a nail sticking out of your tire." I couldn't believe it! Low oil and a nail in my tire! I was not meant to make this trip. There was not enough time to repair the tire and catch up with the caravan of parents.

Sadly, I drove home. Why did this happen? I needed this trip desperately! Then God began to stir my heart to get into His Word. I couldn't stop! I read, cried, and rejoiced until I was full. I did this all weekend! It was at this time that I realized God had allowed my car dilemma to keep me captive at home so He could speak to me, illuminate Himself to me, and begin a beautiful work in my life! Being in His presence brought me closer to Him than I had ever been before.

So when it seems like everything is going wrong, just hang on! God just may be using this to bring you into a sweeter, closer relationship with Him!

Tammy Loyd

18 JOSHUA'S ORDERS

"Be strong and of a good courage: for unto this people shalt thou divide for an inheritance the land, which I sware unto their fathers to give them" (Joshua 1:6).

Right after Moses died, God commanded Joshua to pick up where Moses left off. It was a big job! It was what Joshua had lived his whole life for. Over and over again, God commanded Joshua to "be strong and of a good courage." He had to have strength and courage to obey God and to trust God. God promised Joshua that He would never leave him, forsake him, or fail him. What a picture of a faithful friend and leader!

In all His instruction, the only physical action that God commanded Joshua was: "This book of the law shall not depart out of thy mouth; but thou shalt meditate therein day and night, that thou mayest observe to do according to all that is written therein: for then thou shalt make thy way prosperous, and then thou shalt have good success" (Joshua 1:8).

God's Word is the key to strength, courage, obedience, and ultimately success! That is what I want in my life. How good it is to know that God and His Word will be faithful to help me be successful!

Anne DeKoker

19 THE COMFORTER AS OUR DAILY GUIDE

"If ye love me, keep my commandments. And I will pray the Father, and he shall give you another Comforter, that he may abide with you for ever; Even the Spirit of truth; whom the world cannot receive, because it seeth him not, neither knoweth him: but ye know him; for he dwelleth with you, and shall be in you. I will not leave you comfortless: I will come to you. But the Comforter, which is the Holy Ghost, whom the Father will send in my name, he shall teach you all things, and bring all things to your remembrance, whatsoever I have said unto you" (John 14:15-18, 26).

The Holy Spirit is a Guiding Hand that helps us and comforts us through our everyday trials. How the Holy Spirit ministers to us daily remains a mystery to most of us, yet we accept His leadership through faith. I would like to share about the Holy Spirit's ministry in my own life.

Some years ago, my mother became ill, and her health deteriorated to the point that the family knew she could not survive. With several family members gathered at her bedside in those final moments, she clearly spoke to us, "Have you ever heard such beautiful trumpet sounds in your life?" There was no music playing, yet she heard the trumpets of that heavenly orchestra, playing the processional for her entry into heaven.

When my father passed on to his reward, my family was at his bedside, too, except for me. Daddy roused, sat up in bed, and told the unseen Presence, "I can't go yet. My daughter has not arrived." Soon afterwards, I did arrive, and in less than an hour, Daddy went home to be with Jesus.

The unfortunate people who do not have Jesus in their lives would not believe these stories. Yet they are true, and almost every Christian can tell similar stories. We believe them because we are Christians, and we accept by faith that God is, was, and always will be. We also accept that the Holy

Spirit, or Comforter, leads and directs our lives through faith. There is not a single action that we do that can be concealed from Him; not a single word escapes our lips that He does not hear. What a marvelous comfort just to know that He cares!

Shelia St. John

20 DON'T ASK IF YOU DON'T MEAN IT

"But he giveth more grace. Wherefore he saith, God resisteth the proud, but giveth grace unto the humble" (James 4:6).

On occasion, I will ask the Lord to give me a particular word from the pulpit to study for the week. In most cases, it becomes a word that deals with a flaw in my character.

One Sunday, the word was "humility." That evening I went to work with my Bible, trusty notepad, and pen. Late into the night I came across a passage in the book of James that stood out from all the rest. Now it was time to ask the Lord why this particular passage was so important. He brought to mind an incident where I had to tell a friend that what she was involved in was wrong. Even though I was right in what I said, it was my attitude that needed forgiveness. I thought, "Okay, Lord, if I'm going to go to my friend, confess my wrong, and get forgiveness, You have her call me and I'll do it." The next morning before 7 a.m., my friend called and invited me over for lunch! I had to go to her in person. The relationship was mended, the lunch was great, and I learned a valuable lesson: Don't ask if you don't mean it!

Vanessa Nicholson

21 BE IN YOUR PLACE

"A man hath joy by the answer of his mouth: and a word spoken in due season, how good is it!" (Proverbs 15:23).

I have taught kindergarten at church for six years now, and every Sunday is a special treat to come to see what the Lord is doing in these little children's bright eyes and lives.

On one particular Sunday, I had a bad morning. With three children of my own, I was running extremely late, because my little boy, who was just over a year old, had been sick during the night. I woke up late and hurried my other two children along to get ready for church, but we were really late.

When I arrived at church to teach my class, I was not feeling very beautiful or prepared to meet those little faces awaiting me. My class time began, and I was trying my hardest to play catch-up and make sure the children did not notice that I was tired, sleepy, and weary in my well doing. Just about the time I was feeling my worst, I felt a little boy's arms around my legs. He was in the middle of the biggest hug he could give. I looked down and said, "Thank you for my hug," and he looked at me with his bright eyes and said, "You are beautiful." I thanked him, and he went about his day, playing.

I was left standing there with tears in my eyes and love in my heart renewed for all those little children. It was just as if God had hugged me tight and said, "I know you're tired and weary, but you are beautiful to me." I will never be the same. God always knows just what we need, and when we need it. I am glad I was in my place that day to receive what He had for me.

Mitzi Sims Oaks

22 DELIGHT

"If thou turn away thy foot from the sabbath, from doing thy pleasure on my holy day; and call the sabbath a delight, the holy of the Lord, honourable; and shalt honour him, not doing thine own ways, nor finding thine own pleasure, nor speaking thine own words: Then shalt thou delight thyself in the Lord; and I will cause thee to ride upon the high places of the earth, and feed thee with the heritage of Jacob thy father: for the mouth of the Lord hath spoken it" (Isaiah 58:13-14).

We have all heard Psalm 37:4 quoted many times: "Delight thyself also in the Lord; and he shall give thee the desires of thine heart." We all want the desires of our heart. The key in that verse is delighting in the Lord. I wonder how we should "delight" ourselves in the Lord. I guessed that the obvious – praying, daily Bible study, going to church, etc. – delighted Him. Is there anything else?

That led me on a search. As I studied, I tried to see beyond the verses I was reading to a deeper meaning. I just knew I would find a secret way of delighting Him that would maybe take me years to find. Well, it was not long before I came upon Isaiah 58:13-14. In clear, concise, easy-to-understand English, the verses say, "…and shalt honour him, not doing thine own ways, nor finding thine own pleasure, nor speaking thine own words: Then shalt thou delight thyself in the Lord…" Could that be the answer I was looking for: emptying ourselves of our stuff, filling our hearts with His words, His ways, and His pleasures?

I believe that delighting the Lord is more than just going through the motions of serving Him. I think it's all about changing our selfish hearts, and we can only do that with the help of His Spirit. I'm working on it!

Danna Harbin

23 God Is Faithful

"Faithful is he that calleth you, who also will do it" (I Thessalonians 5:24).

When the Lord calls, we should go, and that is what we did back in the summer of 1994 to Kiev, Ukraine. God's faithfulness — praise the Lord — is not limited to our measure of faith, because He is always true to His Word. When my faith wavered, He became my Rock of deliverance and encouraged me every step of the way. The Lord was there when my spiritual plate spilled over with doubt, fear, and enormous stress as I battled with the Russian language, home schooling, and a totally new way of life in a foreign country.

That first year, we opened our home to Russian language lessons three days a week, to Ukrainian translators five days a week, to an open-door ministry for people in our neighborhood, as well as Sunday morning services and Saturday visitation. There were many times that people would come to our home for spiritual guidance or fellowship. We knew that was what God wanted. Yet deep in my heart, I still battled a fear of not being able to succeed in this new ministry.

Despite the mice invasions, the shortage of water and electricity, freezing temperatures, attempted break-ins, and illnesses, we knew that we were in the center of God's will. Discouragement is Satan's tool to stop or hinder God's work, and that is something I diligently prayed to overcome. Our God is the God of the living and the Lord of victories.

When people say that prayer works miracles, they are absolutely right! People back in our supporting churches were praying, and we could feel the wheels of faith turning. We saw our Sunday services grow with more than 50 children accepting Christ as Savior. Little by little, our Russian language progressed, and we could see God's mighty hand at work. I became convinced that through trials our Lord is always with us, and that He never forsakes His children, especially during those difficult times.

He is faithful to accomplish through us what He wants to establish here on earth. What He wants is our faithfulness! May we always be where He wants us and trust Him for those things we cannot accomplish on our own.

Eve Williamson
Missionary to Ukraine

24 An Instrument Of Righteousness

"...even so now yield your members servants to righteousness unto holiness" (Romans 6:19).

Several years ago, a friend and I were walking regularly in the early hours of the day. It was our custom to rise at 4 a.m. and walk for an hour on the streets of the city we lived in. We dressed for the weather and always carried flashlights. We shared many thoughts as we began our day together. Our friendship grew as we walked together in the darkness. It was on one of these walks that she asked Jesus to become her Savior and Lord.

As a new Christian myself, I had completed evangelism training a few weeks before. During this training, there did not arise a time to present the Gospel to anyone. Every day I had tucked my Bible in my pocket, praying for the opportunity to share with her. For some reason, I had not put my Bible in my pocket on this day, and we were discussing eternal life and the assurance of being in Heaven when we die. The one day that I needed it, I did not have it with me.

As I searched my mind for the words to say and the Scripture to quote, I prayed for the Holy Spirit to bring to remembrance the verses. The Holy Spirit took over quoting all the Scripture that was needed and put the desire in her heart to receive Jesus. She was the first salvation where God used me as the instrument of righteousness.

God showed me that all He needs is a willing and

submissive heart. A dear lady told me once: "Always keep your mind, heart, and hands centered on God. When God needs a servant to use, he will use you." How sad, to discover in Heaven, the blessings God had for you and someone else received because you were not ready.

Jane Whitt

25 RUNNING THE RACE

"...let us run with patience the race that is set before us, Looking unto Jesus the author and finisher of our faith..." (Hebrews 12:1-2).

In any race, the runners have assigned lanes in which they must run. Their eyes are on the finishing tape, not on the spectators or other runners. In order to finish well, they must run with all their might. The Word of God has some very good examples of this:

Peter's mother-in-law was ill with a fever. Christ healed her, and she ministered to a group of visitors. This would include washing feet, cooking food, etc. What a willingness to disregard self! (Matthew 8:14-15)

Dorcas was another "runner." In Acts 9:36-39, we read of the garments she made for others and her death. Peter prayed, and she was raised from the dead. What an unselfish service to others!

In John 12:2, we read that *Martha* served the guests supper. This was a big meal, not a snack. What a caring attitude!

John 12:3 states that *Mary* anointed Jesus' feet with a pound of spikenard, a very costly ointment and perfume. Then she wiped His feet with her hair. What an act of worship!

Don't discount the daily routine as nothing. None of these ladies preached sermons or wrote epistles. Remember, the Lord keeps track of little things as well as great. Matthew

10:42 mentions giving a cup of water in Jesus' name. Are you giving it your all in your line of service?

Elsie James
Missionary to Japan

26 IF GOD BE FOR US, WHO CAN BE AGAINST US?

"...and nothing shall by any means hurt you" (Luke 10:19).

God has allowed my husband and me to be a part of a team to go into other countries to evangelize or teach discipleship on several occasions.

Several years ago, my husband went to Albania with a team to evangelize. As the days passed, my concern for his safety grew. Then one night, I awoke about 2 a.m., feeling so worried and stressed I could hardly breathe. I prayed for him and the team. I was still too restless to sleep, and I decided to get up and study the Bible lesson I would be teaching the children on the following Sunday.

The lesson was "The Good Samaritan," and the text began in Luke 10:24. Not wanting to miss any of the concepts, I began reading in verse 1. The Scriptures read: "After these things the Lord appointed other seventy also, and sent them two and two before his face into every city and place, whither he himself would come." In verse 19 "...and nothing shall by any means hurt you." I knew then in my heart that my husband was fine, and I was able to sleep and rest.

A few years later, we went to the Philippines with a team. We were in a camp outside the city. The ladies were staying in a small straw hut, and we were sleeping on a mattress on the floor. One night, I was awakened by something pulling my hair. It was dark, and I decided that maybe a kitten was reaching through the straw wall. I put my head to the center of the room and went back to sleep. A few minutes later, it woke me again. Something was scratching my foot and pulling my hair! I woke the other girls, and we turned on the light to see big rats run up the ceiling.

The guards outside told us that this was a common occurrence, and there was nothing they could do. A frightened, helpless feeling swept over me, and as I cried out in my heart to the Lord, He brought the Scriptures in Luke 10:1-19 back to my remembrance. I shared it with the girls, and we prayed, believing God's promise – and went back to sleep! The rats never bothered us again.

If God be for us, who can be against us?

Barbara Allred

27 GOD NEVER BLINKS

"For I will set mine eyes upon them for good..." (Jeremiah 24:6).

I know you have heard the saying, "out of the mouths of babes." Although he's not really a baby anymore, my son seems to have such wisdom from God! My Father teaches me through my son over and over.

The other day, as we were driving down the road, he noticed what I have always assumed is a reflection of the moon visible during the day. He was commenting on the design of the craters that look like a face and said, "You know, the man in the moon might be God's face watching over us. He never blinks."

Then it hit me that God never misses so much as the blink of an eye of what comes to us. He sees everything that happens to us. How comforting it is to know that my Father never misses anything concerning His children! He continually sets His eyes on us for good. What a wonderful thought to think that God never blinks!

Regina Hudson

28 THE ONLY ONE

"But Noah found grace in the eyes of the Lord" (Genesis 6:8).

Does it sometimes seem that you are the only Christian at work or among your friends and relatives? Does that matter? It did not take Adam and Eve's descendants long to become totally selfish and wicked. Every thought was evil.

By the time of Genesis 6, God was sorry He had ever made man and made plans to destroy them all. Out of all the people on earth at the time, Noah was the only one who found grace in God's sight. When Noah's kids came home from school whining, "But Mom, everybody's doing it," they were telling the truth! Genesis 6:9 tells us that Noah was a just man and that he walked with God. He believed God's warning about the coming destruction and did what God told him to do, no matter what the consequences.

Noah proceeded to spend the next century of his life building the ark. A massive structure like the ark was not something quickly constructed or easily hidden in one's backyard. What deep conviction, courage, and strength of character he had! Were his sons embarrassed by this odd fellow? Apparently not, because they worked alongside him and followed him into the ark. Noah and his family must have endured unimaginable taunts, jokes, and ridicule of the whole world.

Where were Noah's grandparents, aunts, and uncles? They chose to go along with the world and died terrible deaths. Noah preached and warned people of the flood, and in 100 years he had no converts to show for it, except for his sons and their wives.

Is it okay to be the only one doing right? Yes, it is! Can you endure the teasing? Yes, you can! Keep on doing right.

Laurie Hurt

29 Helping Others Through Pain

"Blessed be God, even the Father of our Lord Jesus Christ, the Father of mercies, and the God of all comfort; Who comforteth us in all our tribulation, that we may be able to comfort them which are in any trouble, by the comfort wherewith we ourselves are comforted of God" (II Corinthians 1:3-4).

In July 1985, I found a lump in my breast. I went immediately to my doctor, who sent me to a surgeon. After the test results were negative for cancer, he suggested we just watch it. After a year of praying for God to give me peace about my condition, it never came. I returned to my doctor, who ordered a biopsy. Three days later, I was told I had breast cancer, which required a mastectomy.

The Sunday before my surgery, my family and I went to church together as always. Brother Rex Terry led the choir in "How Great Thou Art." This message touched my heart, even though I had heard this song so many times before. My family and I went to the altar and prayed to God for His healing power, His comforting Spirit, and His protection for me during surgery.

The first thing I remember when I woke up in recovery was the song "How Great Thou Art." I felt like this was the answer to my prayers, that God was in control of my life, and no matter what happened He would get me through it. I have come through some even harder things since then, but through it all, God taught me the true meaning of dependence on Him and what prayer really means.

I have since been able to help many other women who have gone through a similar experience. I know God sometimes puts us in situations so we will be able to help others in need.

Frances Bonner

30 THE CAT IN THE HAT

"So teach us to number our days, that we may apply our hearts unto wisdom" (Psalm 90:12).

While going through a closet of old books, I came across the famous Dr. Seuss book, *THE CAT IN THE HAT*. In case you don't remember, the cat comes to visit and makes havoc of the house. There was a time when I could have recited every page of that rhyming book, because my children asked over and over for it to be read.

It was then that I realized that I would never again read that book to my two boys, now ages 12 and 15. I don't even remember when I read it for the last time. Did I read it hurriedly, so I could finish some housework? Or did I laugh at the silly cat and enjoy the look of wonder in my boys' eyes? If only a neon sign would have appeared and said, "Dawn, enjoy this, you will never have this moment again with your sons."

It's funny; things are like that in life. We somehow stop one thing and start another, passing from one phase to another, without even realizing that it has ended. Maybe that is why it is important to celebrate birthdays, graduations, and anniversaries. When they come, we pause just long enough to realize that one year is over, and another is ready to begin.

All the times of our life are special. The two boys who used to love *THE CAT IN THE HAT* are now athletes, interested in cars, and thinking about what they want to be when they grow up. Help me Lord to remember the past, enjoy the present, and look to the future as life moves quickly on.

Dawn Terry

31 God, I Feel So Far From You

"For God, who commanded the light to shine out of darkness, hath shined in our hearts, to give the light of the knowledge of the glory of God in the face of Jesus Christ" (II Corinthians 4:6).

I was having a particularly hard day. My husband and I had an argument, and my girls were acting up. It was just not a good day. We were driving down the road, and I was staring out the window just so that I would not have to talk to him or the girls. I was so mad. Part of me wanted to have it out, but the other part knew the best thing to do was pray and ask for God's guidance.

The moon was full, and it caught my eye. It was so beautiful. I just stared at it and finally I prayed. "God, I feel so far from you. I need to see You now! I really need You to reveal Yourself to me." As I prayed and stared at the moon, there were times when we would pass a knoll of trees. I could barely see the moon through them, but I knew it was there. We would come to a field, and there the moon would be, shining just as it was before. Other times, we would pass groves of trees where the moon was fully obscured. Once again, we would pass another field, and the moon was shining just as brightly as it had before.

Then I realized God was talking to me through the moon and the trees. There are times in my life that I can see Him just as plain as day, then I let a few "trees" come between Him and me. I would still see Him, but not as clearly. Then there are days I let the "trees" come completely between Him and me, and I cannot see Him at all. Whether it be unconfessed sin or not sitting with Him in His Word, it put barriers between us. He answered my prayer right there that day. I know He is there, shining like that full moon all the time. I am the one who moves. But when we need Him most, He is there. All we have to do is come to Him and ask His forgiveness.

If you are feeling far from God, ask Him to reveal what "trees" are blocking you from seeing Him and just wait to see what He has in store. Like that moon, He is always shining bright, waiting for you.

Georgeann Hept

1 Quiet Time

"Be still, and know that I am God..." (Psalm 46:10).

Did you ever hear the phrase, "So quiet you could hear a pin drop?" Have you ever stopped in total silence and rested awhile in the presence of the Lord? Our world is in total chaos, just as our lives get at times. Maybe that is because we do not give the Lord our full attention.

We need to stop during our daily routines and just lean on the Lord, rest in His love, and feel the power of His holy presence. How different our lives could be by giving Him total adoration! In His Word, God reminds us that He can still the tumults in our lives if we just daily stop and rest quietly with Him: "Which by his strength setteth fast the mountains; being girded with power: Which stilleth the noise of the seas, the noise of their waves, and the tumult of the people" (Psalm 65:6-7). Harriet B. Stowe wrote:

Alone with thee amid the mystic shadows,
The solemn hush of nature's newly born,
Alone with thee in breathless adoration,
In the calm dew and freshness of the morn.

Yes, we could make a difference in our daily lives, if only we just stopped and had that quiet time with our Lord.

Martha H. Knight

2 The Clouded Future

"And who is he that will harm you, if ye be followers of that which is good?" (I Peter 3:13).

Have you ever felt afraid of what the future holds for you? Did you ever wonder if what you are presently doing could be totally changed in a matter of days? I saw my whole future changed in a matter of two months!

On my way back to Africa for my third term, my mission board suggested that I stop off in France to perfect my French. Missionaries with French diplomas would be able to teach in public schools. This would also permit our mission to open a private school that would be approved by the state.

After spending two terms on the field, my life was clearly cut out for me. Soon I would have my diplomas and would be on my way back to my mission field. And then it happened! Coming out of school one day at noon hour, I stopped suddenly, face to face, with my future husband! We were both under the same mission board. Arthur had been in Czechoslovakia while I was in Africa, and neither of us knew that the other one was now in Paris, or even in France.

It wasn't easy to say "yes" when he proposed to me, and I didn't give my answer for two months. I wanted to be sure that my ministry in Africa was over and that now I was to completely change my life's plans, which is not easy! The Lord showed me that I must always be ready to follow Him, even if it means a whole change in life's dreams. We must always be listening to Him and ready to obey no matter what it costs!

Irene Sommerville
Missionary to France

3 MARY'S WAY VS. MARTHA'S WAY

"And Jesus answered and said unto her, Martha, Martha, thou art careful and troubled about many things: But one thing is needful: and Mary hath chosen that good part, which shall not be taken away from her" (Luke 10:41-42).

I was excited about the weekend ahead. A getaway to the lake would include food, fun, games, testimonies, and spending time with friends. Everyone had arrived and dinner had been served, and now it was time for the nightly devotion.

The speaker began to talk about Martha and Mary and how Mary simply spent time with Jesus while Martha worried about all the work that needed to be done. I briefly thought to myself, "I know this story. I wish they would talk about something else."

As soon as that thought crossed my mind, God began to speak to me. He said, "You are just like Martha. Sometimes you run around just getting stuff done, and you don't even take time to know that I am your God." Wow! The next morning during my Bible reading, I read Psalm 73:20-28, and God again confirmed that I was a Martha.

As I continued to read, God continued to speak to me. He showed me that I may be a Martha, but with His help I can become a Mary. I will be able to know Who God is, and I will be able to know the still, small voice of the Lord. When I am obedient in this area of my life, I can recognize that it is of God, and then I can give Him the glory that He deserves. In your life today and every day, strive to be a Mary.

Alison Schug

4 SUBMISSION

"Wives, submit yourselves unto your own husbands, as unto the Lord. For the husband is the head of the wife, even as Christ is the head of the church: and he is the saviour of the body. Therefore as the church is subject unto Christ, so let the wives be to their own husbands in every thing" (Ephesians 5:22-24).

This is a verse most wives do not really want to hear. I know, because I was one of them. This view totally contradicts the view of the world, which is that women are to be independent and able to live on their own. They do not need a man to tell them what to do. Wow! That is totally different from what God tells us to do. He said that wives are to submit to their husbands.

He says this for a reason. Have you ever been a part of a group with two leaders? It's not much fun, is it? There needs to be a defined leader in the home. This in no way means women do not contribute to marriage decisions, but there should be a defined leader. When I finally submitted to God by submitting to my husband, things in my marriage began to change. Instead of it being me against him, we worked together. My husband was more open to me, because he was not having to defend himself and his position as a leader.

My relationship with God also improved. I was obeying God, and since I was submissive to my husband, it was easier to be submissive to God. Ladies, God has a reason for all that He writes in the Bible. Trust Him, and He will bless you.

Gayle Krohe

5 CHRIST'S LOVE SUSTAINS US

"Beareth all things, believeth all things, hopeth all things, endureth all things" (I Corinthians 13:7).

After my friend proudly took me to see her new craft shop, she insisted that I choose something to take to Korea as a reminder of her friendship. I chose a plaque with the words of I Corinthians 13:7. Little did I know how that little wooden plaque with those words of love and encouragement from God's Word would sustain me during our family's greatest crisis.

For two years, our daughter was very sick, mentally and physically. Day by day, she got worse. My husband and I could not leave her alone or even allow our other children to watch her. Our family was deeply affected. We were beginning our second term and starting a new church. When I went out to teach or do church work, my husband stayed home. When I came in, he would go out and preach or teach, and I stayed home. We could not do much together or function as a normal family.

Every day as I worked around the house and watched our daughter's health deteriorate, I read and re-read those words: "Beareth all things, believeth all things, hopeth all things, endureth all things." God truly gave me strength to bear all things. He increased my faith so I could believe in His will and healing powers. Hope never failed to lift me above the crisis! His Word gave me strength to endure the hard time we were experiencing. In God's perfect timing, we were able to get help for our daughter. God's love never fails!

Reba Dutton
Missionary to Korea

6 FROM FATHER TO DAUGHTER

"That Christ may dwell in your hearts by faith; that ye, being rooted and grounded in love" (Ephesians 3:17).

When our daughter, Britney, was 17, our youth department went through the "True Loves Waits" series. Afterwards, they signed a "pledge of purity" card, promising to stay sexually pure until marriage. It was suggested that the fathers take their daughters out on a date and give them a special gift to commemorate their pledge. It could be anything — maybe something engraved, like a bracelet or necklace. What my husband, Ken, did meant so much to Britney that I thought I would share it.

Ken bought Britney a silver, one-quarter carat diamond cluster ring and presented it to her on Valentine's Day along with a precious love letter. She was so excited and surprised! Here is that letter:

To my beautiful Britney, (my little worm)

I love you so much. You are such a wonderful gift from God. You have made me so happy, and I am so proud of you. I love who you are. I wanted to give you something very special today. I wanted to be the one who gave you your first diamond. I hope you love it and will wear it. This is to represent my feelings for you and our special relationship. I chose this ring (with your mother's help) to represent your value and beauty. The small stones are for all the many joys you have brought and all the ones to come (your mother's words when we saw it at the store). This ring is a symbol of your commitment to God and to me. A commitment to stay pure and holy until your wedding night. I know you belong to God, but He has given you to me to love, protect, and care for. You are mine until the day I give you away to the man God has chosen for you to marry. I hope that you will wear this to remind you, until the day it is replaced with an engagement ring. Never forget how much I love you. You will always be my little worm.

Love, Dad

O Father, thank You for giving Britney such a wonderful dad. They have such an awesome relationship. I love them both so much. Please, bless all the fathers for they are a reflection of You. Please help Britney to keep her commitment.

Jennifer Barnett

7 ATTITUDE ADJUSTMENT

"Set a watch, O Lord, before my mouth; keep the door of my lips. Incline not my heart to any evil thing, to practice wicked works with men that work iniquity: and let me not eat of their dainties" (Psalm 141:3-4).

I worked with a woman that could not get along with anyone, unless they worked in higher management. No matter how you tried, it never worked. Everyone has a person in his or her life that fits this description. It may be a co-worker, a family member, or even a church member.

Well, it seemed to be my turn for her attention. After several months of conflict, I decided it was time to take action to end this problem. I had been sharing my problem with God, but I had not asked Him to take care of it for me. It was time for me to let God handle her, and I knew just what was needed — some good hard "Scripture for thought." I knew it had to come from God.

I kept asking Him to show me the Scripture on what to say and do in this situation. I knew my strength was in God and His Word, and He always gave to me what I needed. Finally, during my daily Bible reading he gave me Psalm 141:3-4.

I laughed and cried when I read it. The good hard "Scripture for thought" was from my Father to me and not to her. It changed my attitude and was just what I needed. It reminded me that God works in His children, and I am His.

Nora Byrd

8 Being An Armourbearer

"And Jonathan said to the young man that bare his armour, Come, and let us go over unto the garrison of these uncircumcised: it may be that the Lord will work for us: for there is no restraint to the Lord to save by many or by few. And his armourbearer said unto him, Do all that is in thine heart: turn thee; behold, I am with thee according to thy heart. And Jonathan climbed up upon his hands and upon his feet, and his armourbearer after him: and they fell before Jonathan; and his armourbearer slew after him" (I Samuel 14:6-7, 13).

Two against an army – not the best of odds if you ask me! The Philistines have set up camp, and Saul should be getting ready to go to battle with them. Saul did not keep the commandment of the Lord, and he is in pretty big trouble. The only weapons to be found belong to Saul and Jonathan. Jonathan takes off, with his armourbearer at his side, and prepares to fight this Philistine army.

In today's culture, we don't think much about armourbearers. But for Jonathan, his armourbearer was his closest ally. *WEBSTER'S DICTIONARY* defines an armourbearer as someone who carried the armor or weapons for a warrior. When Jonathan told his armourbearer what the plan was, the immediate response he received was, "Do all that is in thine heart...I am with thee," no questions asked. The armourbearer believed so much in Jonathan's walk with God that he was willing to follow him into what seemed to be suicide. He not only followed him into battle, but he also fought the battle with him. Because of his faithfulness, he lived to tell the story of how God used the two of them to smite the Philistines.

So what does this mean to us as women? Several years ago, I was challenged to seek out a woman of God that was fighting in today's spiritual battle, someone who was a warrior for Christ and was not afraid to step out on a limb for Him. I found that person, and I knew right away that I could follow her and fight in the battle alongside her. I trust her walk with Christ, to follow her even when it seems that we are headed into the heaviest part of the battle.

Are you bearing anyone's armor today? If not, seek out a warrior, someone who believes God can use the two of you to deliver a nation, and be an armourbearer for her. To my warrior, it's a privilege to fight in the battle with you. Do all that is in thine heart. I am with thee.

Cassie Belbey

9 ARE YOU WILLING TO SACRIFICE?

"If any man serve me, let him follow me; and where I am, there shall also my servant be: if any man serve me, him will my Father honour" (John 12:26).

Robby was a beautiful little boy – full of life and a joy to be around. He always tried to please you and made you feel so proud to be a part of his life. His grades were as good as his behavior. His smile was so captivating, and he was always happy to see you.

Sometime in the spring, the teacher was talking about how proud she was of the children, and she knew they would all be ready for second grade. Robby began having small problems. His work was not finished quite like it always had been. He was also doing little things that he had not done before. The teacher was getting concerned, but Robby did not seem to know why there was such a change.

At home, Robby asked his mom if he had to go to second grade, because he didn't want to go. During their conversation, his mom figured out this was his way of getting to stay where he was happy and content. If he was bad, the teacher would have to keep him. In his small way, he sacrificed to keep what was dear to him.

In my life, what is so dear to me? How badly do I want what is important? Am I willing to sacrifice? Can I be committed to do what the Lord says to obtain what He has in store for me? The Lord's blessings are more numerous than I can imagine and more wonderful than words can even express.

Sandra McKeehan

10 God, I Want A Banana!

"Therefore take no thought, saying, What shall we eat? or, What shall we drink? ... But seek ye first the kingdom of God, and his righteousness; and all these things shall be added unto you" (Matthew 6:31 & 33).

Tanya was tired. She had put in a long day at work and was on her way home when she remembered there was the weekly ladies' meeting at the church. She enjoyed the interaction with the other women. As a new Christian, she had learned much about Jesus Christ as they all studied the Bible together. Tanya debated, "Should I attend tonight or not?"

Just then, Tanya spied some beautiful yellow bananas. A vendor was sitting on the street on her upside-down pail, calling to the pedestrians to stop and buy her bananas. "They look delicious!" Tanya remarked to herself. "I want one!"

Tanya approached the vendor and asked, "How much is one of the bananas?" The lady answered, "One banana will cost you one lei, 50 bani." Tanya counted her money. She had exactly one lei, 25 bani. "Please let me have a banana for 25 bani less; I don't have any more money," begged Tanya. "Absolutely not!" the vendor emphatically retorted. "I am not in the business of giving away bananas!" Tanya prayed, "Oh God, I want a banana. Please give me a banana." Although Tanya walked the streets to find a banana for the amount of money she had in her hand, she was always refused.

"Well," debated Tanya. "Should I even make the effort to attend the ladies' meeting at church tonight? I'm tired and want a banana, and God didn't even answer my prayer!" Suddenly Tanya decided, "Banana or no banana, I'm going to church!" She hurried to the meeting, hoping she wouldn't be late.

They had a guest speaker that evening. Tanya listened to the message of God's provision for our needs and even our wants. "Well, she doesn't understand," mused Tanya. "She doesn't understand that God doesn't give us what we want. I learned that tonight when I craved a banana!" The speaker finished and made a closing announcement: "As I was preparing my speech this week, I felt led of God to fill a bag of goodies for each of you ladies. My assistants will distribute them now. Enjoy!"

The bags were quickly passed out. Tanya reached for her sack, wondering what it contained. Opening the bag, she spied a huge orange. "Wow!" she thought. "What a treat! I could never afford this!" There was also a large red apple, shined to perfection; two gourmet chocolates wrapped in colorful foil; and last but not least, at the bottom lay a beautiful yellow banana! "God did hear my prayer," Tanya wept with delight. "And He even gave me more than I asked for! Am I ever glad I put Him first and didn't go home in a huff when I thought He wasn't listening to me! How much I would have missed!"

God sees the secret desires of our hearts and gives us the gifts He deems best. In fact, He often gives us much more than our needs; He also knows our wants. What a loving, heavenly Father we have, and all because of the great sacrifice of His Son, the Lord Jesus Christ. What can we lack?

Loreen Ittermann
Missionary to Moldova

11 LOVE YOUR NEIGHBORS

"By this shall all men know that ye are my disciples, if ye have love one to another" (John 13:35).

Before my quiet time with the Lord, I always ask God to show me something out of place in my life. One day while reading out of Psalms, God really spoke to my heart. In Psalm 35, David talked about rewarding evil with good. He said,

"They rewarded me evil for good to the spoiling of my soul. But as for me, when they were sick, my clothing was sack-cloth: I humbled my soul with fasting; and my prayer returned into mine own bosom" (Psalm 35:12-13).

Then I thought about my neighbors. They are unkind and are not the sort of people you think you should be around. I realized, however, from this passage that they needed my example and prayers. I am probably the only Bible they have seen. I was also convicted about not being very friendly toward them. I do not know if they are all healthy or not. What kind of Christian does not know if their neighbors are ill?

Lord, help me to be a good neighbor and pray for those who do evil to me. Help me to always be forgiving and to not judge.

Sandy Smith

12 SHARING GOD'S LOVE

"Beloved, let us love one another: for love is of God; and every one that loveth is born of God, and knoweth God" (I John 4:7).

I have an older brother who lives by himself and is an introvert. Even though he lives 400 miles away from me, I make sure that I tell him I love him every time I talk to him on the phone, and when I see him in person, I make sure he gets a big hug from me. He doesn't always respond, and sometimes I know it makes him feel awkward, but I can see that it means a lot to him.

He made me start thinking of how many people I come into contact with who haven't had that same kindness. People who haven't heard the words "I love you" or received a hug or a touch from another person in a while or maybe never. We all want to be loved and to feel needed by others. God's Word tells us He is no respecter of persons. He loves each and every one, even the ones we name loveless.

How many people do we come into contact with daily who have never experienced God's love? What kind of changes would we see in others if we were willing to reach out and share God's love? It really doesn't take that much extra time to go that extra step. Share God's love today.

Dear Lord, help me today to show Your love to everyone I meet. Teach me to love others as You do.

Sarah Partin

13 ARE YOU SPEAKING MY LANGUAGE?

"Though I speak with the tongues of men and of angels, and have not charity, I am become as sounding brass, or a tinkling cymbal" (I Corinthians 13:1).

One summer I came across an interesting book, *THE FIVE LOVE LANGUAGES*. As I began reading this book, I realized how very important it is for me to learn to speak the correct language of love, not only to my husband, but also to my children and grandchildren. I am a gift giver, so it was not surprising to me when I found out that my language of love is gifts. It doesn't have to be expensive or even material. A gift of time or just being thought of in a special way interprets love to me. Does my family understand this language, or do I sound like a tinkling cymbal?

Now that we have a Spanish ministry growing in our church, I can see the vast need of being able to speak in the language that is familiar. Communication is hindered in an unbelievable way when the language barrier is staring you in the face. One of our dear ladies continues to say to me, "Oh, Ms. Katy, please speak Spanish!" My only reply is a promise that I will continue to try. I feel helpless when there is something I would like to say to her and equally helpless when there is something that she desires to say to me.

In John 13:34, we are told, "A new commandment I give

unto you, That ye love one another; as I have loved you, that ye also love one another." God has never had any trouble speaking our language. He knows exactly what to say to us, and He knows how to say it so that we can understand.

Dear God, please help us to see the cries of those around us begging us to please speak their love language and show them Christ in us in a way they can clearly understand.

Katy Ripley

14 WHAT IS LOVE?

"For God so loved the world, that he gave his only begotten Son, that whosoever believeth in him should not perish, but have everlasting life" (John 3:16).

Do we understand love? I don't think a person has lived who fully understands the love of God. To me, John 3:16 says it all. God loves me, and He gave his only Son for my sins. I have given a lot of thought to how we say "I love you," and it is just words. Do we love the people of the world? I know it is hard to do, but I am praying that I can do it more than I have.

In Ephesians 3:17-19, the Apostle Paul sought to give the measurements of God's love: "That Christ may dwell in your hearts by faith; that ye, being rooted and grounded in love, May be able to comprehend with all saints what is the breadth, and length, and depth, and height; And to know the love of Christ, which passeth knowledge, that ye might be filled with all the fulness of God."

Can any of us describe love any better than God does from His own Word? God so loved the world!

Marvaline Smith

15 ANGELS WATCHING OVER ME

"For he shall give his angels charge over thee, to keep thee in all thy ways" (Psalm 91:11).

Several years ago, Mama, my son, and I were driving in the country. As I was preparing to make a turn onto another road, I put my turn signal on and began to slow down. I did not realize my turn signal was broken, and I did not notice the large gravel truck speeding up behind us. Suddenly, I heard a voice in my head say, "Look up." At that moment, I saw the truck in my rearview mirror and made a fast turn. Mama, who was holding the dashboard, said, "Didn't you take that turn a little fast?" She didn't see the truck, but my son and Someone else did.

Another time we were in an unusual, dangerous circumstance that occurred when our son was a baby. I was on the way to purchase a car seat for him. He was sitting in the front seat in an infant carrier that he had almost outgrown. It was a beautiful, clear day with very little traffic. I began to drive up a sharp incline with a steep embankment on my side of the road. At that point, I heard a voice say, "Slow down." Just as I slowed down, a young man in a car came speeding over the hill in the middle of the road directly toward us. I managed to pull to the side and get out of his way. Our son was thrown to the floor, but he was only shaken up, not hurt. All I could think of was that we could have gone down that embankment or been hit head-on by that car if I had not slowed down when I did.

Heavenly Father, we love You and thank You so much for the protection You give freely to those who are saved through the precious blood of Your Son, Jesus Christ, Who died so we could live forever in Your love. We thank You, Lord, for all the many blessings You give us, even though we are not worthy. Still You love us and bless us. We thank You and honor You through Your precious Son, Jesus.

Pat Porter

16 Burnout

"...weeping may endure for a night, but joy cometh in the morning" (Psalm 30:5).

It was the summer of 2001, and after working in the church for almost four years with many responsibilities, my health began to give me problems. I believed erroneously that "good" stress would not hurt the body – I loved everything I was doing! But all of my activities were taking their toll. I had high blood pressure, and I was always feeling stressed, although I didn't know why. We sought help from all kinds of doctors, but none gave me the relief I needed. Finally, after two weeks of almost no sleep and the horrible side effects of that, such as depression, weight loss, and panic attacks, I gave in to some medication that I did not want to take.

During this time, my husband did not know what to do with me. I had never acted this way before. He would not let me out of his sight or would ask someone from the church to stay with me. One of the women was an invaluable friend and help. She rubbed my back and feet to help me relax, but most of all she was my friend and prayed for me.

Little by little, I began to feel normal again. Through all of those dark days I knew the Lord was with me, and I felt this was to be a pruning and growing experience. What a learning adventure I have had! It has given me greater confidence in the Lord's control of my life.

Aloha Vance
Missionary to Canada

17 I'D RATHER BE HERE WITH YOU

"…in the shadow of thy wings will I make my refuge…" (Psalm 57:1).

My heart was stirred by the message in the following story, and how easily it can be adapted to our daily Christian walk. First of all, to me it states so beautifully, from a child's standpoint, just how we should be following our Lord in order to have the close, loving relationship with Him that He desires for His children. Secondly, whatever this mother in the story was doing, she was making an impression on her son. He could not possibly follow so closely that she could step on his toes without his taking note of her words, actions, and attitude. He felt comfortable and safe right wherever she was, close to her, touching her, and under her wings of love. That's where we are safe and loved – close to our Lord.

On My Heels

My three year old was on my heels no matter where I went. Whenever I stopped to do something and turned back around, I would trip over him. I patiently suggested fun activities to keep him occupied. But he simply smiled an innocent smile and said, "Oh, that's all right, Mommy. I'd rather be here with you." Then he continued to bounce happily along behind me. After stepping on his toes for the fifth time, I began to lose patience. When I asked him why he was acting this way, he looked up at me with sweet green eyes and said, "Well, Mommy, my Sunday School teacher told me to walk in Jesus' footsteps. I can't see Him, so I'm walking in yours."

Author Unknown

In the Scriptures, Jesus spoke of Himself as our friend. We all know that the relationship between two friends is one of security, protection, and love. There has never been a closer relationship than that of Jesus and His Father. We must have the heartfelt desire to be so close to our Savior that we emulate His relationship with His Father as He stated in John 5:19: "...The Son can do nothing of himself, but what he seeth the Father do: for what things soever he doeth, these also doeth the Son likewise." Jesus was telling us here that He was watching the Father, and whatever He (the Father) was doing, He did it also. One cannot watch another without being close to them. Obviously, we can't physically see our heavenly Father, but we can watch through studying the Scriptures, prayer, worship, ministry, etc. Do we desire to be in His Word (where He is)? Do we long for prayer at the throne (where He resides)? Do we "bounce happily along," meditating, and communing with Him moment by moment? Psalm 104:34 says, "My meditation of him shall be sweet: I will be glad in the Lord."

Are we daily heeding our Savior's words in John 12:26? "If any man serve me, let him follow me; and where I am, there shall also my servant be...." How it must thrill our Savior when He sees in our lives the desire to be close to Him! Do we as God's children have the desire that the little boy had, so that we can sincerely tell our Savior, "I'd rather be here with you?"

Anita Williams

18 I WISH, I WISH

"Not that I speak in respect of want: for I have learned, in whatsoever state I am, therewith to be content" (Philippians 4:11).

One day when I was playing with my granddaughter, she said, "Mi-Mi, I wish you were a young girl!" I laughed and said, "I wish I was also, but I am not, so you will have to enjoy playing with me just the way I am."

We are familiar with the song, "When You Wish Upon A

Star." As Christians, we sometimes wish that things were different: I wish I had more money, I wish I had a different job, and I wish I had a new car. The list could go on forever. We are so caught up wanting things to be different or wanting something else that we often forget to enjoy the moment we are living in at the present. We are blessed with food, clothes, a warm home, and all of the wonderful things we have because of knowing the Lord. We have the peace and joy of the Lord, the security of our future, and blessings beyond measure.

The next time you find yourself wishing, stop and enjoy the moment God has given you. May we learn to live Philippians 4:11.

Pat Bishop
Wife of Ron Bishop
SCORE International

19 THE POWER OF NO PRAYER

"...God forbid that I should sin against the Lord in ceasing to pray for you..." (I Samuel 12:23).

Since my salvation in May 1993, I have experienced the power of prayer. I have seen people healed because of prayer. I have seen many lives turned around because someone was praying. I have seen people give their lives to Jesus because someone loved them enough to pray for them. I have even had the awesome experience of praying with several people to accept Jesus into their hearts to become Lord of their lives. The lesson I have just recently learned is the power of no prayer.

I have learned that not praying for those we love leaves an open door of opportunity for Satan to destroy their lives. I learned this by reading *THE POWER OF A PRAYING WIFE* by

Stormie Omartian. I bought the book thinking it would tell me how to pray for my husband, and how I would change him through my prayers. I was not expecting what I got from it.

It has shown me how I need to change! I have fallen short as a wife, friend, and prayer partner for the most significant person in my life, other than the Lord Jesus Christ. I'm not saying that I didn't pray for my husband, but my prayers were so vague. I realized that there were so many areas of need that I never brought up in prayer. Those areas included his fears, his relationships, his past, his emotions, his fatherhood, and his future. The list goes on and on. It did not occur to me that he might have weaknesses or struggles in these areas and so many more. I now see how he fights a war in his mind daily with a world of temptations facing him each day.

I realized that by not praying for him, I was leaving a major gap open for Satan to work and try to destroy our marriage and our family. I have asked my husband to forgive me, and he did. I have promised to lift him up in prayer every day to block out the power of no prayer and to bathe him in the power of love through Jesus Christ our Lord.

I can't fix all that is wrong in our hearts and lives, but God can! It is my job to pray. Then God will do the work.

Kelly Jones

20 NOTHING IS TOO HARD FOR HIM

"Behold, I am the Lord, the God of all flesh: is there any thing too hard for me?" (Jeremiah 32:27).

Before we left for England, a dear friend of mine framed several Bible verses she had done in calligraphy as a gift for our family. She had chosen several of our favorite verses. However, she chose one on her own and wrote it on a small card. I placed that small, unframed calligraphy card on my kitchen window, where it has been for many years. That verse was Jeremiah 32:27. Little did she know how much God would use that verse to impact my life. All through life we face difficult challenges and changes, whether it be moving to a new culture, a new ministry, or a new job, or dealing with an empty nest or the death of a loved one. So many times we go through life in our own strength. We pray and say we leave burdens at the foot of the cross, yet we get up, pick them up, and carry them with us.

God will perform His perfect work in our lives. We must learn that we can do nothing apart from God. We must learn to rest in His love and draw strength from His power. We serve the God of all flesh. Nothing is too hard for Him.

Debbie Woodard
Missionary to England

21 HEART OF WORSHIP

"Although the fig tree shall not blossom, neither shall fruit be in the vines; the labour of the olive shall fail, and the fields shall yield no meat; the flock shall be cut off from the fold, and there shall be no herd in the stalls: Yet I will rejoice in the Lord, I will joy in the God of my salvation" (Habakkuk 3:17-18).

I often pray, "God give me the heart for Your desire in my life. Help me to see through Your eyes. Give me Your vision." My whole heart's desire is to have a heart of worship. Habakkuk 2:3 says, "For the vision is yet an appointed time, but at the end it shall speak, and not lie: though it tarry, wait for it; because it will surely come, it will not tarry."

I believe my actions and reactions to everyday life are a measure of my obedience, my faith, my trust in God's vision, and ultimately my heart of worship. When I lose sight of Him for any reason, it affects my heart of worship. It could be easy to lose God's vision if I do not trust Him, because I'm facing a trial or I think He does not hear my prayer. My flesh's tendency is to take over, but I realize that losing sight of Him is a reflection of areas in my life where I lack spiritual growth.

God is God. He does not change. He is the same yesterday, today, and forever. I want to have a true heart of worship — praising His name and trusting His vision, whether it carries me through the mountains or the valleys. He is worthy of my whole heart and unconditional worship.

Cyndi Copeland

22 PREVENTING TEMPTATION

"There hath no temptation taken you but such as is common to man: but God is faithful, who will not suffer you to be tempted above that ye are able; but will with the temptation also make a way to escape, that ye may be able to bear it" (I Corinthians 10:13).

"If you find yourself in a questionable situation, get out immediately." As a high school teacher, I have conveyed this quote many times to my students. My own children can also recall hearing this statement in our home. I would explain to them if a situation took place that was not in their control to call home immediately. They would not be in trouble if they called for a way out.

For example: My son is given permission to visit one of his friends in the neighborhood on a Saturday afternoon. His friend's older brother comes home from college with his roommate in tow These older boys are up to no good. My son, knowing the possibilities of trouble coming, is to call home immediately for me or his dad to come and get him. He has found a way out and follows through. If he lingers there knowingly and curiously waiting to see what will transpire, judgment from his mom and dad will be severe and quick!

As a mom, to think my children would never face temptation is foolishness. Did you know the opposite meaning of foolishness is wisdom? Wisdom would be to train up our children in His ways. Our responsibility as moms is to give our children "tools" to use not only while they are in our homes, but most importantly when they are out from under our authority. Teach them now while they are young that you are there for them, and help them to have a mindset that prevention outweighs consequences!

Dear Lord, help me to instill into my children that they need to live a life honorable to You. Help me to lift them up in prayer to You daily, and for my life to be lived in a way to be an example for them.

Denise Phillips

23 VISION OF AN EAGLE OR A CHICKEN

"But as for you, ye thought evil against me; but God meant it unto good, to bring to pass, as it is this day, to save much people alive" (Genesis 50:20).

Every day God gives me a choice concerning the way I will view things. An illustration used by Brother Jeff Adams, Pastor of Kansas City Baptist Temple, included the comparison of the vision of a chicken and an eagle. A chicken wanders around on the ground and only sees things at eye level and at a short distance. An eagle soars in the sky and sees a wide view of things below. I try to keep this illustration in my memory as a reminder to stay focused on Christ and not the circumstances.

My mom and stepdad lost their house to a fire a few years ago. To add to the loss, it was on Christmas Eve. Two days later, my stepdad had a heart attack. Some may think, "What could be worse?" But God is faithful to turn what the Devil means for bad into something that will bring glory unto the name of the Lord. That came a few months later when my stepdad received Christ as His Savior.

Just as the eagle in the illustration could see the wide view, Christ knows the big picture of our lives. He reminds me that He has just asked me to trust and obey Him. When the path is not clear, He has promised us that His Word would be a lamp to guide us to the next step.

Amanda McKay

24 LOVE BEGETS LOVE

"We love him, because he first loved us" (I John 4:19).

"I love you," he said, as we sat side by side on the floor of his apartment. My face must have lost all its color, as I remained motionless and speechless. I had to respond, but how? I knew he loved me. I could see it in his gentle patience with my sometimes overwhelming enthusiasm. So what was the problem? I'd said it back to plenty of other well-meaning boys. It was teenage etiquette, but things were different now. God had changed my heart, and I was determined this relationship would be different. I wouldn't echo those words until I was sure he was Mr. Right.

Just as I was about to explain my hesitation, he took my hand and whispered softly, "It's okay. You don't have to say it back." Tears began to roll down my face. How blessed I was! Here sat a wonderful man who loved me, regardless of my feelings for him.

We remained silent for what seemed like forever. This must have been what John meant when he said, "We love him, because he first loved us" (I John 4:19). Apart from God, we haven't the ability to truly love anyone. We, like I was in those teenaged relationships, are just in it for the benefits. God loves us because of Who He is, not for who we are or what we can do for Him. He is love, and love begets love.

Needless to say, it wasn't very long before I was able to tell Mr. Right that I loved him, too. Since that day, we've had three little ones with whom to share that love. Each of us uses those three little words as often as we can!

Melissa Whitt, wife of Michael Whitt
Pastor of Calvary Baptist Church
Cottonwood, Alabama

25 God Keeps His Commitments

"And said, By myself I have sworn, saith the Lord, for because thou hast done this thing, and hast not withheld thy son, thine only son: That in blessing I will bless thee..." (Genesis 22:16-17).

During my troubled marriage, I had committed my life to Jesus. Obviously I had made a mess of things trying to run my own life, so I turned everything over to His control—my finances, my career plans, and especially my children. After my divorce, my first concern was to find a good church. In particular, I wanted one with an Awana program and Christian friends for my 12-year-old daughter and 9-year-old son. I thought I knew just the right one, but setting aside my own thoughts, I asked God to reveal His plan to me. He led me to a small inner-city church. I was appalled. This was not at all what I had in mind.

Realistically, my children would never make friends with the wild kids from the projects. I was certain that they would be so frightened at their first sight of the drug addicts, the alcoholics, and prostitutes attending the services that they would refuse to come back with me. Most of all, their father would turn this against me in our custody battle. He had already filed papers claiming that I was an unfit mother. This would just convince the judge that he was right. Without exaggeration, I was risking the loss of my children. It was a decision I agonized over, but God kept reminding me, "You gave me your children. You said you'd go wherever I sent you." I had to keep my commitment, so I joined that poor little church.

I didn't lose my children, and my children loved that church. They exhilarated in the vitality, the raw honesty, and the stark exposure to another side of life. They were baptized in that church and developed teaching and leadership skills, compassion, and values for what's really important in life. I kept my commitment to God, and He kept His to my children.

Joanna McAbee

26 LET YOUR LIGHT SHINE

"Ye are the light of the world. A city that is set on an hill cannot be hid. Neither do men light a candle, and put it under a bushel, but on a candlestick; and it giveth light unto all that are in the house. Let your light so shine before men, that they may see your good works, and glorify your Father which is in heaven" (Matthew 5:14-16).

When I was living away from home for the first time during my freshman year at Auburn University, my mom regularly sent me care packages filled with homemade goodies. As a college student who survived on pizza and the vending machine, I was always grateful for these expressions of love, and my friends were, too. Whenever a package came, I had to pick it up at the campus post office in the middle of the quad. As I walked back to my dorm and up three flights of stairs to my room – lugging a big, brown box – I got lots of curious stares. For the rest of the day, my friends poked their heads in my room, looking for a handout. I was always happy to share, because my mom always sent too much. To all the girls who lived in Owen Hall that year, there was no question that my mom loved me, and she gave me something special to share.

Isn't that a perfect picture of God's love for us? He loved us so much that He sent His Son to die for us, and that's a gift that should be as obvious in our lives as those big boxes I carried across campus. God's Word tells us in Matthew 5:14-16 to let our light shine before men. That means other people should see our light, be curious about it, and look for a handout. Just like my mom's care packages, Jesus Christ is a gift worth sharing.

Dear Lord, thank You for my mom's love and all the gifts she has given me. The most important gift she ever gave me was telling me about Your Son. Help me to let my light shine, so I can share that gift with others.

Dawn Kent

27 Why Does God Allow Problems In Your Life?

"And he said unto me, My grace is sufficient for thee: for my strength is made perfect in weakness. Most gladly therefore will I rather glory in my infirmities, that the power of Christ may rest upon me" (II Corinthians 12:9).

On the mission field, we're always faced with problems and have one choice: to let them defeat us or let them build us. God is trying to say something when He permits problems to come into our lives. It all depends on how you respond to them. Most people fail to see how God wants to use problems for good in their lives. We react foolishly and resent them rather than stopping to consider what benefit they might bring. Consider five ways God wants to use our problems:

To direct us – God often lights fires under us to get us moving, motivate us to change, and point us in a new direction. Is God trying to get your attention right now? (Proverbs 20:30)

To inspect us – People are like tea bags. If we want to know what's inside them, just drop them into hot water. Is God testing your faith with a problem? What does it reveal about you? (James 1:2-3)

To correct us – Some lessons we learn only through pain and failure. Just like when you were told not to touch something hot, you didn't listen, and you got burned. Sometimes we only learn the value of our health, money, or relationships by losing them. (Psalm 119:71-72)

To protect us – Problems can be a blessing in disguise if it prevents us from being harmed by something more serious. (Genesis 50:20)

To perfect us – Problems, when responded to correctly, are character builders. God is far more interested in your character than your comfort. Your relationship to God and your character are the only two things you're going to take with you into eternity. (Romans 5:3-4)

God is at work in your life – even if you don't recognize or understand it. It's much easier and profitable if you see what He's trying to teach you, and what you can learn from Him, rather than to figure out a solution on your own. Set your thoughts not on the storm, but on the one who rules over the storm.

Sue Laparra
Missionary to Guatemala

28 MY CALL TO OBEDIENCE

"And thou shalt love the Lord thy God with all thine heart, and with all thy soul, and with all thy might" (Deuteronomy 6:5).

As Christians, we are commanded to obey. This command has never been more clear to me than it has been recently.

What happens when God gives you the "desires of your heart" and then tests you to find out if He is still "number one" in your life? "Would you give up that which is so precious to you in order to prove to me that I come first?" "Will you obey Me by letting Me decide what is best for you and your life?" These are questions God posed to me recently. I wanted to question what God was asking of me. What I found was that when I stopped trying to figure it out on my own, and stopped struggling against God and obeyed Him, He gave me a peace that passes all understanding. I still didn't understand His reasoning for the "test," but I accepted it and obeyed.

Two weeks later, during my daily Bible reading in Deuteronomy 6-11, God graciously answered my questions. In these chapters shortly before entering the Promised Land, Moses is giving an overview of what God had done for the children of Israel. He reminds them that the first commandment is to love God with all of their heart, soul, and might. I thought of Abraham and how God asked him to give up Isaac, the one person so dear to his heart. Because of Abraham's obedience, God spared Isaac. I realized that God understands how much it hurts to give up someone precious to us; He gave His Son that He loved so much. Jesus responded in obedience to His Father's will. "Who am I?" I asked myself, "to question my faithful Father when He calls for my obedience?"

The story ends on a happy note, for in chapter 11, we see the blessings that come from obedience. This Scripture confirms what we should remember; our Father knows what's best for us, and when we don't understand and don't see His plan, when we can't trace His hand, we must trust His heart.

Cheryl McCurley

29 THE HANDS OF GOD

"God hath spoken once; twice have I heard this; that power belongeth unto God" (Psalm 62:11).

The hands of God are greater
Than our human hands of clay,
For they can handle any problem
That comes to us each day.

We fume and fret, and worry more
When a conflict does arise,
While all the time the hands of God
Could be brushing the clouds from our skies

How often have we prayed and said,
"It's in the Master's hands,"
But then we snatch our burden back
And begin to fret again?

Don't we see that God's hands are powerful
And can meet our every need;
They can even solve our problems
Before them we ever see.

So we never have to hurry
Over future dates and plans
And we never have to worry
Because it's all in God's strong hands.

Margaret Hoskins Dellinger

When You Thought I Wasn't Looking

When you thought I wasn't looking, I saw you hang my first painting on the refrigerator, and I immediately wanted to paint another one.

When you thought I wasn't looking, I saw you feed a stray cat, and I learned that it was good to be kind to animals.

When you thought I wasn't looking, I saw you make my favorite cake for me, and I learned that the little things can be the special things in life.

When you thought I wasn't looking, I heard you say a prayer, and I knew there is a God I could always talk to and I learned to trust in God.

When you thought I wasn't looking, I saw you make a meal and take it to a friend who was sick, and I learned that we all have to help take care of each other.

When you thought I wasn't looking, I saw you give of your time and money to help people who had nothing, and I learned that those who have something should give to those who don't.

When you thought I wasn't looking, I saw you take care of our house and everyone in it, and I learned we have to take care of what we are given.

When you thought I wasn't looking, I saw how you handled your responsibilities, even when you didn't feel good, and I learned that I would have to be responsible when I grow up.

When you thought I wasn't looking, I saw tears come from your eyes, and I learned that sometimes things hurt, but it's all right to cry.

When you thought I wasn't looking, I saw that you cared, and I wanted to be everything that I could be.

When you thought I wasn't looking, I learned most of life's lessons that I need to know to be a good and productive person when I grow up.

When you thought I wasn't looking, I looked at you and wanted to say, "Thanks for all the things I saw, when you thought I wasn't looking."

1 ARE THE EYES THE WINDOWS TO OUR SOUL?

"...for out of the abundance of the heart the mouth speaketh" (Matthew 12:34).

I think we have all heard the saying, "The eyes are the windows to our soul." This has always made sense to me, because I used to think you could tell a lot about people by the expression on their face.

However, there came a week in my life that taught me to change my way of thinking. Because of a rare accident, I had to have my eyes bandaged up. No one was able to see my eyes, and I was unable to see anyone. I realized once again how important it is to not judge anyone. We are unable to see into their hearts to the real person inside.

Following my accident, I prayed that I would not be legally blind. God was showing me that His desire is that I am not spiritually blind. Over and over, verses came to mind about seeing. In Exodus 3, God reveals Himself through the burning bush in verse 7, saying, "...I have surely seen the affliction of my people which are in Egypt...." God wanted Moses to see what He saw. In the life of Saul of Tarsus, God took away his sight to get his attention while on the road to Damascus.

It was obvious to me that the Lord was leading me to focus on my sight that year. Getting fitted with His glasses will no doubt help me view life and others from a new perspective. In Matthew, God tells us that "out of the abundance of the heart the mouth speaketh." We are using the sense of hearing not seeing to comprehend what is in someone's heart. My prayer is that God will allow me to see the world through His eyes with love and compassion for His children.

Tammy Gordon

2 Waiting On The Lord

"The Lord is good unto them that wait for him, to the soul that seeketh him" (Lamentations 3:25).

The Lord used this verse to give me peace and hope in my life. This may sound silly to some, but a few years ago I had this itch to get married. I was about 22 or 23 years old, and it seemed as if all of my girlfriends were getting married. I had a boyfriend, a college degree, and a job, so in my mind, the timing was perfect. One day I was feeling discouraged and a little frustrated about it, so I mentioned it to my boyfriend. He was not upset that I brought it up, but he didn't really respond in any way, so I still wasn't satisfied. That night, when I was reading in Lamentations, this verse jumped off the page. At that time, God was telling me that He was going to be good to me if I would just wait on Him and continue to seek His face. After reading that, I had so much patience and peace about the future, because the Lord told me through His precious Word to wait on Him and seek Him.

Now, a couple of years later, I have been married for a year and a half, and the Lord has been good to me, just as He said He would. If I do get discouraged any time in the future, I know that I can think back to God's Word in Lamentations 3:25 and remember how the Lord comforted me with that verse.

What are you waiting on the Lord for? For me, at that time, it was marriage. But for you, it could be a job, a house, or a child. Whatever it is, God knows about it. Just wait for His timing and His guidance, because He has a perfect plan for your life. You find that plan by staying faithful to Him and His Word and walking with Him each day.

Stacy DeKoker

3 You Should Have Been There

"Wherefore God also hath highly exalted him, and given him a name which is above every name: That at the name of Jesus every knee should bow, of things in heaven, and things in earth, and things under the earth; And that every tongue should confess that Jesus Christ is Lord, to the glory of God the Father" (Philippians 2:9-11).

Have you ever had someone tell you about the winning play of a game you missed? You try to get into the excitement of the moment as they describe it for you, and then they tell you, "You should have been there."

Perhaps someone is trying to tell you about a funny event. They keep laughing as they try to relate the story, and you just can't get into the moment of it, and then they say, "You should have been there."

What about someone telling you about a church service where God was working? You try to feel the sweet spirit of the service, but you are told, "You should have been there."

There is one event that brings me to tears when I try to imagine it. That moment is when I am finally in the presence of Jesus. My mind cannot comprehend what it will be like to finally experience true worship when I fall before my blessed Lord and Savior. We sing songs of praise and worship and are stirred, but that does not come close to what it will be like. Philippians 2:9-11 tells us that there will be a day when "every knee should bow."

No longer will I be bound by the limitations of this flesh. No longer will the things of the world distract me. I can focus totally on giving Him the honor and praise due Him! No one will be able to say, "You should have been there." I will be there!

Terri Gilliam

4 A Touch From God

"For our light affliction, which is but for a moment, worketh for us a far more exceeding and eternal weight of glory; While we look not at the things which are seen, but at the things which are not seen: for the things which are seen are temporal; but the things which are not seen are eternal" (II Corinthians 4:17-18).

In September 1996, I went to the doctor because I was hurting all over. He said I had fibromyalgia, and for six years, I took strong medicine four times a day. All I did was sleep, and I got so tired of taking medicine. I finally went to another doctor who gave me some medicine that would help me, and it did not make me so sleepy. Besides advising me to eat right and exercise, this doctor also prayed with me every time I was hurting.

I prayed that God would heal my pain, and in October 2002, I was referred to a surgeon who removed my gallbladder. Since then, I have been pain free.

I thank God for healing me and for giving me a Christian doctor and friend in Christ.

Helen Helms

5 Don't Look Back

"Remember Lot's wife" (Luke 17:32).

As a missionary in Zambia, God has taught me a valuable lesson from the national ladies. Of course, it did not happen overnight.

The Zambian women have a very difficult life. They work very hard in their fields each morning. They live without electricity and running water. Most of the time, there is sickness, hunger, and death all around them. Their little mud huts usually do not have the comfort of a bed, couch, pillows, or blankets. They sleep on dirt floors or straw mats, and they cook their food over an open fire. Life expectancy for the people in Zambia is 36 years of age, so death is an everyday part of life.

The Christian ladies in Zambia are amazing. One of our churches asked me to teach a ladies' Bible conference, which went on for three days and three nights. This is one of their favorite things to do. They will travel by foot for miles to go and sleep on the ground and eat very little just to fellowship with their Christian friends and hear the Word of God. I have learned more from them than they have ever learned from me. After each lesson, they responded as innocent children who loved their Father with all their hearts. Day after day, they were so excited about being there! I felt so ashamed at times because I was uncomfortable! It was the hot season, and we were not in an air-conditioned church with padded pews. The Lord was showing me the reason they love Him so sweetly. They do not have all the cares of this world cluttering up their lives and pushing God out.

Jesus tells us in Luke 17:32 to remember Lot's wife. She was married to a wealthy man who years before had split with his Uncle Abraham to live in Sodom. I imagine once they moved to the wicked city, it was uncomfortable for them. But as she set up her new house and things, she tolerated it. Week after week, month after month, getting used to her surroundings, she probably started becoming more comfortable with all the sin. Maybe she even became a part of the sin herself. All this was changed one day. As Lot sat in the gate of the city, the Bible says that his heart was vexed. He probably longed for his old life or maybe longed for a life without all the sin that beset him each and every day. That day, two angels showed up, and he took them to his house. God was going to destroy the city, and the angels had come to see if there were any righteous people in the city. The angels had come to get Lot and his family out of the city. God had mercy on them and gave them a way to escape. God required only that they not look back. The angels literally had to take the family by the hand because they were dragging their feet, wanting to stay just a bit longer. As they ran away from the city, Lot looked around for his wife. Then he spotted a white pillar of salt — a silhouette of a woman looking in the direction of Sodom. What caused her to look back?

I believe she could have looked back because she had her treasures back there — her children, her house, and all her stuff. I do not believe she had a relationship with God. She was more concerned with a life of pleasure and ease. Perhaps all these things caused her feet to slow and her head to turn. Now Jesus uses her for a bad example. He does not even call her by name. Do not look back. Look ahead today. What can we do to lay up treasures in Heaven to show our Savior we love Him with all our hearts and souls? When we live for Him, He is with us and directs our paths. When we think of Lot's wife, what things should we learn from her?

Have a relationship with God. Know Him and trust Him, so that you are not conformed to this world (Romans 12:1-2).

Be satisfied with what you have. Be thankful. Don't covet. Lay up treasures in Heaven, so you are not drawn to the things of the world (Luke 12:31-34).

Be in subjection to the authority God has set up. Follow your Lord, your husband, and your pastor.

God has shown me why the Zambian ladies can love Him so sweetly and with such a pure heart. It is because they have so little. He is their Father Whom they need, and they put their trust in Him every minute of every day.

Becky Bonner
Missionary to Zambia

6 SAVED BY FAITH, NOT BY SERVICE

"And he said to the woman, Thy faith hath saved thee; go in peace" (Luke 7:50).

After first reading about the woman who anointed Jesus' feet with oil in Luke 7:36-50, I thought, "What a sweet story of this woman's love for Jesus!" However, God has a way of making us see what He intended in His Word.

I read this passage days before Brother Doug Ripley preached it, but I did not realize how it was written for me until after the sermon. This event describes how I ought to serve God and how I desperately want to serve Him. The verses show that this woman gave no thought to her surroundings. She served God without worry of who was watching, what they might say, or how they might think of her. She also served with humility and passion. She submitted to washing our Master's feet, and she did so with expensive oil and her own hair.

Her example shows me that it is truly not our service that saves us — it's our faith. Only a strong faith could make a woman use her crown of hair — her most prized possession — to wash a part of the body that is considered dirty. Faith allows one to put aside fleshly desires and truly obey the will of God.

I want to serve Him this way, with total submission and without regard for self or others. I want my service to be a reflection of my faith.

Jennifer Screws

7 HE STRENGTHENS ME

"I can do all things through Christ which strengtheneth me" (Philippians 4:13).

In August 1994, Mom and I were washing dishes together at her house, chatting about different things. Out of the blue, Mom said: "You have dealt with more hardships at your young age than I have in all of my life, and I wish I could take all the pain away." Then she just cried. I was 28 years old then, and I didn't really think about what she said at the time, but over the years it has kept coming back to me.

You see, from 1986 to 1994, I experienced a lot of bad things in my life. It was a very confusing time, because all my life I had served the Lord, and I thought He had forgotten about me. My parents raised me in church. I even lived next door to the church. I was there literally every time the door was open.

My family was a singing group, and we traveled on Friday and Saturday nights to sing just about anywhere. My parents loved to praise the Lord, and so did I. When I asked Jesus into my heart, my life was changed, and it gave me a greater desire to do more for Christ than I already had done. I guess I had lived a life of serving the Lord to some extent and didn't really know it. I really believed the protection of the Lord Jesus Christ was with me because He was with me all the time, even before I had asked Him into my heart, and because of my parents having personal relationships with Jesus Christ.

Every now and then since that time in 1994, I have thought about what mom said, and in the same thought God has given me Philippians 4:13. Now as I look back, I really understand how my mom felt by wanting to take away my pain, but Christ actually did it for me. Through this whole time of heartache, God was actually giving me a tremendous amount of strength to deal with it all. I see now His strength, guidance, grace, protection, and many other ways the Lord worked in me. It is difficult to let go of the past, but God has taken it from me. I give all the glory and praise to my Lord and Savior Jesus Christ for all of it. I truly know the strength and power of the Lord.

Thank You, God, for Your strength for each and every day.

Laura Vest

8 DRIVE YOUR STAKE

"For whosoever shall call upon the name of the Lord shall be saved" (Romans 10:13).

After we joined Decatur Baptist Church, we got involved in ministry, and everything seemed to be going great. I had a good marriage, a great job, and I was pregnant with my daughter, Olivia. However, something was missing! I went through the motions in church, my marriage, and my job, but I felt lost inside! Most days I didn't know if I was coming or going! I was miserable, but I couldn't pinpoint why. Finally, in tears one night, I confided my feelings to my husband. I was ready to quit church, because I couldn't see the use of attending. I was getting nothing out of it.

We called our department director, and he came over that Saturday, which was October 31, 1992. He went through the plan of salvation. I knew that I had been saved at an early age, but what I needed was assurance of my salvation. I was raised in a Southern Baptist church and was saved when I was nine years old. I could remember my sister telling me one Saturday night that she didn't like me and neither did Jesus. After my dad got out of the shower, I went to tell on my sister. It didn't bother me that she hated me, but the thought that maybe Jesus hated me was more than I could stand. My dad shared the plan of salvation with me, and I accepted Christ as my Savior that night.

My department director helped me see that what I was going through was a battle with the Devil. You see, it's not until we start serving God that the Devil tries to get in our way. The Devil was trying to convince me that I was too young when I got saved, and I was falling for it because I couldn't remember the exact date. The Devil used this to confuse me and to try to convince me that I couldn't be saved. In my heart, I knew better. Through prayer and receiving assurance on that Halloween day, I settled the issue once and for all. I drove a spiritual stake that day, and all I have to do when I doubt is go back to that day and remember the stake I drove. I know that I have a home in Heaven when I die.

Pam Williams

9 HE IS WITH ME

"...lo, I am with you alway, even unto the end of the world. Amen" (Matthew 28:20).

Many times, life on the mission field is trying, difficult, and lonely. If it were not for the promises of the Word of God, a missionary could not bear up under the pressure. Matthew 28:20 was David Livingstone's favorite verse. Through much of the turmoil of his ministry in dark Africa, he would say, " 'lo, I am with you alway, even unto the end of the world' is the word of a gentleman of the strictest and most sacred honor, so there's an end of it!" This promise keeps us at our post of duty, knowing that God walks with us every step of our way, even if it is in the shadows.

As missionaries and servants of our great God, we must realize that we are doing this duty to fulfill His commandment for our lives. Luke 17:10 says, "So likewise ye, when ye shall have done all those things which are commanded you, say, We are unprofitable servants: we have done that which was our duty to do." Most of the time, we do what we do for the Lord out of a sense of responsibility or for rewards. However, if one does a close study of the word "duty," he will find that to do one's duty is to serve the Master with a sense of joy because of our love for Him. Whether we're on the mission field or serving at an insignificant post somewhere else, our duty brings glory to God if we do it with love and joy in our hearts.

Let us determine to do our duty with love and joy in serving our Lord. Somehow the trials, struggles, and heart-aches of life do not seem so enormous, knowing He is in the shadows.

Peggy Baker
Missionary to Nicaragua

10 PEACE

"Likewise the Spirit also helpeth our infirmities: for we know not what we should pray for as we ought: but the Spirit itself maketh intercession for us with groanings which cannot be uttered. And he that searcheth the hearts knoweth what is the mind of the Spirit, because he maketh intercession for the saints according to the will of God" (Romans 8:26-27).

I recently experienced an extremely hard test of my faith and trust in the Lord. I could have taken this test and failed by being angry, bitter, and discouraged. Instead, I passed this test because of my relationship with Jesus. I approached this test with joy, hope, and peace.

In Romans 8, the Apostle Paul talks about how our flesh can conflict with the Holy Spirit. I knew that I did not want my flesh to be in the way of what the Lord was going to do in my life. This test was needed in my life. Otherwise, God would not have allowed it to happen.

Romans 8:26 tells us that the Holy Spirit helps our infirmities, which could be a sickness, broken family, disabili-ty, lost loved one, or the death of a loved one. Whatever our infirmity, the Holy Spirit is there to help us according to God's will. If our relationship with the Lord is right, then we can have peace in any test we go through.

God is in control of our lives! We need to keep our relationship with the Lord fresh and new, so we can pass our tests and grow in Him.

Jenny Jones

11 WHEN ALL IS GONE

"I am the true vine, and my Father is the husbandman. Every branch in me that beareth not fruit he taketh away: and every branch that beareth fruit, he purgeth it, that it may bring forth more fruit" (John 15:1-2).

One of the greatest and most fulfilling times in my life found me at my church, singing in the choir, giving my money to missions, teaching in children's church and Awana, homeschooling my children, and doing all the work I could do for God. At this time, our finances, job insecurity, debt, and dream of a better lifestyle led us to search for new opportunities. We prayed fervently, sought God's will, made a decision, and found ourselves away from home with none of these things that were valuable to us.

We attended a small church with no choir, no children's church, no homeschooling, no friends, and a lot of pain. It hurt to see that all my work and the things I cherished were left behind. I felt an emptiness for all those things, and I tried to fill the void with activities and good deeds. Nothing worked.

Then Jesus spoke to me through John 15:1-2. I understood then that my children, choir, and church were not my fruit but His, and I needed to make room for more fruit. The Father had to prune away all that pride and self-sufficiency to make room for humility and total dependence on Him, just as the branch depends on the vine.

The pain associated with the loss of what was so dear to me gave place for something more precious and beautiful than I ever imagined. I found a closer relationship with my Father that was more meaningful and full of surprises.

Elena Moore

12 SINGING WITH GRACE

"And let the peace of God rule in your hearts, to the which also ye are called in one body; and be ye thankful. Let the word of Christ dwell in you richly and in all wisdom; teaching and admonishing one another in psalms and hymns and spiritual songs, singing with grace in your hearts to the Lord" (Colossians 3:15-16).

The morning that our family was awakened by gunfire and rockets blasting nearby was one of disbelief and great sorrow. I had just flown into Abidjan, Ivory Coast's capital city, the night before. Michelle, our oldest child, was a freshman in college, and I had been in the States for five weeks helping her settle in. My husband, Jeff, and our other two daughters had driven four hours from our home in Bouake to meet me at the airport. Six hours later, deep into the African night, the entire structure of Ivory Coast shifted dangerously as well-organized dissidents took over our town of Bouake and another more northern city and attempted to also take Abidjan.

To make a long story short, we were never allowed to go back to Bouake to collect things from our house there. The girls were never able to say goodbye to friends or retrieve their most special treasures from their rooms. I, too, was struggling with the loss of our home, the special things there, and our ministry opportunities.

During those ten days in Abidjan after the war started, a song came to my family's mind. The tension and uncertainty of each new day was telling on us. However, because of God's grace, we were able to continually sing this song: "God will make a way, when there seems to be no way; He works in ways we cannot see — He will make a way for me. He will be my guide, hold me closely to His side. With joy and strength for each new day, He will make a way ...He will make a way!"

We had a cat named Bubba, and he was still stranded in our house in Bouake. With the raging war and people fleeing in panic, our hearts broke to realize that we would have to leave Bubba there alone. Stefanie, our middle daughter, had bought Bubba for $1 six years earlier in another African town. He had become a very special part of our family.

Because of the deterioration in the country's infrastructure, we were asked to evacuate as quickly as possible. Other missionaries were trying to get out of other cities also. Our plane was to depart on a Saturday. As we continued to pray, monitor the situation, and sing our song, we watched God unfold an absolutely unplanned, but fantastic, way for Bubba to come to us. He was actually evacuated with a British family who was willing to bring him to Abidjan, even with all the stress and tension they had on them. Within 18 hours of our departure for the States, Bubba was in our arms!

We were not able to retrieve anything else from our home in Bouake and probably never will. However, when we stroke Bubba's soft fur and hear his contented purring, we continue to sing for joy! God does indeed work in ways that we cannot understand, but He has promised grace for singing, even when times are hard!

Do you need grace today to face a situation? Ask God to send it on the wings of a song!

Kim Abernethy
Missionary to Ivory Coast

13 LIFE MORE ABUNDANTLY

"The thief cometh not, but for to steal, and to kill, and to destroy: I am come that they might have life, and that they might have it more abundantly" (John 10:10).

One of the hardest things I had to learn was how to control my negative thoughts. When this happens, I believe the worst of myself. I also believe the worst of everyone and everything. One of our Bible study lessons included II Corinthians 10:5, which says, "Casting down imaginations, and every high thing that exalteth itself against the knowledge of God, and bringing into captivity every thought to the obedience of Christ."

The first time I really paid attention to my problem with negative thoughts, it was a real struggle, because the thoughts seemed real. Sometime later, John 10:10 came to mind, as I allowed this to come into play in my life. I watched the care group that I am a part of become a more abundant group. The relationships grew, the ladies bonded, and now they are all being discipled. Being on the other side, I can now say it was worth it all.

Deborah Allen

14 GOD'S CHILD, THEN HIS SERVANT

"But he himself went a day's journey into the wilderness, and came and sat down under a juniper tree: and he requested for himself that he might die; and said, It is enough; now, O Lord, take away my life; for I am not better than my fathers" (I Kings 19:4).

"Poor, poor me," moaned Elijah, as he sat under the juniper tree, "I'm ready to die." Of course, I am paraphrasing, but this was his state of mind as the account of I Kings 19 unfolds. God had just used this man, Elijah, to lead one of the most dynamic and powerful worship experiences in history. The mighty prophet called down fire from Heaven, demonstrating God's omnipotence and causing all people present (including not just Israel, but also 800 false prophets) to fall on their faces and confess that Jehovah was the only true God. You would think after such an awesome display of God's power that absolutely nothing could distress or frighten Elijah. But when Queen Jezebel sent word that he was at the top of her hit list, Elijah melted into a puddle of unbelief, proving his humanity.

What a comforting thought it is that even a warrior of God such as Elijah could get discouraged! I'm sure he felt as if God had abandoned Him, a feeling we've all experienced at some time or another. But it's vital in those times to remember that abandoning His prize creation (that would be us) is not God's nature. He promises that He will never leave or forsake us (Hebrews 13:5). In Isaiah 49:15-16, God makes another great promise: "Can a woman forget her sucking child....yea, they may forget, yet will I not forget thee. Behold, I have graven thee upon the palms of my hands...." Wow! God can't forget me because I'm engraved on His hands.

In his book *THE UNQUENCHABLE WORSHIPPER,* Matt Redman describes how God feels about us: "As a servant I was dispensable. Servants come and go, and God can choose any of us to do any job in His kingdom...But as a son and as a child of God, I was indispensable. There could never be another me. A child is irreplaceable." That knowledge of God's love for me is so overwhelming! God is first concerned about me as His child. Then He begins in me the process of becoming His servant.

Just like Elijah, we are humans that God wants to manifest His power through. But sinking into self-pity and forgetting the promises of God's constant faithfulness to us diminishes His ability to show Himself strong in our behalf. II Chronicles 16:9 says that God is desperately searching the earth to find a heart that is bent toward Him so that He can reveal His might through them.

Isaiah 58:10-11 gives us a challenge: "And if thou draw out thy soul to the hungry, and satisfy the afflicted soul; then shall thy light rise in obscurity, and thy darkness be as the noon day: And the Lord shall guide thee continually, and satisfy thy soul in drought...." Be that liaison for the Lord! Ask God to give you someone to minister to, so you can divert your attention off your own problems. Send someone a card, treat someone to lunch, or just tell someone you were thinking about them and praying for them. Turn your pity party into a celebration of God's willingness and ability to touch another life through you.

Suzanne Spiers

15 Easier To Learn — Harder To Live

"Be ye followers of me, even as I also am of Christ" (I Corinthians 11:1).

I'm sure that there are many of us who struggle with learning God's Word for ourselves while trying to teach and train our children in the process. For me, learning God's Word is much easier than living God's Word. It appears that the apple doesn't fall far from the tree.

When our boys were small, about first and fourth grades, we were out by the pool enjoying the cool water on a hot summer day. The boys were in the pool swimming, having a good time. Clay was playing with a float when Seth decided he wanted the float for himself. He tried everything he could think of to get that float. But when all failed he said, "Be ye kind one to another." Clay, with his teeth clenched and a look that could kill, responded, "Do good to them that hate you."

Hearing this, I pulled them aside to explain the true purpose of God's Word. While I was speaking to them, I was reminded just how loving and patient our heavenly Father is with His children. Thank You, Lord, for being patient with me when I learn Your Word but fail to live it.

Lorrie Austin

16 My Failures...God's Faithfulness

"Jesus Christ the same yesterday, and today, and for ever" (Hebrews 13:8).

Have you ever wrote something on your schedule or made a promise and could not keep it? Was it not kept intentionally or accidentally? This summer, when piano lessons were at an irregular schedule for our children, I got the days mixed up. The day I thought we had lessons, the teacher called to find out what had happened the day before. I felt so bad because I had the right day written on the calendar.

Once again, I was reminded of keeping promises when

our son was doing an assignment for language in school. The lesson was to write a paragraph for the following questions: You told your soccer coach you would be at practice, but your best friend invited you to go camping. What should you do? Why? This can be a difficult task for a nine-year-old boy.

How thankful I am for God's never-ending, never-failing and never-changing promises. By reading His Word, I receive new strength and mercy for the day. Truly, all our needs are provided by the awesome God we serve. It is so clearly expressed by the hymn, "Great Is Thy Faithfulness." Try reading or singing the words and think through the meaning of each line.

God is always faithful, even when I let Him down. He knows our needs even before we ask. At times there are needs that we are unaware of, yet He knows all and provides accordingly. My heart is so grateful and can loudly sing, great is Thy faithfulness!

Rebecca Miyashita
Missionary to Japan

17 CHRIST IS ALL I NEED

"And he said unto me, My grace is sufficient for thee: for my strength is made perfect in weakness. Most gladly therefore will I rather glory in my infirmities, that the power of Christ may rest upon me" (II Corinthians 12:9).

One afternoon I heard a co-worker coming down the hallway sobbing uncontrollably. I hurried down to meet her and find out what was wrong. She was crying so hard that I could hardly understand what she was saying to me. I finally made out that her brother left her a message saying that her mother had brain cancer and that she needed to come home. I tried to reassure her and told her of different people I knew personally that had brain cancer and recovered totally. She began to calm down and realized she needed to find out more about her mother's condition. My co-worker is a single parent and looks to her mother in times of difficulty. She said, "I don't know what I'll do without my mother. I need her." I then told her that God wants us to rely on Him for our needs, not our parents. No matter what the outcome of her mother's medical condition, she would be all right if she put her trust in the Lord.

A few weeks later, I called my father's hospital room to find out the results of some tests he was having. He said he had a large mass in his left lung, and his prognosis was not very good. He told me that he had sent my mother home to rest, and he told me to call her so she could tell me more. He said he needed time to pray. I frantically tried to reach my mother at home, but there was no answer. I began to cry. My husband asked me what was wrong. I began to tell him and heard myself saying, "Daddy can't die! I need him!" When I calmed down, God began to speak to my heart. The statement, "I need my dad," rang through my mind. God reminded me of my words of encouragement to my co-worker a few weeks earlier. When I finally accepted that I didn't need my dad, even though I really wanted to keep him around awhile longer, God's amazing grace came and comforted my heart.

My father passed away three months later. Through all the decisions and preparations that one has to go through to say goodbye to a loved one, God's grace was there every minute, giving me strength and comfort as only He can. Christ is truly all I need!

Mindy Monroe

18 ARE YOU WORTH YOUR SALT?

"Ye are the salt of the earth: but if the salt have lost his savour, wherewith shall it be salted? it is thenceforth good for nothing, but to be cast out, and to be trodden under foot of men" (Matthew 5:13).

For more than four years in a ladies' Bible study group at our church, we studied the various names of God and Christ. From this study I gained a deep security of knowing Who God is and all He has done and continues to do for me. When we finally finished, I felt we needed to balance this study by learning the various names for believers in the Bible. Wow! We are called so many things, and each name gives great insight into what our personal relationship with the Lord and Savior should and could be.

One of the names we are called is "salt." At one time, because of its scarcity and the work it took to mine it, salt was considered a precious commodity. You have probably heard the saying, "he is not worth his salt." That common expression means one's work does not measure up to his pay. Our word "salary" shares a common root with the word "salt." Salt does many things: preserves food, flavors food, and stimulates thirst. It also has many medical benefits. Salt has also traditionally symbolized friendship that is pure, loyal, faithful, obedient, and committed.

God wants us to be the salt of the earth, meaning our presence should be purifying and healing to those with whom we come in contact. Our lives should stimulate a thirst in others to know more about our Lord and Savior. Just as the Bible teaches that God is a loyal and faithful friend committed to fulfilling His promises, our commitment to our heavenly Father should be just as pure, loyal, faithful, and obedient. Dear Lord, make me worth my salt.

Cheryl Adams, wife of Jeff Adams
Pastor of Kansas City Baptist Temple

19 PRETTY INSIDE

"Out of the mouth of babes and sucklings hast thou ordained strength because of thine enemies, that thou mightest still the enemy and the avenger" (Psalm 8:2).

When our granddaughter Julie was four years old, she told me her dad said she was the prettiest girl in her class. I agree with her dad! I told Julie that her hair, her eyes, her complexion, and her smile make her pretty on the outside, but that there are two pretties.

With a puzzled look on her face, she asked me, "Meemaw, what is the other pretty?" I told her it was pretty inside. It was the way she acted. Did she obey her dad and mom, or did she disobey? Did she talk sweetly to them, or were her words mean? Did she have fun with her brother and sister, or did she fight with them and call them names? Did she share, or was she selfish? Was she kind to her family and her friends? I said, "Julie, doing right makes us pretty inside, and that is the most important pretty."

She stared at me for a few minutes. Then she said, "Meemaw, you aren't pretty outside, but you are really pretty inside; and that's the most important pretty, isn't it?" Lord, please help me to always use every opportunity You give me to teach lessons to our grandchildren. Please help me to live a life that will always be pretty inside to others.

Cherrio Cyphers

20 DECISION MAKING WITH GOD

"He that trusteth in his own heart is a fool: but whoso walketh wisely, he shall be delivered" (Proverbs 28:26).

Are we aware of how many hundreds or thousands of decisions we make daily? Your decisions may range from the simplest form, such as "What am I going to wear today?" to a life-changing experience. If life were black and white, and obedience was as easy as doing one thing or its exact opposite, how much would we truly have to trust our heavenly Father? Are we holding God's hand through the gray areas of decision making? When we let go, life becomes complex.

God only wants to make the solutions simple, but it's the trusting part where we get tangled up. Have we stopped to think that God has one perfect thing He wants each of us doing at any given time? If we are trusting Him, He can reveal His will to us.

This verse has been our family's claim for 12 years as we have served Him overseas. What wonderful blessings we have received from trusting Him! There are adversities faced by everyone in different measures, but God can see us through. Just don't let go! I don't know if I would lean on Him if life were only black and white. How about you?

Anne White
Missionary to Singapore

21 I'M AMAZED

"That Christ may dwell in your hearts by faith; that ye, being rooted and grounded in love, May be able to comprehend with all saints what is the breadth, and length, and depth, and height; And to know the love of Christ, which passeth knowledge, that ye might be filled with all the fulness of God" (Ephesians 3:17-19).

When I think back to all the things that God has done in my life, I'm amazed. I could never figure out why God would give up His Son, because I could never give up either of mine. When I realized that I was the reason He gave up His Son, I was overwhelmed. How could it be that He would die for me?

Even though I was the guilty one, He became the sacrifice for me, so that I could have a chance to go on living. Now, no matter what I've done, I'm forgiven and protected by His mighty hand. What had I done to earn such a gift that He would be my Savior? I had not done anything. It was His amazing love and saving grace.

I'll never understand why He would love someone like me that much. His love, grace, mercy, and faithfulness still amaze me, and there is no way that I can repay Him for all that He has done for me. All I can do is offer Him my praise and worship and tell others about His amazing love. He makes me whole, and my life would be nothing without Him. In all that I do, I want to honor and glorify God because of what He has done for me.

Shannon Kelley

22 TAKE A SIT SOMETIMES

"Who can find a virtuous woman? for her price is far above rubies" (Proverbs 31:10).

My granddaughter Mary Christine's favorite verses are Proverbs 31:10-31. When she was five years old, I asked her what she would like to hear for her bedtime Bible reading, and she jumped up and down and exclaimed, "Read me about the virtuous woman!" She said, in her animated way, "Oh, she makes pretty clothes for her family, puts bandages on their hurts, and gets up early to cook their food! She makes things to sell, and her children call her blessed!" I then read Proverbs 31:10-31 to her.

My thoughts went back many years ago to my beloved grandmother, the most virtuous lady I have ever known. There was always time for helping make the cake and lick the spoons, for taking a walk in the woods and picking berries, or for making custard for snow cream. Every day she labored over an old wood stove to cook huge meals for a huge family. After those wonderful meals, Grandma Pearl always went to her old rickety rocking chair in the corner of the room for a sit and gave us her undivided attention for a little storytelling.

In today's busy lifestyle, it is hard to find time to make memories with our children and grandchildren, or to do something that is simply thoughtful for others. Take a sit sometimes and do as Deuteronomy 4:9 tells us: "Only take heed to thyself, and keep thy soul diligently, lest thou forget the things which thine eyes have seen, and lest they depart from thy heart all the days of thy life: but teach them thy sons, and thy sons' sons."

Christine Maddox

23 THROUGH THE STORM

"Then they cry unto the Lord in their trouble, and he bringeth them out of their distresses. He maketh the storm a calm, so that the waves thereof are still. Then are they glad because they be quiet, so he bringeth them unto their desired haven" (Psalm 107:28-30).

How I love to sit inside a cozy house and watch a good thunderstorm! The wind blows its fury, tearing down whatever is in its path, while the rain batters every rooftop and pane of glass. It's safe here, inside the fortress; but what happens when we are forced to meet the storm head-on?

We lade ourselves with protective clothing and a determination in our hearts. But as we walk through it, we soon become weary. We feel the cold and the wet seep through to the bone. Our eyes become blinded, and we are brought to our knees. The darkness is so thick we can feel it. Crying out for help is useless, as no one will hear us. So how do we pray? God, please make the storm go away; or, Lord, please help me through this. Then, just when we think it cannot get any worse, the hail comes. All we want to do now is hide away until the storm passes us by. In the distance we hear a noise. Thunder! As we listen to its mighty roar, we look up from our knees and wait. Great streaks of light break from the sky, giving us those few seconds to get up, find our bearings, and look ahead to where we need to go. We no longer feel the cold and dampness as we have new hope and light to see us through.

The Father guides our way through the rest of the storm. God may not always calm the storm, but He will go through it with us!

Katrina Reid
Missionary to Scotland

24 KEEP IT SIMPLE

"But grow in grace, and in the knowledge of our Lord and Saviour Jesus Christ. To him be glory both now and for ever. Amen" (II Peter 3:18).

Back before everyone had a computer and before email replaced sending a handwritten note, I took a class to learn about computers. One of the first things the instructor taught us was the term KISS, which translates "Keep It Simple, Stupid." For some reason, this modest statement confounds most people. We often want to make things more complicated than necessary. However, somehow this simple phrase helped me get back on track in my spiritual growth.

I received my salvation late in life, and after the initial exuberance waned this awesome weight overcame me. Others around me were more knowledgeable than I was about the Bible and the wonderful Lord I was now serving. I was overwhelmed with the notion that I had to catch up with them.

Since receiving Jesus into my life, I have been diagnosed with an incurable debilitating disease, which saps my energy. Until then, I had been working and living a fairly normal life. Why would this happen now? Before my salvation, bitterness and blame would have been my response. Much to my amazement, this diagnosis made me focus on my relationship with my Father in Heaven. I finally realized what "keep it simple" really means. Our Lord does not want us to jump through hoops for Him 24 hours a day, seven days a week, to prove ourselves to Him. He made us and loves us unconditionally. In return, He wants our love, commitment, and faithfulness to Him above all else, and the rest will fall into place according to our individual strengths and abilities. This is not so complicated after all!

Dear Lord, I love You so much and look forward to loving and honoring You forever in Heaven. I don't deserve anything because of my sinful nature, and for this I am truly repentant. I know You love me unconditionally and gave Your Son so I might live forever with You. I am thankful for this, as well as all my other blessings. I ask that Your Holy Spirit stay with me and help me to grow in grace and knowledge of You until we meet face to face.

Janet Gilliland

25 A FATHER'S TIME

"The ungodly are not so: but are like the chaff which the wind driveth away" (Psalm 1:4).

I cannot remember a time my family didn't attend church somewhere. So as a little girl I looked forward to that one week during the summer for Vacation Bible School. One particular year seemed to be hard because we had to memorize whole chapters of the Bible instead of just verses. One evening, my dad and I sat on the front porch steps talking about things as we did a lot of times. I had what I thought was a big question for him. What was chaff?

With a very confident voice, he explained: "Jo Ann, see that wheat growing across the road? They harvest that wheat by cutting it and then taking the heads, which have seeds in them that are encased in a protective outer coat. They don't want that outer coat, so they have to get rid of it to get at the heart where the good part of the seed is located. In Bible times, they placed it on sheets or blankets and tossed it into the air where the wind would blow away the unwanted outer coat. Therefore, the ungodly are not so, but are like the wind that tosses them to and fro. You want to be like the heart of the seed, pure so God can use you to further His kingdom."

If my father had not taken the time to explain to me, I wonder where I would be today? That is so like our heavenly Father. He gives us so much time and attention. If we are very still and listen, He explains things to us in His own time.

Jo Ann Shelton

26 GROWING PAINS

"The righteous shall flourish like the palm tree: he shall grow like a cedar in Lebanon. Those that be planted in the house of the Lord shall flourish in the courts of our God. They shall still bring forth fruit in old age; they shall be fat and flourishing" (Psalm 92:12-14).

There is a song I remember singing when I attended church at People's Baptist Church in Corpus Christi, Texas. The chorus said, "Don't give up on the brink of a miracle, Don't give in, God is still on your side, Don't give up on the brink of a miracle, Don't give in, God is still on His throne."

There is much comfort in these words and much comfort when I sing them in my heart to the Lord. I am happy that God saved my life, because I realize that I never had a life until I was saved. I recently celebrated six years of sobriety. I feel as though I never drank or did drugs, because the grace of Almighty God has set me free.

During the time that I was drinking and on drugs, my son helped me and prayed for me. For this, I thank him. I truly believe that he is the reason that my life was spared. God answered his prayers. I know that I cannot control the outcome of my son's life, but I thank God that He will give security in knowing that He will take care of him. Making decisions for my son is not as easy now as it was when he was younger, and he must learn to trust God on his own. As moms, we need to earnestly pray for our children that we will be the examples before them that we should be. God promises us wisdom if we will ask, and every day our desire should be that our Father in Heaven will use us as tools in our children's lives.

I thank God for the husband that He has given to me - a man who cares deeply for me. We need to pray for our marriages that they will be strong, and that we will be committed to being the women that God would have us to be. I have seen the damage that is caused by broken marriages. Not only do the adults suffer, but also the children. Every day we should renew our desire to be the wives and mothers that God, in His Word, admonishes us to be, so that our families will be strong, loving, and serving God will all of their hearts.

Shelley Graham

27 A Fulfilled Life

"His lord said unto him, Well done, thou good and faithful servant: thou hast been faithful over a few things, I will make thee ruler over many things: enter thou into the joy of thy lord" (Matthew 25:21).

My calm, professional demeanor crumbled as my babysitter explained how my son fell and hit his head, and she could not stop the bleeding. As I ran for the front door of the pharmacy, peeling off my white coat and badge, I transformed into a frantic mom in a matter of seconds. I did not have my usual transition time to go from one role to another, from pharmacist to wife and mother.

I love all my roles. Even though they are very different from one another, each role helps me in the other. As a mother, I have compassion for my patients, especially the tired moms of sick children and the exasperated person taking care of an elderly patient. And at the end of a work day, I can hug my healthy children and count my blessings.

God's intentions for the roles in our lives are given to us through the talents and gifts He has blessed us with. If we let Him, He will direct us toward these natural abilities. We will often be most fulfilled when we use these talents and are comfortable and competent at what we are doing. Squeezing into a position or role not right for you can be frustrating for you and everyone around you.

I expect a lifelong struggle as my life changes and God has more plans for me. Occasionally, my balancing act crashes among my relationship with my husband, my patience with my children, or my decisions at work. Usually, these trials and tribulations occur because I have left the pathway God has laid out for me. Later, after a lot of tears and prayers, I find my way again.

Be good at what you do. Be good at something. If it is God's will, you can look ahead to when you will ultimately be rewarded with this message: "Well done, thou good and faithful servant."

Nerissa Appleton

28 My Shepherd

"The Lord is my shepherd; I shall not want. He maketh me to lie down in green pastures: he leadeth me beside the still waters. He restoreth my soul: he leadeth me in the paths of righteousness for his name's sake. Yea, though I walk through the valley of the shadow of death, I will fear no evil: for thou art with me; thy rod and thy staff they comfort me. Thou preparest a table before me in the presence of mine enemies: thou anointest my head with oil; my cup runneth over. Surely goodness and mercy shall follow me all the days of my life: and I will dwell in the house of the Lord for ever" (Psalm 23).

Recently, while studying the life of David, I was reminded of Psalm 23 and the way it blesses my heart again and again. The words, "The Lord is my shepherd," bring such comfort. By putting emphasis on the word "my" it makes the entire Psalm very personal. The word "shepherd" carries with it thoughts of tenderness, security, and provision, and yet it means nothing unless I can say, "The Lord is my shepherd."

We as born again believers are not immune to discouragement, sadness, pain, or the feeling of being inadequate when surrounded by situations in which we have no control. It is during these times that we especially need to go to our favorite portions of Scripture and let them guide us, heal our hurts, and be a source of comfort to us. Matthew 11:28-30 says, "Come unto me, all ye that labour and are heavy laden, and I will give you rest. Take my yoke upon you, and learn of me; for I am meek and lowly in heart: and ye shall find rest unto your souls. For my yoke is easy, and my burden is light."

We are so blessed to have God's Word and its wonderful promises. Let's claim them and keep them in our hearts, strengthening us in our daily walk with the Lord.

Jo Ann Huggins

29 YES, YOU HAVE THE RIGHT NUMBER

"These things have I written unto you that believe on the name of the Son of God; that ye may know that ye have eternal life, and that ye may believe on the name of the Son of God" (I John 5:13).

On Sunday, January 5, 2003, I received a phone call, and the lady asked to speak to Cherrie. I told her she had the wrong number, and she said okay and hung up. About five minutes later, the phone rang again, and this time the lady said, "Phyllis?" I said yes, and then she said she was my Aunt Myrtle, who lives in Mississippi. She had been trying to get in touch with my brother, Jimmy, who is terminally ill. She told me she had written my sister-in-law's name next to my phone number. That was why she asked for Cherrie when she called the first time.

I gave her my brother's phone number. We started talking about him, and I told her I had talked to him about the Lord the last time I had seen him, but I wasn't sure if he was saved or not. We talked about eternity being a long time if you went to Hell, and if you went there, you didn't get another chance to accept Jesus Christ as your Savior. I told her that I had sent him the "Romans Road" to salvation that I had also sent her. My aunt told me she had prayed the prayer, but didn't feel saved, and didn't know if she was or not. I told her that if she told the Lord she was a sinner and wanted Jesus to come into her heart and life and become her Lord and Savior, and meant it with all her heart, that He would. I told her to read I John, and she would know that if she accepted Him, she was saved.

I told her that God does not lie. If Satan tried to tell her she was lost, tell him he is a liar, and get away from her in the name of Jesus Christ. After we finished talking, the Lord put it on my heart to share with her the Discipleship 1 lessons regarding salvation and eternal security. I sent her the information the next day.

Coincidence that she called me instead of my brother? I don't think so. God's hand was all over the situation.

Phyllis Todd

30 BLESSINGS FROM BROKENNESS

"And we know that all things work together for good to them that love God, to them who are the called according to his purpose" (Romans 8:28).

How might someone experience blessings from brokenness? Oftentimes, we find ourselves experiencing pain, hurt, bitterness, and perhaps resentment during times of brokenness. Situations in our lives cause us to experience brokenness. Perhaps it is a divorce that we did not ask for; or maybe a loved one has died unexpectedly. Maybe a spouse has lost a job, or a child is abusing drugs. Whatever the situation may be, we truly can experience blessings from brokenness. Brokenness is an opportunity. It is an opportunity for spiritual growth. It is an opportunity to see God working in our lives. It is living by faith and knowing God is changing our hearts and minds. Brokenness is a time to gain knowledge, understanding, and wisdom. It is during these times that God wants us to totally rely on Him to handle our burdens.

Many of us have a tendency to reject trials and hardships for fear of the unknown. We don't want to experience difficulty because of how it might make us feel: sad, hurt, lonely, or anxious. It is during these times, however, that He makes His presence known to us.

During my divorce, God embraced me with His loving arms and comforted me during that difficult time. He has strengthened me and has given me a new life since I rededicated my life to Him in January 1999. I have truly experienced His unconditional love. My life is forevermore changed.

I encourage you today to examine times in your life when you experienced brokenness. I'm sure you received a blessing from it. The brokenness I have experienced has made my relationship with God more intimate now than ever before. As I approach times of difficulty today, I am reminded of how He loves me and protects me. I am often reminded, "this too shall pass."

Tracey Prince

31 SHOES TELL MANY STORIES

"He hath shewed thee, O man, what is good; and what doth the Lord require of thee, but to do justly, and to love mercy, and to walk humbly with thy God?" (Micah 6:8).

When people come to our house, one of the first things they notice is the cubicles of shoes on the back porch. Shoes can tell many stories, especially in a family of ten. Since we were saved, we have always trusted God to guide each step we take, which brought us to the Dominican Republic more than eight years ago. We pray we can guide the feet that fit these shoes to walk humbly with God all their lives.

The smallest shoes are the Mickey Mouse sneakers and the G.I. Joe sandals. We need to guide them from the very beginning and many times carry them through their first years.

The shoes of the pre-teen and teen girls sometimes look very grown-up. That is how girls want to be at this age. They need love, care, understanding, and guidance from Mom and Dad as we teach them God's Word.

Next we see baseball cleats, worn-out tennis shoes, and sandals that belong to the teen boys. They will be tempted in many ways at this time in their lives, and as parents, we need to help direct their steps with God's counsel and wisdom. The oldest will soon be walking the halls of college. We suddenly remember his first steps and pray for him as he takes his first steps out on his own.

A mother's shoes are usually pretty worn out as she performs many tasks, both easy and difficult. If she does it all with love and God's help, He will bless her abundantly. I would never trade the paths these shoes have trod.

The last pair of shoes are those that preach the Gospel. They have gone many places and probably will go many more. These shoes have a great responsibility of spiritually guiding our family. Most of our children have come to know and love the Lord Jesus because of the paths our feet have walked and are still walking.

Take a good look at your shoes. What story are they telling about you, your relationship with God, your position as mother or wife? Our shoes do tell a story.

Barb Grenon
Missionary to the Dominican Republic

"And the Lord God said, It is not good that man should be alone; I will make him an help meet for him. And out of the ground the Lord God formed every beast of the field, and every fowl of the air; and brought them unto Adam to see what he would call them: and whatsoever Adam called every living creature, that was the name thereof. And Adam gave names to all cattle, and to all fowl of the air, and to every beast of the field; but for Adam there was not found an help meet for him. And the Lord God caused a deep sleep to fall upon Adam, and he slept: and he took one of his ribs, and closed up the flesh instead thereof; And the rib, which the Lord God had taken from man, made he a woman, and brought her unto the man. And Adam said, This is now bone of my bones, and flesh of my flesh: she shall be called Woman, because she was taken out of Man. Therefore shall a man leave his father and his mother, and shall cleave unto his wife: and they shall be one flesh."

(Genesis 2:18-24)

1 He Will Not Let Go

"I therefore so run, not as uncertainly; so fight I, not as one that beateth the air" (I Corinthians 9:26).

Some years ago on a hot summer day in South Florida, a little boy decided to go for a swim in the old swimming hole behind his house. In a hurry to dive into the cool water, he ran out the back door and jumped in. As he swam toward the middle of the lake, he did not realize an alligator was swimming toward the shore.

In the house, his mother looked out the window and saw the two as they got closer and closer together. Terrified, she ran toward the water, yelling to her son. Hearing her voice, the boy became alarmed and made a U-turn to swim to his mother. It was too late. Just as he reached her, the alligator reached him. From the dock, the mother grabbed her little boy by the arms as the alligator snatched his legs, beginning an incredible tug-of-war. The alligator was much stronger than the mother, but she was too passionate to let go.

A farmer driving by heard the mother's screams, raced from his truck with a gun, and shot the alligator. After weeks and weeks in the hospital, the little boy survived. The alligator's vicious attack scarred his legs. On his arms were deep scratches where his mother's fingernails dug into his flesh as she hung onto him. The newspaper reporter who interviewed the boy after the trauma asked if he would show him his scars. The boy lifted his pant leg. Then, with obvious pride, he said to the reporter, "But I have great scars on my arms, too. I have them because my mom wouldn't let go."

You and I can identify with that little boy. We have scars, too. They're not from an alligator but from a painful past. Some of those scars are unsightly and have caused us deep regret. But some wounds are there because God refused to let go. In the midst of our struggles, He's been holding onto us. The Scripture teaches that God loves us, and we are His children. He wants to protect us and provide for us in every way. But sometimes we foolishly wade into dangerous situations. The swimming hole of life is filled with peril, and we forget that the enemy is waiting to attack. That's when the tug-of-war begins. If you have the scars of His love on your arms, be very grateful. He did not let go and never will.

Sylvia Hancock

2 I Want To Be Just Like You

"And these words, which I command thee this day, shall be in thine heart: And thou shalt teach them diligently unto thy children, and shalt talk of them when thou sittest in thine house, and when thou walkest by the way, and when thou liest down, and when thou risest up" (Deuteronomy 6:6-7).

This is a letter I wrote in August 2002 to my niece Melissa Baker and her husband, Jeff. At the time, their twin girls, Kaitlin Diane and Ashley Caroline, were one year old.

Dear Missy,

At church this morning our new babies were dedicated. They were so cute! I thought about your girls when a soloist, Jason Steele, sang this song for the parents and grandparents who are working together to raise those little ones. The words of the song so touched my heart that I wanted to send them to you. I am changing the words to fit your beauties, but the meaning is the same. The song is titled, "I Want To Be Just Like You."

Lord, I want to be just like You,
'Cause they want to be just like me;
I want to be a holy example,
For their innocent eyes to see;
Help me be a living Bible, Lord,
That my little girls can read;
I want to be just like You,
'Cause they want to be like me.

Awesome responsibility, that of raising children! When

you hold one in your arms, you hold a soul for which you are responsible. You are responsible for the training they receive or do not receive in their lives. Awesome that God would entrust that to us, isn't it? We need His help every day. I'll pray with you for yours, because there were people who prayed with me for mine. Enjoy them every day of their lives and work with them so that they will know Him. I love you and respect the job you and Jeff and the grandparents are doing with your girls. God entrusts the special gift of children to special people.

Love, Aunt Carolyn

Carolyn Hogan

3 He Will Lead The Way

"Trust in the Lord with all thine heart; and lean not unto thine own understanding. In all thy ways acknowledge him, and he shall direct thy paths" (Proverbs 3:5-6).

Being married is hard work! However, being married to an unsaved person makes for triple the work and many more prayers. When I found a church home at Decatur Baptist Church, all I wanted was to share it with my husband. After weeks of nagging, begging, and praying for Dustin, I was frustrated with him and with God.

One day, I was praying and told God that I was giving up the fight, because I could not get Dustin to go to church. Then He reminded me of Proverbs 3:5-6. I was supposed to trust in God and let Him lead the way. So that's exactly what I did. I felt as though I should lay low and quietly show Dustin my relationship with God. If I did that, Dustin would see my happiness in the Lord.

Being submissive to God and to Dustin sure paid off! A few weeks later, Dustin was saved and began his new life. Daily, I enjoy watching him grow and become a wonderful spiritual leader and godly husband. How I praise the Lord for giving me a new husband! Now we are both new creatures in

Christ, and we are growing together. Trusting in God to lead Dustin and me in the right direction has changed both of our lives for the better. It's nice to rely on God to lead the way.

Theresa Dickens

4 THERE IS A LAD HERE

"There is a lad here, which hath five barley loaves, and two small fishes: but what are they among so many?" (John 6:9).

What an exciting day! Today he was going to spend the entire day on the hillside listening to Jesus. He can't believe the day is finally here. What a great day! As usual, his mother was busy in the kitchen getting breakfast ready and singing a happy tune. With a smile on his face, he quickly dressed and hurried to the kitchen to get his morning hugs from his mom and dad. His dad had to rush off to work, and his mom had to stay home with his younger brother and sister, but as soon as breakfast was over his great day of adventure would begin.

As he hurried out the door, his mom gave him another quick hug and whispered in his ear: "I put a little extra food in your lunch basket. God has blessed us so much I wanted you to be able to share with your friends. Please, son, have a great day!"

There was a huge crowd that day on the hillside waiting to hear what Jesus was teaching. Many of the people had traveled for hours, maybe even days. But it was worth it! Andrew, Simon Peter's brother, was walking through the crowd greeting everyone and sharing the excitement of being close to Jesus. As he walked through the crowd he couldn't help but stop and speak to the special lad standing in front of him. "Hello, sir," the young lad said. He spoke with such excitement that Andrew could only smile. "I have come to listen to Jesus. Did you come to hear him, too?" the lad asked. Andrew nodded and quickly noticed the lunch basket sitting on the lad's lap. Following his eyes, the lad smiled and said,

"My mom told me as I left home today that she packed some extra food so that I could share with my friends. Would you like some?" Andrew was speechless! When Andrew finally found his voice, he asked the young lad to please come with him, because he wanted him to meet someone.

As Andrew walked up to Jesus and Simon Peter, he heard Peter say, "Two hundred pennyworth of bread is not sufficient for them, that every one of them may take a little." Peter looked at the large crowd continuing to gather around them. Andrew quickly spoke up and said, "There is a lad here, which hath five barley loaves, and two small fishes: but what are they among so many?"

As we know, Jesus took this lunch and fed the multitude. But what if this lad's mother had not prepared the lunch? What if she had only put in enough for her son and not one bite over? What if this lad had not been taught the importance of sharing? What if this lad had not been there on that hillside to see Jesus that day?

Are we enabling our children to be used of God? Are they faithful in their place? Are we teaching them to look for opportunities to serve?

God, please use my children and grandchildren. May I do my part to have them prepared to be used by You. I realize there is nothing greater in this world than to be able to be used of God.

Katy Ripley

5 How Do You Do This?

"The Lord will give strength unto his people; the Lord will bless his people with peace" (Psalm 29:11).

About eight or nine years ago, I began looking for a change within the local bank where I had been working for about 15 years. After being denied the change, I explored other options and enrolled at a local college to begin a degree towards nursing. Upon graduating in 1998, I got a job in the emergency room at Decatur General Hospital. It was a big change from banking!

For about the first three weeks I was there, I remember having thoughts like, "I've made a big mistake," "I don't think I'm going to be able to do this," and "I'm going to go back to school and do something else." Well, just as I had made it through school by the grace of God, I made it through my introductory period and now enjoy an exciting career in the E.R.

A few months ago, as I was adjusting the oxygen cannula in the nose of my dying aunt, she looked at me with sunken eyes and weakly asked, "How do you do this?" Inside, my answer was the same as it has been countless times, "Only by the grace of God."

Lisa Pensworth

6 THE MIRACLE OF THE BROKEN ELBOW

"For my thoughts are not your thoughts, neither are your ways my ways, saith the Lord" (Isaiah 55:8).

One thing an American missionary fears most about living in a Third World country is the dread of becoming ill or having an accident that requires a trip to the hospital. The medical care available is primitive at best. One prays often for good health and an accident-free life. However, God does not always see things our way. That day arrived for me when I fell on a cement floor and broke my elbow. Of all times, this happened on the first day of Christmas vacation! It was difficult enough being separated from friends and family during the holidays, but to begin this season with a broken elbow was more than I could imagine. However, we can always trust God to take any situation and turn it around for His glory, and that is exactly what He did.

I was rushed to the emergency hospital where my elbow was x-rayed with equipment that looked as if it had performed 60 or 70 years of service. But the picture was clear. The bones where my elbow bends were broken. It did not look good. The doctor was knowledgeable, and he set the bones with a heavy plaster cast. He sent me home with instructions to be very careful, because these types of breaks usually require surgery. The pain was intense for several days; then I settled into the inconvenience of having to manage with a cast. People were praying, and God was healing. In two and a half weeks, much to the amazement of the doctors involved, my bones were knit together in perfect order, and the cast was removed.

Much praise and glory was given to God, and that was a witness to everyone. When a bone specialist in the States heard about it, he, too, exclaimed, "That truly was a miracle of God!" The first day of the Christmas holidays began with the broken elbow, and interestingly enough, the cast was removed on the last day of the vacation. The ministry did not suffer, and God was praised! Let us all accept those experiences that God sends our way and ask Him to glorify Himself through our trials and sufferings. After all, didn't He create us to glorify Him?

Loreen Ittermann
Missionary to Moldova

7 A MESSAGE IN A SONG

"For this God is our God for ever and ever: he will be our guide even unto death" (Psalm 48:14).

Being a part of the music ministry has been a blessing in my life since the first time I sang in the choir. I am deeply moved by the messages in our songs. I guess I thought that just because I was enjoying coming to church and being a part of a ministry, that everyone else in my family was, too.

However, our family had many struggles with our teenage children, and I started thinking that I should step down from the choir. I thought it would be good for me to sit in the pew with them if they came to church. But every time I had these thoughts, a song or chorus came to mind, reminding me that the choir is a ministry, and that that is where God wanted me to be. I prayed that God would guide me and keep me faithful in my ministry.

Recently, after receiving some bad news, I prayed and asked the Lord to give me courage and strength through the following days. Once again, our ever faithful Lord and Savior gave me the words I needed to hear and sing out loud: "I don't know about tomorrow. I just live from day to day…I don't worry over the future, for I know what Jesus said. And today I'll walk beside Him, for He knows what is ahead."

The best part is that I know Who holds tomorrow, and I know Who holds my hand. These are the words from one of my favorite songs, and they ring so true, as God has taught me so many times. Praise the Lord for His mercy and love.

Tina Hill

8 THE OFFENDED BROTHER

"It is good neither to eat flesh, nor to drink wine, nor any thing whereby thy brother stumbleth, or is offended, or is made weak" (Romans 14:21).

Here is a sound biblical principle given to us as Christians to help us evaluate whether or not to engage in certain practices, which are neither explicitly endorsed nor prohibited in Scripture. The question is not whether the practice will hurt the stronger Christian who engages in it, but whether his or her example might offend, mislead, or discourage a weaker brother or sister.

This matter of giving offense is quite serious in God's sight. "Give none offence, neither to the Jews, nor to the

Gentiles, nor to the church of God" (I Corinthians 10:32). The problem addressed in this passage, which is that of eating meat purchased from temple markets after it had been offered to idols, is not an issue for Christians today, but it was a very real problem to new believers in the first century. The principle given by Paul for deciding that issue is still valid for other issues today, such as clothing, entertainment, recreational games, smoking, etc. As Paul expressed it: "But take heed lest by any means this liberty of your's become a stumblingblock to them that are weak. But when ye sin so against the brethren, and wound their weak conscience, ye sin against Christ. Wherefore, if meat make my brother to offend, I will eat no flesh while the world standeth, lest I make my brother to offend" (I Corinthians 8:9,12,13).

On the other side of the coin, the stronger Christian should be careful to not take personal offense at something done by a fellow believer. Psalm 119:165 says: "Great peace have they which love thy law: and nothing shall offend them." The rule for a mature, sincere, concerned Christian is to seek diligently to neither give offense, nor take offense on any personal issue, by God's grace. Sometimes these are not easy. God help us to be alert concerning these issues. May our children see victory in the way we handle them.

Katherine Fretwell

9 He Promises Protection

"I will lift up mine eyes unto the hills, from whence cometh my help. My help cometh from the Lord, which made heaven and earth" (Psalm 121:1-2).

A few months ago, I was driving back from a short trip I had taken to Acapulco to take care of several things. I had been there to take care of a youth pastor's wife who just had a baby. I was also there to bring back some of their belongings to Chalco, where they would come to receive training so they could leave for a foreign country as missionaries. I wanted to be there to assist her in whatever she needed. To make room for their stuff, I had to take out all the seats in my van and leave them at home. I was scared. Although I have traveled plenty, I have never driven to a destination alone.

I left on Saturday and made it there without any problems. On Sunday I was in church and then spent a week taking care of this dear lady. On Thursday morning when my time in Acapulco was over, I left there with my van filled to the top. I couldn't even see through the back window. If I was scared on my way over there, I was terrified on my way back. Driving conditions would be different because of the weight and poor visibility on a highway with many curves. I left about 7:45 a.m. and drove and drove and drove. I finally made it to Mexico City and still had to drive two hours to get to my destination in Chalco. I was afraid of being stopped by cops or having an accident on the freeway. The two-hour drive went by, and I finally pulled into my garage, thinking everything was fine.

We were unloading the van and putting everything inside the house when I noticed that the front right tire was totally flat. I was speechless! When did this happen? I told my husband, and we had to believe that this happened while I was alone on the curvy road. So why didn't I have a terrible accident? There is only one reason. The Lord had taken care of me. I believe Psalm 121:1-2 with all my heart, and I give thanks to God for keeping His promise of protection in my life on that day.

Lori Brown
Missionary to Mexico

10 God's Perfect Plan

"Let not your heart be troubled: ye believe in God, believe also in me" (John 14:1).

What continually amazes me is how the Lord's perfect plan unfolds before my very eyes on a daily basis. As I look back, I delight in the wisdom of the strategies He has orchestrated thus far. So why worry about anything?

Here are two things which I claim daily. The first one is: "Remind me, Lord, that there isn't anything that can possibly happen today that we can't handle together." The second one is: "Remind me, Lord, to dream the impossible, for with You nothing is impossible." So, every day is extraordinary and is an amazing revelation of His infinite aspirations for me. But the awesome part is when I recollect the "what, when, why, who, and how" of yesterdays that finalize only one piece of the immense puzzle of my pilgrimage. And all I do is believe, obey, and serve Him. Wow! That's breathtaking! Yes, I understand fully Who is in charge, and when I daydream of the future I beam with anticipation.

By placing my will in God's hands, I believe I can be as the mustard seed and increase my faith daily, stretching forward to illustrate His omnipotence, everlasting mercy, and unconditional love. Now that I live in China, I realize that my geographical position may bring more challenges to my faith in God's protection and leading, but praise the Lord, He is always the same.

Cadie Palmer
Missionary to China

11 HAVING GREAT FRIENDS IN CHRIST

"I thank God, whom I serve from my forefathers with pure conscience, that without ceasing I have remembrance of thee in my prayers night and day" (II Timothy 1:3).

I have been a member of Decatur Baptist Church for a long time. When I started attending the church, it was called Moulton Heights Baptist Church, because that is the community in which the church was located. When the church outgrew the facilities, it purchased land on the southwest side of the city. After the new church was built, the name was changed to Decatur Baptist, and that was a special time in the life of the church.

My first Sunday at church was also someone else's first Sunday. That was Brother Doug Ripley. He said that he planned on being in Decatur for a long time. I decided to make that a part of my life, too. We both have had many wonderful years with God's help.

When I began attending church, my son Steve was only three years old. He loved to sing and would get up in front of church and sing "Jesus Loves Me." Everyone just loved it and could not believe that a little fellow would be able to sing so well in front of such a large crowd.

I have so many pleasant memories of attending church, and my church family is a great blessing in my life. I'm proud to know I have great friends in Christ. My prayer is that we, as a church family, can continue to be a blessing to each other.

Dear God, thank You for giving me a warm church family. May I be a blessing to others as they are a blessing to me.

Ruby McCulloch

12 Embrace Adversity, Become A Victor

"Bless the Lord, O my soul, and forget not all his benefits: Who forgiveth all thine iniquities; who healeth all thy diseases; Who redeemeth thy life from destruction; who crowneth thee with lovingkindness and tender mercies; Who satisfieth thy mouth with good things..." (Psalm 103:2-5).

My definition of adversity is any situation in which I have no power or control. Throughout my life, I have had my share of stumblingblocks, but I overcame these situations without much difficulty.

Three years ago, I truly thought I was in the midst of a progression of trials. In ten months we buried seven members of our family. One of those was my husband of 40 years. I was a victim, alone, and no one could understand the grief I was experiencing. Advice, kindness, consideration, and generosity were shown by many, but they could not console me. I needed to relieve my hurt and depression. That year was my year of adversity. Determined to understand why all of this was occurring in my life, I turned to my Bible and found some answers. What a wake-up call I had! Scales were removed from my eyes! I was living and depending on myself, not on Jesus. I now survive and thrive on God's promises, and my heart and mind have changed into what the Holy Spirit wants them to be. I am a victor, never alone, because the Spirit is with me always. I live for Jesus, and one day I will experience to the fullest God's gift, eternal life. You can also.

Peggy Sheffield

13 When Do Bad Times Turn Good?

"And we know that all things work together for good to them that love God, to them who are the called according to his purpose" (Romans 8:28).

We've all heard Romans 8:28, but what does that verse mean exactly? My dad was dying in March 1999, and people quoted that verse to me a lot. I just couldn't understand what good could possibly come out of losing my dad. I would go to the hospital every day, hoping and praying for a miracle.

I would stand back and watch my mom take care of my dad with such unconditional love and a selfless attitude. No matter how tired or stressed she was, his needs came first. At one time, he was in the Intensive Care Unit for eight straight days and was very restless and unresponsive to my brothers and me. My mom would come in and just take his hand, and we could see a peace come over him. I never thought that I would ever want to get married again, but by watching the love and care my mom showed my dad and the way my dad had such a peace just knowing she was there made me want that kind of relationship one day.

My dad died on March 30, 1999, and I met my husband in May of that same year. God showed me through the illness and death of my dad that marriage can be a wonderful thing. Had I not gone through this great trial in my life, I would have missed one of the greatest blessings of my life, my husband. I praise God for the good times and the bad. His Word is true — all things do work together for good.

Katie Tumlin

14 PARENTING ISN'T FOR COWARDS

"Lo, children are an heritage of the Lord: and the fruit of the womb is his reward. As arrows are in the hand of a mighty man; so are children of the youth" (Psalm 127:3-4).

I read the other day in *READERS DIGEST* a quote that stated, "Parenting is part joy and part guerrilla warfare." I had to laugh because, as a popular saying goes, "Been there, done that." I have many precious memories of my children that are forever locked away in my heart. I also recall doing battle on the front line: teaching my young about the word "no," to obey at all times, and what was good and evil. Many hours have been dedicated to fighting the battle that they may grow up to have a desire to be godly and to live a life that would be pleasing to Him.

The one area that I lacked was to completely rely on my "Superior" for guidance and wisdom. Too many times I went to Him for damage control. As mothers, we have a responsibility to Him in raising the children He has loaned to us. What better place to do battle than on our knees, a place that Satan hates to see the Almighty's soldiers fighting in intercession.

Christian books on parenting are great tools, but God and His Word are the final authority. Are you a young mother with small children? If so, now is the time to begin a routine of daily intercession of guidance and wisdom. Are you a mother of teens and in great need of wisdom or possibly damage control? God is there with His arms open just for you! Go to Him, sit at His feet, and seek out His wisdom!

Dear Lord, help me to be faithful in seeking Your will and wisdom in my life and in my children's lives. Forgive me when I rely on my own strength. Thank you for the precious children you have loaned to me.

Denise Phillips

15 THINGS HAPPEN FOR A REASON

"Finally, be ye all of one mind, having compassion one of another, love as brethren, be pitiful, be courteous" (I Peter 3:8).

It was a typical day in my life as a schoolteacher. I got up, got ready for school, and got to work at 7:20 a.m. I was busy in my classroom getting things ready before the kids arrived when I heard a knock on my classroom door. One of my students and his mother, Ann, were outside wanting to speak with me, and I invited both of them into my classroom where we could talk privately. My student, Joseph, had been forgetting to do his homework, and he wasn't getting important things signed from his mother. She was there to explain why. She told me her mother was sick with cancer, and things were not looking great at all. Her time was consumed with taking care of her mother. Ann further explained that she hadn't been around Joseph as much as she would have liked. His older sister had been helping take care of him.

Ann started crying as she continued talking about her mother. The entire conversation began to focus totally on her situation. I don't consider myself the best counselor in the world, so I just sat there, listened, and let her talk. The emotional pain was evident by the expressions on her face. She was scared her mother was going to die. Yet she was exhausted from taking care of her, too.

After several minutes passed, the Lord laid on my heart what I was to say to this mother. In many ways, I could relate to her personal situation. I began sharing my story with her. A year before this conversation, my own mother had been diagnosed with cancer and was given three months to live. It was a nightmare to hear the news at first. I shared how my mother had been in the hospital for two months and then came home and required total care. I remembered working all day, taking turns with my brother spending the night, and taking care of Mom throughout the night. I remember not knowing if my mother was going to live and the emotional pain that caused in my life.

It was during this conversation that Ann, Joseph, and I bonded in a way we would never forget. I asked Ann if she believed in prayer, and if she would mind if I prayed with her and Joseph. She said she didn't mind. We held hands in my classroom, and I prayed for Ann's family, her mother, and the entire situation.

After she left, I realized why I had gone through what I did with my mother. Things happen for a reason in our lives, even when they don't make sense. God brought to my attention that I had an unbelievable amount of comfort and compassion I could give to other people because of my experience with my mom's cancer. Not only could I sympathize with people, but I also could empathize. I'm so thankful for the lesson God taught me in this situation.

Susan Hogan

16 Learning Patience

"And the servant of the Lord must not strive; but be gentle unto all men, apt to teach, patient" (II Timothy 2:24).

To people in a fast moving, do-it-my-way society, patience is often a lost art. Yet patience is one quality God desires of us as we respond to situations in our lives. For example, a right response to a delayed flight or a harsh word speaks volumes to observers. But what about the more urgent matter of waiting on God for an answer to prayer? What about when struggles come?

Psalm 62:5 says, "My soul, wait thou only upon God; for my expectation is from him." Waiting on God is not a time period of doing nothing. It is a time period to acknowledge that God is in control. He knows the questions I have and the struggles I am experiencing. He cares. He is making me more like Him and teaching me more about Himself. Waiting on God is looking to Him and His Word with an expectancy of what He will do. It is trusting His timing.

Hebrews 12:1 challenges me to run with patience the race that is set before me. During the difficult times, I must keep on doing what I know is God's will. This includes rejoicing and giving thanks, which is only possible when I look to God for answers and comfort in the Scriptures and in prayer. During the difficult times, I need to evaluate if there is a lesson to learn or a change to be made. Then, as a young child with a loving Father, I simply must trust Him.

Kathy Stark
Missionary to Uganda

17 THE EYE OF THE STORM

"And now I exhort you to be of good cheer..." (Acts 27:22).

When I was 11 weeks pregnant and exhausted from the day, I went to bed only to be awakened in the middle of the night. As I lay in bed, God spoke to my heart to read over the Sunday School lesson I was to teach the next day. He impressed upon my heart the lesson was for me! So I hesitantly obeyed and re-read this lesson in a new light — scrutinizing every word and praying to see God's lesson for me.

The story takes place with Paul on a ship in a horrible storm, which threatened to take the lives of everyone onboard. But God spoke to Paul in the middle of the night (sound familiar?) and told him that he and everyone onboard would survive this storm. They would not only survive, but they would also become building blocks for faith and character. Others would come to know Christ because of their faith in this experience. God did not say He would take the storm away — He simply chose to show His presence and ride through it with Paul, comforting him and holding him in His arms.

God loved me so much that He chose to prepare me through His Word for the trials coming my way. The next day, I told my husband, Ken, about my precious moments with God, and that in some shape or form God was going to give us a storm in our life. That following week, on August 24, 2002, God welcomed our baby into His loving arms when I miscarried. And on November 11, 2002, after another miscarriage, He welcomed another one. I have not reached the shore yet, but while I'm still in the center of the storm, I find such peace and calmness in knowing that His loving presence in my life is truly all that I need.

Just as Paul learned, I also am learning more love, faith, and character, and my prayer is that others will come to know my Father better through this process. I have promised Him that I will glorify Him through this experience. Now I want to challenge you to pay close attention when God speaks to your heart. He might want to prepare you for an upcoming storm. Be careful to not be angry if God answers "no" to taking away your storm. He wants us to see that His presence and peace are often found in the eye of the storm.

Geri Frances Harris

18 THE BATTLE FOUGHT

"Saying, Father, if thou be willing, remove this cup from me: nevertheless not my will, but thine, be done" (Luke 22:42).

My heavenly Father came today
    And spoke His will to me,
But I rebelled against His way
    And prayed, "Lord, let me be."

My desires were not contained therein
    As I surveyed His plans;
I argued with Him, "Change your will –
    This one I will not have!"

I cried and begged but fast He stood
    And so I fought His will;
With angry words and busy hands
    His verdict I tried to repeal.

But kick as I would against the pricks
    God would not let me win;
For those to Him their lives commit,
    Only His best He'll send.

Weary at last, no strength was left,
    I succumbed, accepted His will;
To my surprise I then found rest
    And contentment my heart filled.

I fought with God, ashamed to say
    His will I tried to defy;
But I can say, "Praise God for this,
    He won the battle – not I."

Margaret Hoskins Dellinger

19 A PROVERBS 31 WOMAN

"Who can find a virtuous woman? for her price is far above rubies" (Proverbs 31:10).

Here are 13 "eggscellant" ways to improve life in your little nest:

Pray for your husband every day. Thank God for his strengths, and pray for his weaknesses. Make God your first priority and your husband second, every day.

Before arguing, ask yourself, "What's the argument about, and is it really worth hurt feelings?"

Don't nag. If your man doesn't do something you want him to do, such as help around the house or with the children, make simple suggestions and pray!

Don't skip church, even to be together. You need the stability, consistency, and teaching.

Don't take for granted your finances. Communicate and agree upon a budget and the guidelines to keep you within the budget. Don't secretly spend on little things, because they add up.

Don't hold sex over your husband's head! It is not a bargaining tool.

Don't say no to sex just because you're not in the mood. Get in the mood. The moral to this rule is: "If he can't get it at home, there is always someplace else he can get it."

Dress up and fix up for your husband. He loves to look at you that way. Most of the women he sees all day long at work look that way!

Don't talk down about his family. If there is something that bothers you about them, talk constructively and lovingly. It is human nature to defend your family when attacked. Don't attack!

Interest yourself in his interests. Let him talk about what he likes to do. Communicate!

Build him up! Tell him how much and why you love him. Talk about how good he makes you feel and what a wonderful husband he is. Compliment him on his strengths. When you build up a person's strengths instead of beating them with their weaknesses, they will naturally want to turn their weaknesses into strengths.

Allow and expect him to be the spiritual leader. If he doesn't want to take the initiative, gently give it to him without pushing or nagging.

Submit to him with no strings attached!

Sabrina Boshell

20 I CAN DO ALL THINGS

"I can do all things through Christ which strengtheneth me" (Philippians 4:13).

In this verse, Paul is saying that he can do everything, from being poor to living like a king, through Jesus Who gave him the strength to handle anything. This was not an expression of pride in his own abilities, but an example of the strength Christ provides.

This is my life's verse. My mom helped me choose it when I was invited to participate in the Pre-Teen Alabama Pageant to compete for scholarships with other girls from the state. I was invited to participate because of my good grades and extracurricular activities. This invitation was an honor and very exciting for me, because it was very difficult to make the grades that I did. School does not come easy for me, and I usually come home with a headache every day. Don't get me wrong. I don't make bad grades, but in order to achieve the A's and B's that I make, I have to try harder than a lot of my friends do. I know they don't understand. However, I do know that it is through God's strength that I am able to do it, not on my own.

There are people who are smarter, funnier, stronger, more athletic, and more talented than I am, but that doesn't matter to me. I know God made me the way I am, and He made me just the way He wanted me to be. He chose everything about me, like the color of my hair and eyes. He gave me special talents and abilities that I can excel in. I could not achieve things without encouragement from my parents and friends, but above all I need Christ. I believe with all of my heart that I can achieve anything I want to, as long as I ask Christ to help me.

Amanda Barnette

21 VENGEANCE IS MINE SAITH THE LORD

"...Vengeance belongeth unto me, I will recompense, saith the Lord..." (Hebrews 10:30).

As principal of our Christian Day School in Nicaragua, I was working with the teachers to have the best Christian education we could for the children who were enrolled in the school. In the midst of all this, a national pastor became jealous of my work in the school and began to give false testimony to some of the church people and parents of the school children. I talked with him and tried to work out our differences. He would not listen. The pastor thought that I was getting rich from the school. This was a lie. The children were paying $1.40 a month for tuition. I did not receive a salary, and I was always helping with the finances of the school. Other lies followed until I was ready to give up and return to the States. A Christian lawyer told me that I could have the pastor put in prison if I wished to do so. I told the lawyer that I wanted to leave it in the hands of the Lord and that He would take care of the problem.

I felt that I was not wanted and it was time to leave. Another pastor came to me, and we had a long discussion about the problem. This pastor asked me how many people lived in the city of Managua. At that time, there were about 485,000 people. Then he asked me how many people attended the church where the problem existed. There were about 285. He then asked how many would be left in the city if we subtracted 285 from 485,000. Considering the large number of unreached people in Managua, I chose to stay in Nicaragua but leave the school. I decided to work elsewhere and let the Lord handle the vengeance.

In time, the insulting pastor suffered a mental breakdown and had to be hospitalized for treatment. After many months of treatment, when he was on his way back to good mental health, he came to the school where I was working and asked my forgiveness for what he had done. I accepted his apology.

I am telling you this to remind you of God's gracious care for His children when they come to Him in distress. God always answers our prayers in His own special way.

Martha Kunberger
Retired Missionary from Nicaragua

22 UNDER THE SHADOW

"I will say of the Lord, He is my refuge and my fortress: my God; in him will I trust" (Psalm 91:2).

Every morning at the breakfast table before school, I would recite a little of Psalm 91 until I had memorized it all. I was a fourth-grader and a young Christian. My mother listened, prompting me when I would forget a word here or there. She knew this was a portion of Scripture that would bring me encouragement, peace, and hope in the times of life that would seem so hopeless.

Now I was about to become a mother myself. An Army wife, alone in a foreign country, I was expecting our first child. It was during the Kosovo conflict, and more experienced Army wives told me not to expect to see my husband for a year. But I refused to give in to that idea. I just couldn't conceive of it. Not only that, but how much danger was he in? Were they really safe out there on that muddy airstrip in Tirane, especially when every major news network was reporting live from there just about as soon as our forces were in place? I thought, "God, what are You doing? Will he be all right?"

Then turning to the Word, I found comfort once again in those precious words of Psalm 91. "He is my refuge and my fortress…Thou shalt not be afraid for the terror by night; nor for the arrow that flieth by day…There shall no evil befall thee, neither shall any plague come nigh thy dwelling." The word "dwelling" literally means "tent." My husband, Brian, was living in a tent for three months. The comfort I felt after reading those words was indescribable. I was reminded that Almighty God, our loving heavenly Father, was protecting both of us, and He would not allow any harm to come to Brian, because Brian was dwelling in the "secret place of the most High." I rested that night knowing that God was in control. God is faithful to His Word. Rest in that assurance. When we are dwelling in that secret place, we are under the shadow of His wing!

Cecelia Hagood

23 MOTHER'S BUTTON BOX

"She seeketh wool, and flax, and worketh willingly with her hands" (Proverbs 31:13).

Mother is a precious Christian lady who loves the Lord and her family. She was always working with her hands – sewing, cooking, cleaning, or doing whatever needed to be done when I was growing up. One day, I asked, "Mother, don't you ever want to just do nothing?" She answered, "Oh, no, there are always things to be done." As I grew older, I found out that is so true. Being a wife and mother means there are always things waiting to be done. Mother made our clothes, mostly from cloth that came from the cow's feed sacks. Mother also had a button box filled with buttons from clothes we had outgrown or worn out. Mother would pour out the buttons, looking for the right size and color for the garment she was making. Many nights, she would sit up making dresses for me or cowboy shirts for my brothers. Sometimes we needed them, and sometimes she made them so we would have something to wear for a special occasion. Other things, like old jewelry or a pen, would also find their way into the button box. We didn't have a lot, but mother made our home happy and as comfortable as she could.

Mother is now 84 years old, and four years ago she had a stroke, which affected her speech and motor skills. She is not able to sew, quilt, write letters, or read, which were some of her favorite things to do. She still has a beautiful smile and a sparkle in her eyes. Some of the few things she can say are, "I love you, darling," and "in Jesus' name" at the end of a prayer. She radiates joy to each person who knows her. God is good to have given me a mother that loves the Lord and that taught her children to love Him, too. She recently went to her button box and struggled as she sewed a button on my dad's shirt. This brought joy and tears to my eyes to know she is still trying to serve the ones she loves. This is a poem my mother wrote several years ago:

MY OLD BUTTON BOX

By Paunee Hall Honley

One day I went to my button box to find a button for my vest.
I poured out all my buttons to see which one was best.
As I looked through the collection my thoughts wander back.
Articles nudged my recollection; all colors yellow, red, and black.
There was Grandma's broken brooch and Daddy's old fountain pen,
Button off daughter's baby dress I haven't thought of since "Lord knows when,"
A button from a Cub Scout shirt, a bow tie from a skit, a zipper from a skirt,
Oh yes, a snap from a cowboy's shirt.
Now as I look through this pile of junk,
My mind wanders back. I think of my three sons sleeping on their bunk.
And my only daughter, I see her in her gathered skirt with so many petticoats.
Oh she was so pert.
Now they are married and gone away.
I am left to remember how it was in other days.
It all began with my old button box.
I put it away now and remember it again at another date.

Louise Anglin
Rock of Ages Prison Ministry

24 How God Speaks To Bradley

"And when he putteth forth his own sheep, he goeth before them, and the sheep follow him: for they know his voice" (John 10:4).

One day while we were riding in the car, my five year old, Bradley, said, "Mom, do you know that God speaks to me in my head?" I said, "Yes, that is how we know what God wants us to do. He speaks to our hearts and our minds." Then I asked Bradley, "What is God saying to you?" Bradley said, "Well, how should I know? He is speaking Spanish!"

I think many of us have felt like Bradley. We have tried to listen to the voice of God. Yet with our inhibitions and preconceived ideas, it is hard to truly understand what He is saying. But God promised us that if we, as His children, stay in His Word, we will know His voice.

Anita Blunier

25 Through Trials and Tribulations

"Fear none of those things which thou shalt suffer: behold, the devil shall cast some of you into prison, that ye may be tried; and ye shall have tribulation ten days: be thou faithful unto death, and I will give thee a crown of life" (Revelation 2:10).

In 2000, I thought my life had come to an end. I was faced with the biggest tragedy a mother would ever want to face. My son, Michael, was playing basketball on a church team. As we were watching him play one day, Michael jumped up to block a shot and fell on the court. My husband and I just sat there, thinking he had just gotten the wind knocked out of him or twisted his ankle, but that wasn't the case. I ran up to my son and saw him covered with sweat, because he was in so much pain. Seeing his leg so disfigured, I knew something very bad had happened.

Later on, we got to the hospital, had x-rays taken, and talked to the doctors. We found out that Michael had a tumor in his bone, which was why it broke. At that moment, it felt like somebody stabbed me in my heart. I thought, "My son could be dying. Why would God let this happen?"

I know that God had a reason for my family to go through this trial. Revelation 2:10 says, "Fear none of those things which thou shalt suffer..." Only in Heaven will we know if God allowed Michael to break his leg so we could find out early about the tumor. That knowledge saved his leg and maybe his life. God showed me that when I have trials and tribulations, it is proof of my faith, and that God uses my trials and tribulations to make me more like Jesus Christ.

Sandy Micklow

26 WHO AM I?

"Better it is to be of an humble spirit with the lowly, than to divide the spoil with the proud" (Proverbs 16:19).

Have you ever wondered why you were chosen for a specific task or why God used you in a certain situation? Perhaps your questioning stemmed from curiosity, or better still, maybe from humility. Humility is a tremendous attribute for a Christian to possess. However, most of us do not possess a humble spirit. When we think we do, we probably do not. Someone once said that a humble man agrees with his critics.

A perfect example of this remarkable Christian virtue is found in the life of David. It is likely that David's humility began in his youth. As a shepherd, he learned to perform menial, humble tasks. In Saul's kingdom, David became the king's own personal servant and musician. David learned to tend to the needs of others.

Later in his life, when David was named king of Israel, he maintained his humility. When God promised that He would establish his throne forever, David was surprised and asked, "...Who am I, O Lord God? and what is my house, that thou hast brought me hitherto?" (II Samuel 7:18).

Imagine that! David was already king of Israel and a very respected man. Yet he still asked, "Who am I?" instead of,

"Who else but me?" It is very likely that David's humility was the thing that allowed God to use him in a tremendous way.

Lord, help me to be truly humble. Use me as You see fit for Your glory, and help me to sincerely ask, "Who, me?"

Melissa K. Roe
Missionary to Cuba

27 I Am Blessed

"That they may teach the young women to be sober, to love their husbands, to love their children" (Titus 2:4)

In 1992, I was recovering from a divorce of a 32-year marriage, from which you never really recover. Soon after that, our church made a change from all lecture classes taught by men to tables in each department with ladies teaching ladies and men teaching men. Brother Doug Ripley called me to ask if I would teach in the young married department, and the Lord gave me Titus 2:4. I had taught a ladies class for many years before coming to Decatur Baptist Church, but at this time I did not want to teach. All I wanted to do was sit and listen. I knew I had been a good wife, and the Lord put a burden on my heart that made me realize I could teach young married ladies to be the wives God wants them to be.

Over the past ten years, God has blessed me with some of the finest young ladies who have helped me more than they will ever know. I teach them to leave their father and mother and to cleave to their husband. I instruct them to put God first in their life, their husband second, and then their children. Then I encourage them to teach their children the same principles. No matter what kind of life they have seen their mother or their grandmother live, they can make a difference using their own life and being the wife God wants them to be.

The Lord has so blessed my life through my teaching ministry. On many days, when I was discouraged, one of the young ladies would call or come by to share their burdens. We would pray, and then I seemed to forget all of my problems. Thank You, Lord, for Your blessings on me.

Shirley White Teal

28 LET GO AND LET GOD

"My brethren, count it all joy when ye fall into divers temptations; Knowing this, that the trying of your faith worketh patience. But let patience have her perfect work, that ye may be perfect and entire, wanting nothing" (James 1:2-4).

Have you ever been at the end of your rope, so to speak, and felt there was no hope, no help, and nowhere to turn? Sometimes we are so determined to do things our way that we won't give up when giving up is the best thing we can do. We should be submissive to God and admit to ourselves that we don't know what to do.

Some people have to hurt more than others do. I am just thankful God loved me enough to let me hurt until I got back on track. There are sufferings that come as a result of trying to live for the Lord the best you know how. James 1:2-4 talks about the trials the followers of Christ will suffer. Romans 8:28 says all things work together for good to them that love the Lord. If you haven't been there, you will. If you are a child of God, He has a plan for your life.

Again, I am thankful each day for all the sufferings I have endured because of what they have taught me. When will all our problems and sufferings end? That happens when we get to Heaven. God is not finished with me yet, and I am learning to trust the Lord with all my heart and lean not on my own understanding (Proverbs 3:5). I am also learning to let go and let God handle my problems.

There is an old song that says, "Where could I go, Oh, where could I go, seeking a refuge for my soul, needing a friend to help me in the end. Where could I go but to the Lord?"

Mary Ann Keeton

29 For You, Mom

"Her children arise up, and call her blessed; her husband also, and he praiseth her" (Proverbs 31:28).

My daughter Tara wrote this for me as a Mother's Day gift in 1993:

Into this world I was born from you.
    Within this world you have carried me through.

As a baby I began,
    And so many times into your loving arms I ran.
I have sought shelter in your love,
    And thanked God for my blessing from above.

I have never wished for another mother, that's true.
    I have never wanted anyone but you.

My friends all envied me so.
    They all wished to my home they could go.
I could stand and be proud of my mother, you see.
    I could always know you truly loved me.

As the years clicked quickly past,
    I never realized how your love stood steadfast.
When I faltered and fell, you picked me up.
    When I began to thirst, you filled my cup.

Grown into a woman now, with children of my own,
    I can now realize how deep your love was sown.

You love my children as no other could.
    You love my children as I always dreamed you would.
Kisses and hugs are a specialty of yours.
    With kisses and hugs the meaning of "grandma" soars.

I have always loved you, my dear Mother, and that you
    should know.
My love will follow you wherever you go.

LaVone Benton

30 God Turns It Into Good

"But as for you, ye thought evil against me; but God meant it unto good, to bring to pass, as it is this day, to save much people alive" (Genesis 50:20).

A few years ago, my husband, Ed, and I invested much of our time training, teaching, and discipling two young girls that were saved under our ministry. We would constantly open the doors of our home to them, as they both did not have the opportunity to live in a Christian home or even a well structured home.

One night, because of bad information, they asked to talk to me. In an arrogant and hurtful way, they attempted to discipline me and scolded me for something they later found out was not true. After discussing the matter for an hour, during which they attacked me many times, I went home crying and brokenhearted. It was hard to explain to my husband through my tears what had happened. How could these sisters in Christ think I could do something like that? For two days, I experienced depression, sadness, and anger, as I remembered the words of those two young girls.

As I began putting things in order of the whole situation and reading my Bible, Genesis 50:20 gave me victory. It became very clear to me that even though they desired something evil against me, God was using it for good, just like He did when Joseph's brothers sold him into slavery. Looking back on this emotional experience, I can see how God has transformed it into something good.

Have you felt attacked, disregarded, and criticized by others? Remember, God can and will transform it into something good. Do not fear. Just sit back and watch how He changes everything around you.

Annita Hoagland
Missionary to Mexico

1 He Is Able

"And seek not ye what ye shall eat, or what ye shall drink, neither be ye of doubtful mind. For all these things do the nations of the world seek after: and your Father knoweth that ye have need of these things. But rather seek ye the kingdom of God; and all these things shall be added unto you. Fear not, little flock; for it is your Father's good pleasure to give you the kingdom" (Luke 12:29-32).

A few years ago, the Lord taught me very clearly that He is able to provide for all of my needs. My family was preparing to come back to the United States on furlough after serving as missionaries in Brazil for our first term. I was born and raised in Brazil as a missionary kid, and my husband is a native Brazilian, so we were actually leaving rather than coming home. I was very concerned about how we would set up housekeeping, since we had left nothing in the States.

A few weeks before going on furlough, I read Luke 12:29-32. Though I had read that passage a number of times, those verses spoke to me in a special way that day, considering my need. I prayed, "Dear Father, we are striving to put You first in our lives. In these verses, You have told me not to worry, but to trust in You to care for my needs. Though I don't understand how, You will fulfill what You have promised."

I wish I could say that after that prayer, I never worried again. As my parents drove us to the airport in Sao Paulo, I told my mother, "I just don't know what we are going to do! We will need to buy dishes, sheets, pillows, blankets, towels, an iron — everything!"

We traveled by plane all night with our four-year-old and six-month-old daughters. Exhausted from a sleepless night, I wondered what awaited us as we drove in our rented car from Atlanta, Georgia to Greenville, South Carolina. Some friends had already rented a mobile home for us, and I imagined we would need to clean the place up first. And there were all of those things we needed to buy! I knew my husband, Rom, would not be in the mood to go out shopping, but I told him, "I don't know what condition the trailer is in or what all we will need to buy today, but one thing we need urgently is some diapers for Roxanne." He just nodded. I knew he was as exhausted as I was.

We finally arrived in Greenville. When we drove up to our temporary home, I noticed flowers planted around our front door. It warmed my heart to see that someone in our church had taken the time to do that for us. However, I was still unprepared for what awaited us. As I entered the front door, I felt as if I was entering Heaven's gate. People from our church not only cleaned and fixed up the interior of the trailer from top to bottom, but they also had completely furnished the place, all the way down to a full refrigerator and hangers in our closets. They also put in a few decorative touches, and there was even a package of disposable diapers in our baby's size!

God had prepared better for me and my family than I could have dreamed. I guess God was trying to tell me, while I was still in Brazil, that He was taking care of everything. Thank You, God, for once again showing me Your love and care.

Rachel Ribeiro
Missionary to Brazil

2 Sanctify Yourself

"And Joshua said unto the people, Sanctify yourselves: for tomorrow the Lord will do wonders among you" (Joshua 3:5).

Upon reading this verse, God reminded me that sanctify means "to set apart" and that today I need to set myself apart. Today I need to be different, not just from the guys at the bar or the girls at that party, but I even need to be different from Christians who are complacent. I need to be set apart individually to Who Christ is, because I'm not supposed to compare myself to anyone except Christ. He is the standard, and He is perfect. God is so good to me. Why do I ever think of being complacent? Why do I assume God will settle for me doing good and not my best? Complacency sure is foolish of me, and it sure is sin. I need to strive for perfection, because if I do, God has amazing wonders prepared for my tomorrow. If

I don't sanctify myself, then I'll miss out on His blessings. Reading this verse renewed in me a desire to be sanctified, not only because I want those wonders in my life, but also because I really do want to be one that is pleasing to God.

Anne DeKoker

3 Can I Be the One To Tell Her About Jesus?

"Tell ye your children of it, and let your children tell their children, and their children another generation" (Joel 1:3).

One Friday night, I had the joy of having both of my grandchildren, three-year-old Kyleigh and eight-year-old Devin, spend the night with me. Early the next morning, the house was full of laughing and playing. After I fixed them breakfast, I went into my bedroom to get dressed for the day ahead of us. Like most children, they immediately realized that they did not have my attention and came to see what I found to be more important than being with them. I explained to them that I needed to get dressed and that I wouldn't be long. I told them to continue playing their game, and I would be with them all day.

As I was putting on my earrings, Devin came into my room to ask me just one more question. As I turned around and looked at him, he asked, "Grammy, when Kyleigh gets old enough to be saved, can I be the one to pray with her?" Already deep in my Grammy mode to say "yes" to almost anything my grandchildren want, I didn't know what to say. Tears came into my eyes as I hugged him and drew him into my lap to tell him how proud I was of him. I told him what a big honor it is to tell people about Jesus and that he would always be a great example to his cousin, because of Jesus living in his heart. But I told him that praying with Kyleigh is an experience that her mother would want to have.

With a smile on his face, he ran back into the living room, leaving me with my thoughts. God, we must be doing something right for our son's son to want to be the one to introduce our daughter's daughter to Jesus. God, please help me to be as eager as Devin to tell someone about Jesus.

Katy Ripley

4 Faith Brings Peace And Happiness

"Therefore being justified by faith, we have peace with God through our Lord Jesus Christ" (Romans 5:1).

You can ask any woman what she wants, and her answer will be happiness and peace. Most of us never experience this peace. Our lives are always like a whirlwind, because we are always too busy. Even when things are going well, there are still many worries, such as the kids, the house, a job, school, etc. One of the things that God has been showing me in His Word is how to have this internal peace and happiness! It only comes through faith in Him! Only unconditional trust in the Lord will give us complete security, trust, and hope.

We know that Jesus Christ died on the cross for our sins. When we accept Jesus Christ into our hearts, He accepts us just as we are. Think about our heavenly Father – His wisdom, His mercy, and His power. Romans 5:1 says we are justified by faith. If we believe all of this, why aren't we happy? Why don't we experience this internal peace in our daily lives?

The answer is that true faith demands service. Our pastor and leaders have a vision to not only reach our city, but also to reach the world with the Gospel of Christ. This gives us many opportunities to minister. But the most important ministry is the sharing of our faith. If you are single, share your faith with your family and friends. If you are a teen, share your faith at school. If you are married, share your faith with your husband and your children.

Hebrews 11:6 says that without faith, it is impossible to please God. Lord, help me to have faith in You and serve You through my faith, because it is only then that I will experience happiness and peace. May my faith be shown by my service unto You.

Marisol Adanari Tippett

5 KEEP A HUMBLE SPIRIT

"By humility and the fear of the Lord are riches, and honour, and life" (Proverbs 22:4).

Great is your gladness,
And rich your reward,
When you make life's purposes,
The choice of the Lord.

We are humbled again and again. I pray that God will help me to keep a humbled spirit and not be proud.

Last evening, our oldest daughter, Joy, and I gave four orphaned children sweatshirts and sweaters to help keep them a little warmer against the cold. My heart had gone out for the littlest one, Crystal Bell. I have seen her many times in her small ragged dress, two times too small for her. She is about seven or eight years old, but her small size is about the same size as that of my own healthy five year old, Grace.

I gave Crystal a turtleneck and a jumper. I wanted her to feel the same joy and happiness that I feel when I am blessed with something that I need. Then, I gave her sister and two older brothers each a sweater. Little Crystal Bell turned to her older brother, Sam, about 10 to 12 years old. She began speaking excitedly in her native tongue. I asked, "What is she saying?" The interpreter said, "She is telling Sam, now he will have something to protect him from the cold."

I think that there is a good lesson to be learned from this poor, ragged orphan girl. She had nothing and yet she found joy in the blessings of others more than her own. My heart broke. We have so much, and yet we complain and want more. The things that I gave were not even a sacrifice. Lord, help me to be more like the poor, ragged orphan girl!

Beth Ann Severt
Missionary to Zambia

6 AT THE SCULPTOR'S HANDS

"As far as the east is from the west, so far hath he removed our transgressions from us" (Psalm 103:12).

Have you ever gotten to the point and time in your life when you feel you just can't take any more? When you think it can't get any worse, something else happens, and it does! I was at a business meeting not too long ago that totally changed the way that I look at adversities and trials in my life.

The story was told about a sculptor and his block of marble. It takes years for him to chisel away a piece here, hammer away a hunk there, and smooth away a rough edge by knocking or carving, until one day there is a priceless masterpiece waiting to be discovered.

As I began to think about what was said, I came to the conclusion that when adversities and trials come into my life, God, the Master Sculptor, is trying to sculpt me into being who and what He needs me to be for Him. He is molding my character so that I will become more Christ-like. Trust me, I am a hard piece of marble to chisel away at. He had to hammer several times in some areas until I broke. Hardheaded, opinionated, rebellious, temperamental — not exactly a mirror image of Christ-likeness, is it? Every day, God carves away and smoothes a little bit more in these areas of my life. It has not been an easy road, and I regret to say that I have hurt some very special people along the way. But praise God for forgiveness! Most people say forgiveness, but I say "forgetness," because Psalm 103:12 says, "As far as the east is from the west, so far hath he removed our transgressions from us." He forgets – never to be remembered again.

So, the next time you feel you can't take any more, and you are getting chiseled on, hammered on, carved at, and knocked, don't forget that the Master Sculptor is at work. He is fine-tuning those rough areas of our lives, so that one day we will be that priceless masterpiece for His kingdom.

Peggy McKleroy

7 No Short Cuts

"These things have I spoken unto you, that in me ye might have peace. In the world ye shall have tribulation: but be of good cheer; I have overcome the world (John 16:33).

When God wanted to train His first two children not to touch, He did not place the forbidden object out of their reach — He placed the tree of knowledge of good and evil in the midst of the garden, where they would pass it continually. God's purpose was not to save the tree, but to train the couple. By exercising their wills to not eat, they would have learned the meaning of good, as well as evil. Eating was a shortcut to the knowledge God would teach them in His own timing.

God spoke to my heart concerning my desire to take shortcuts, especially during times of hardship. I busy myself in looking for an easier way. God showed me that I needed to stop looking for shortcuts in my attitude and in my mothering skills. His desire for me is to walk through the hard times, no matter what.

God created the universe and everything in it. He sacrificed His perfect Son to give me eternal life. He loves me more than I can comprehend. O God, help me to remain faithful and cheerful as You accomplish Your work in me.

Tammy Gordon

8 GIVING HIM CONTROL

"...for I the Lord thy God am a jealous God, visiting the iniquity of the fathers upon the children unto the third and fourth generation of them that hate me; And shewing mercy unto thousands of them that love me, and keep my commandments" (Exodus 20:5-6).

When my children were young, my daily routine revolved around meeting all of their needs. I made sure they ate a variety of healthy foods and restricted junk food, limited the time they spent watching T.V., and banned video games from the house. I also encouraged outdoor activities, read good books every night at bedtime, and welcomed appropriate friends into our home.

But as my children grew older and more independent, I could no longer control everything they did. One thing that particularly distressed me was my son's emerging pattern of taking on helpless girlfriends. I shuddered at the thought of him marrying such a dependent type of woman. My son had assumed the role of "man of the house" early in life because of my divorce and had always been my knight in shining armor. It was evident that he was simply transferring his care for me to a girlfriend.

During this time, God was revealing my failures to me. I came to realize that I had a big problem. Believing that I was indispensable, I was working myself to death trying to be the caretaker of everyone within reach. As I submitted myself to God's will for my life, He led me to stop trying to be in control and instead to trust in His power. My personal problems resolved, and my life dramatically improved.

After 11 years of singleness, I met and married a wonderful man. Shortly after the wedding, without any advice from me, my son broke up with his girlfriend. They stayed friends, but he established personal boundaries that gave him the space he needed for personal growth. It was evident that my newfound freedom had freed my son as well! As I considered how my psychological state was replicated in my son, I determined to exercise this power for good. I have to keep myself spiritually healthy, not just for myself, but for all the loved ones in my life.

Joanna McAbee

9 A Virtuous Woman

"Who can find a virtuous woman? for her price is far above rubies" (Proverbs 31:10).

Have we forgotten how to be virtuous women? Are we being taught? Are we teaching our daughters, our granddaughters, and other women to be virtuous women?

In *Webster's Dictionary*, virtue is defined as moral excellence and righteousness. Virtuous is defined as displaying virtue; righteousness, endowed with or marked by chastity of a girl or woman; to be pure. The Bible describes a virtuous woman in Proverbs 31:10-31. She is trustworthy, she works willingly with her hands, she is frugal, she helps the poor and needy, she provides for her family, she is kind, she is wise, and she fears the Lord.

As women, we are single, we are wives, we are mothers, and we are grandmothers. The future of our lives, as well as the lives of our children, our grandchildren, our families, and our marriages, rests in large part on the kind of women we choose to be. There is no greater call on our lives than that of being virtuous women. Satan tries to blind us to this truth by telling us that we don't have everything we need, that there's something we're missing out on. But Satan is our enemy, and he wants to destroy our families, our churches, and us.

Once we have accepted Jesus Christ as our Savior, we are to be new women. We are to live our lives in a manner that is above reproach. Dear Lord, help me to be a virtuous woman, and help me to be an example for my daughters, granddaughters, and other women.

Margaret Bond Marble

10 God Watches Over The Sparrows

"Are not two sparrows sold for a farthing? and one of them shall not fall on the ground without your Father" (Matthew 10:29).

Several years ago, my husband and I were asked to go to Germany with a group from our church to teach discipleship. My husband really wanted to go, but I was afraid to fly. I was also afraid to go into a foreign country. I told my husband that I would pray about it, really thinking that I already knew the answer. As I had promised, I started to pray about what God would have me to do. The next day, we had to give our answer. As much as I wanted to, God would not let me say "no" and still have peace. It seemed the Lord was right there with me, and I was faced with the question: "Do I trust Him or not?" I remember saying out loud, "Yes, Lord! I do trust You. I will go."

As we began making preparations to leave in eight weeks, it seemed everything went wrong. First, both of our cars broke down, then the refrigerator broke, our heating system quit, and I got very sick. Just six weeks before we were to board the plane, the doctor found that I had multiple gallstones and said I needed surgery. I told him of my commitment to the trip, and asked if the surgery could be postponed until I returned. The doctor insisted that I not go to Europe before having the surgery. He said if everything went well, I should be able to go on the trip as planned. At this point, I was very concerned, because in three previous surgeries, I had developed complications.

When I left the doctor's office, I was almost in tears. How could we pay for repairs to our cars, the refrigerator, and heating system, and still have money for our trip and my surgery? When I returned home, I walked into the den, leaned against the glass door, and began to cry as I started to talk to the Lord. "Lord, I don't understand why these things are happening! I don't know if it's Satan trying to hinder me and discourage me from going, or if it's You telling me that

You don't want me to go. Please, Lord, I want to do Your will, and I don't know what to do." Just then, two little sparrows came hopping across the patio. Suddenly the Holy Spirit brought to my mind what God says about the sparrows in His Word. I got my Bible and looked up everything I could find about the sparrows. In every case, God was saying how He loved and took care of sparrows, and that He would take care of me.

Four weeks before we left for Germany, I went into the hospital and had my gallbladder removed. They were able to do laser surgery, and for the first time, I had no complications! When my departure day for the trip arrived, I was ready! God had supplied what we needed for all the repairs. I kept up with the team, carried my own baggage, and felt fine. The trip was wonderful, and God taught me many things. It is so wonderful to have a heavenly Father who loves us and takes care of us in every area of our lives!

Barbara Allred

11 THE BEST MOTHER'S DAY GIFT

"And all things, whatsoever ye shall ask in prayer, believing, ye shall receive" (Matthew 21:22).

I want to tell you about the best gift I have ever received on Mother's Day. I have three children, and I love them all dearly. My oldest son, Brandon, stopped going to church when he moved out on his own, and this was hard for me to accept. I wondered where I had gone wrong and what I could have done differently. I talked to him about it at different times, and he said it was his choice. My husband and I both worried about him.

As the years went on, we talked to Brandon about his salvation, and he assured us he got saved when he was six years old. I prayed daily for Brandon, as well as for my other children, Jonathan and Emily, holding onto Matthew 21:22. I know Brandon's dad, brother, and sister prayed for him, too.

We tried inviting him to special services, anything to reach out to him. But only God knew what it would take to bring my son back to Him.

Through some very sad events in Brandon's life, he reached out to God, and God saved him on May 4, 2002. On Mother's Day 2002, Brandon asked me if I would walk with him down the aisle, so he could make a public profession of faith. There was much rejoicing with all three of my children at church on that Mother's Day.

God always heard my prayers, but He answered them in His time and in His way. I hope this will be an encouragement to any mother whose child is going his or her own way instead of God's way. Never stop praying, never stop believing, and never lose hope, because God is faithful.

Janice Blankenship

12 THE BIBLE STUDY LESSON GOD PREPARED FOR ME

"For even hereunto were ye called: because Christ also suffered for us, leaving us an example, that ye should follow his steps" (I Peter 2:21).

One week, I spent more time than usual preparing my Bible study lesson. I was not sure why this lesson on suffering intrigued me so, but it did. God was showing me so much about why we suffer, how He shares in our suffering, and the spiritual growth it brings about in our lives. I was excited about sharing these truths with my care group on Sunday.

As is my usual practice, I rose early that Sunday morning to review the lesson just one more time. As I was finishing, the telephone rang. It was my 21-year-old daughter, Erin, hysterically telling me that her four-week-old baby had died during the night. We later learned that his death was due to Sudden Infant Death Syndrome. My husband, Ron, and I, of course, rushed immediately to Erin's side. Those next several days were very hard. The pain of losing my grandchild continues even today.

I never did get to teach that lesson to my care group, but I now know that it was not for them that God gave me such a strong desire to study it. In His infinite wisdom and mercy, God had been giving me what I needed to be able to endure those tragic, difficult days that lay ahead. What a strength and comfort it was to be able to draw upon those things I had so recently learned, and to be able to share them with my daughter and other family members, who were also grieving. What joy it gives me to know that God loves me so much!

Melanie Cook

13 SOMETIMES YOU JUST HAVE TO LAUGH!

"A merry heart doeth good like a medicine: but a broken spirit drieth the bones" (Proverbs 17:22).

Have you ever had one of those days when you felt that God was telling you to stop, slow down, and enjoy your kids? Well, this is about one of those days for me.

I was in the process of loading our van to head to Gatlinburg, and I was becoming frustrated. My husband was running late, which meant I would have to finish all the loading by myself. My kids were hyper and very excited about leaving, while I was stressed with a capital "S." Johanna was in the kitchen with a Coke in her hand, and I had just warned her to not spill it. Less than ten seconds later, I heard her say, "I spilled it!" Now, even more frustrated and angry, I yelled at her to get something to clean it up. She grabbed her rabbit blanket, and I quickly took it from her and said, "Not your blanket, you will want to sleep with it. Now use your head!"

The next time I turned around, Johanna was on her knees, swishing her hair back and forth on the floor, trying to clean up the Coke. "Johanna! What are you doing?" I cried. She answered, "You told me to use my head!" I threw her a towel and tried very hard to be serious, but it was no use. The situation got the best of me, and I began to laugh as my stress evaporated.

God was showing me that sometimes I just need to chill out. Johanna is only four years old, and I need to take the time to enjoy her at this age. One day, she will be all grown up, and all I will have are these precious memories.

Kellie Halbrooks

14 Prayer Paths

"But thou, when thou prayest, enter into thy closet, and when thou hast shut thy door, pray to thy Father which is in secret; and thy Father which seeth in secret shall reward thee openly" (Matthew 6:6).

Having been a missionary for 25 years, ministering through church planting in South Africa, I've learned a lot through the customs and ways of the natives.

When people in rural areas accept Christ, he or she is taught to select a quiet spot in the bush for his or her daily devotions. As they go there daily, a path is worn in the grass. But the grass grows rapidly. If they miss a day, the grass grows higher. If they continue to miss their quiet time, the path disappears. These prayer paths gauge the spiritual condition of a person.

Do we have distinct prayer paths into God's presence, or has the grass grown over them because we have neglected our quiet times? It has been said of prayer, "The equipment for the inner life of prayer is simple. It consists of a quiet place, a quiet time, and a quiet heart."

These are not easily achieved. Perhaps it is difficult to find a place where we can have solitude and quietness. It may be that our schedules are so full that we have difficulty finding a time to be still before God. There may be so much tension, confusion, and turmoil in our lives that it seems impossible to quiet our hearts in His presence.

Our alone time with God is important. That will lead us

to pray without ceasing. As we pray without ceasing, our lives will be lived in the spirit of prayer as we stay in constant touch with Him.

Rina Venter
Missionary to South Africa

15 My Mother's Trust In God

"Trust in the Lord with all thine heart; and lean not unto thine own understanding. In all thy ways acknowledge him, and he shall direct thy paths" (Proverbs 3:5-6).

My mother was my greatest example of faith and dependence upon God. She was such a blessing, not only to her family, but also to everyone who knew her. I watched as she took care of my dad after he was diagnosed with cancer until he died. Nine years later, she suffered the tragic loss of my brother and never questioned God. Her trust in God, like the kind we are instructed to have in Proverbs 3:5-6, was an incredible example to me.

Mother had her own physical problems, too, and yet her faith never wavered. When the doctor once told her she had three months to live, she said that God had given her a good life, and she was ready to go. God blessed her with ten more years after that. On May 2, 1999, which was a Sunday, God spoke to me during the evening service as the choir sang, "It's Almost Over." He told me it was time for my mother to go home to be with Him, and the following Wednesday, she did.

All of the trials I have faced in my life have been easier because of the faith my mother passed on to me. Lord, help me to trust You like my mother did, and help me to pass that heritage along to my children and grandchildren.

Charlotte Lowery

16 ROSEBUDS ARE FOR SISSIES

"Give her of the fruit of her hands; and let her own works praise her in the gates" (Proverbs 31:31).

It was Mother's Day, and the sanctuary at our little church was teeming with visitors. My husband and I always sat in the back, but we were late that day, and our regular seat was taken. We inched our way across the back aisle, surveying the crowd, and wondered where we would sit. I spied room for two down front, so we made our way down and took the seats.

After the service started, we took a moment to greet visitors. The lady in front of us turned to say hello. She looked at me with a smile and said, "Aren't you Miss Carrie's daughter?" I was surprised, because I did not know who this lady was, and I wondered how she knew my mother. I had grown up in a church across town, and my mother had never been to this church. My husband and I had only attended there for a short while, and there were many people we still had not met.

Then the lady introduced herself as "Rosebud." Tears filled my eyes as I realized this beautiful young mother had once been a gangly little tomboy at the orphanage where Mother worked for many years. "Rosebud's" given name was Kathy Ard, and she came to the orphanage when she was eight years old. Her parents had died in a car accident, and there were no relatives to take her in. Mother loved Kathy, and they bonded right away. Since Kathy was a cute little girl, Mother wanted to dress her in ribbons and lace, but Kathy wanted no part of that. She wanted jeans, sneakers, and a baseball cap. Mother gave Kathy the nickname "Rosebud" to tease her. Kathy would squeal when Mother called her "Rosebud." She would say, "I ain't no rosebud. Rosebuds are for sissies." Mother would always laugh and give her a big hug.

I used to visit the orphanage and take my daughter to play with the other children. I had watched Kathy grow up and finish high school while living there. I never would have guessed how she had changed. She introduced me to her husband and little boy. Her husband's parents were members of the church, and Kathy and her family were visiting for Mother's Day. In those few brief moments, she brought me up to date on her life. She told me what a wonderful influence Mother had been in her life. Mother had died in October the year before while Kathy and her husband were on vacation, and they were unable to attend the funeral.

I had not had any contact with "Rosebud" in several years and often wondered what had happened to her. Seeing her that day and hearing the good things she said about my mother was a wonderful Mother's Day gift to me. I am sure the Lord arranged for us to be just late enough so we would have to sit in those two spaces down front. Otherwise, I probably would not have had the opportunity to see or talk to "Rosebud." My, how she blossomed!

Dianne Stewart

17 THE STABILIZER

"And I will pray the Father, and he shall give you another Comforter, that he may abide with you for ever" (John 14:16).

I live in a country where we have electricity problems all the time, and the power often goes out. Many times, when the power is on, the voltage is low, and that is when a gadget called a stabilizer comes in handy. When the voltage is low, the stabilizer brings it up, and when it is high, the stabilizer brings it down to normal. Appliances would not work properly without the stabilizer.

In our families, we as wives and mothers should be the "stabilizer" for our husbands and children. They would not function properly if we were not there. In John 14:16, God talks about the Holy Spirit as our Comforter. In my family, I would like to think that I serve as the human comforter. Sometimes my husband is down, and I need to encourage him to bring him up. Sometimes my children are upset, and I need to soothe them to calm them down.

Ephesians 6:4 says, "And ye fathers, provoke not your children to wrath: but bring them up in the nurture and admonition of the Lord." It is obvious to me that the warning about provoking children to wrath is directed to fathers. My role as a mother is to encourage him to follow God and work with him to raise our children in harmony. Our families need us, not just for the things we do around the house, but for the comfort we provide. What a sweet blessing it is to be used of God in our families, those we love the most on this earth!

Erla Bartell
Missionary to Albania

18 GOD'S FAVORITE PLACE

"And the peace of God, which passeth all understanding, shall keep your hearts and minds through Christ Jesus" (Philippians 4:7).

I've often wondered as I'm going through a trial, "God, what do you want from me? I feel so alone. Where are you?" One thing that all of us know He wants is for us to have faith, to trust His providential hand in our times of hurt and disappointment. But how do I have faith that moves mountains when I'm blind with pain or confusion? Do I just do my best to muster up this kind of faith?

For a long time, I lived a defeated life, especially when tribulation came along, because I wasn't hitting on the nerve, so to speak, that prompts God to pour out His peace that passes all understanding. Philippians 4:7 tells us that God will give us that depth of peace and that it will guard our hearts and minds. But why does it seem so hard to acquire? Maybe it's because we've left out a key ingredient given to us in Philippians 4:4: "Rejoice in the Lord always: and again I say, Rejoice." We know very well the verses following, about not being anxious and about making known our requests to God. Telling God what I want....I've got that one down! Can I get a witness out there? However, asking God for what we need or desire is just a piece of the "peace-getting" puzzle.

When the Ammonites and the Moabites threatened to

attack Israel in II Chronicles 20, a very fearful King Jehoshaphat immediately asked God what to do. God's response is surprising! Instead of telling them to sharpen their swords or call in extra soldiers, God commanded that they go to the front lines of the battle proclaiming over and over, "Praise the Lord: for his mercy endureth for ever." That's the missing piece! That's what God wants from us as we're in the midst of our struggles: praise, rejoicing in Him. If continually exalting His name is what makes God move, then why are we trying to move Him using our own ways?

I Thessalonians 5:18 says, "In every thing give thanks: for this is the will of God in Christ Jesus concerning you." As I've begun to apply this truth in my life, God has shown up in my dark times of unrest and loneliness. Psalm 139:11 promises, "If I say, Surely the darkness shall cover me; even the night shall be light about me." God loves praise and wherever His praise is sung, there He will be. I've observed one common characteristic among Christians who are the happiest and the most content: they praise God in every situation, good or bad.

The next time life knocks you off your feet and your heart says, "God, what do you want from me?" remember that all He wants is your praise. Start singing a love song to Him, tell Him He's the best thing that ever happened to you and that you can't live without Him, or make a list of things you're thankful for. God loves that kind of stuff! And you'll be amazed how small your problems will look as God shows you how big He is! Never forget, what's over my head is under His feet.

Suzanne Spiers

19 HOLD ME, MOMMY

"Thou wilt keep him in perfect peace, whose mind is stayed on thee: because he trusteth in thee" (Isaiah 26:3).

One day I was washing the dishes, thinking of the rest of the housework and the day's activities that were scheduled. It seemed to be a busy day in which something needed to be done continually, and I was lost in thought when my two-year-old daughter came to me and said, "Hold me, Mommy." My first thought was, "Not now, I have too much work to do." But I picked her up, walked into the living room, and sat down.

As I held Mary's warm little body and rocked her, I felt God remind me of how much I need to keep my mind on Him. As I stroked her soft skin and hair and looked into her loving eyes, I felt a part of Heaven. The verses "Surely goodness and mercy shall follow me all the days of my life..." (Psalm 23:6) and "...the fruit of the womb is his reward" (Psalm 127:3) came to mind.

There is always time for children, who grow up so fast. There is always time for God, while we are here on earth. Peace follows, as I think on Him.

Lisa Watson

20 Something Old, Something New, Something Borrowed, And Something Blue

"And let us not be weary in well doing: for in due season we shall reap, if we faint not" (Galatians 6:9).

There were two little girls, Alice and Janice, who became close friends in first grade and remained friends throughout their adult lives. After high school, they both married and began their families. After Janice gave birth to her first daughter, her grandmother bought the baby a beautiful pastel blue dress trimmed in delicate white lace. The dress was just perfect for the new addition to Janice's family. It was a beautiful dress for a beautiful little girl.

A year later, Alice gave birth to her first daughter. As young mothers do, Janice began to graciously give Alice clothes for her new daughter. Alice was very grateful and adorned her daughter, Allison, in many of the clothes Janice had passed along to her. Of all the clothes, the little blue dress was one of Alice's favorites, and she kept it in perfect condition.

A few years later, Alice's sister-in-law, Ann, had a little girl named Leigh Ann. Alice continued Janice's tradition of passing along clothes, including the little blue dress. Later, Alice had a second daughter, Jamie, and Ann returned the little blue dress. After Jamie, the little blue dress was put into storage.

Thirty-one years later, Janice's daughter, the first little girl to wear the little blue dress, married and conceived a child. According to a sonogram, the baby was a little girl. Alice pulled the little blue dress out of storage and returned it to the original owner.

Janice is my mother, and I was the first little girl to wear the little blue dress. My mother passed away a few months before my daughter Marena was born. Although she never got to hold or see Marena, through her generosity years before, she was able to give my daughter, her granddaughter, a very special little blue dress. The little blue dress is now in storage, again waiting to be worn by another little girl. We do reap what we sow.

Donna Terry

21 ANSWERED PRAYER

"Who is as the wise man? and who knoweth the interpretation of a thing? a man's wisdom maketh his face to shine, and the boldness of his face shall be changed. I counsel thee to keep the king's commandment, and that in regard of the oath of God. Be not hasty to go out of his sight: stand not in an evil thing; for he doeth whatsoever pleaseth him" (Ecclesiastes 8:1-3).

Do you ever wake up in the middle of the night? What do you do? I pray. One night I woke up, so I started praying. I was praying about making a change in one of the ministries I was involved in. I started telling God what I wanted to do, expecting Him to rubber-stamp it so I wouldn't feel bad about the change. I continued to pray for Him to allow me the opportunity to talk to the pastor of this ministry.

As I was praying, God put a verse of Scripture in my head. Instead of getting up and reading it, I drifted back to sleep. The next morning, I didn't read the Scripture God had given me, and I didn't have the opportunity to talk about the change I wanted to make. The following Sunday morning, I read Ecclesiastes 8, the passage God had given me while I prayed that night. Before I began reading, I prayed for God to speak to me through His Word. As I was reading, God all but verbally told me "no." Ecclesiastes 8:1 says, "Who is as the wise man?" I certainly do not think I am a wise woman. Ecclesiastes 8:2 goes on to say, "I counsel thee to keep the king's commandment..." We all should want to keep God's commandments. The big "no" was in verse 3, which says, "Be not hasty to go out of his sight: stand not in an evil thing; for he doeth whatsoever pleaseth him."

Whoa! Whatsover pleaseth him, that was it! I was telling God what I wanted and what was pleasing to me. Boy, did that change my heart! I decided to be exactly where He wants me to be, not where I want to be. I know that if I had changed my ministry, I would have still been serving Him, but I would not have been where He wanted me to be.

Amanda McKee

22 IS YOUR FAITH SHOWING?

"Wherefore seeing we also are compassed about with so great a cloud of witnesses...let us run with patience the race that is set before us, Looking unto Jesus, the author and finisher of our faith..." (Hebrews 12:1-2).

About a year ago, I visited my mother, who had been critically ill and in and out of the Intensive Care Unit. Rheumatoid arthritis had severely crippled her body, and she was bedridden most of the time. She felt as if she was of no use to God or our church, because she couldn't be involved in ministry. I told her that God was using her and that she truly was an inspiration to everyone that knew her. Although she listened, I could see the discouragement in her eyes.

Then God did something so special for her. On Grandparents Day at Decatur Heritage Christian Academy, where my children attended school, the senior class had been given an assignment to write a report or a poem on a person of integrity. Displayed on the bulletin board, among all of the papers on presidents, patriots, and Bible saints, was a poem about my mother, Joyce Stutts. Jerrell Vinson, a student she barely knew, had written the poem, and God used it to bless my hurting mother:

Joyce Stutts: A Person Of Integrity

Their grandmother's hands are stuck like glue,
    Carved like the veins in her hands were blue;
She stumbles trying to put one foot down to walk;
    She has not eaten in days for her face is pale as chalk.
She is not very tall in height;
    She depends on her physician, Jesus Christ,
But when her sickness ever has her feeling blue,
    She picks up the Good Book and knows what to do.
She comes to our games and she's a good fan;
    She comes to support her grandchildren when she can.
She's an old-fashioned lady like no other;
    She's a wonderful friend and better — a mother;
She has her happy days and times of sweet sorrow,
    Living each day, not promised tomorrow.
She knows life is not easy and is full of hurt,
    But every Sunday tries to make it to church.
She is full of life and life she enjoys,
    She brightens the day of little girls and boys.
She is full of the Word and full of love;
    I guess she's trying to be an example of God up above.
She has been through all of life's toils and strife,
    That's why she's a big influence in many people's lives.
Even though her days on earth aren't long,
    The memories of this woman will forever go on.
She's a good example of how a Christian needs to be,
    Because she has integrity.

Dear heavenly Father, thank You for touching my mother's heart in a way that only You could. Thank You for inspiring this boy to write this for her. Help us to remember that we all have our own race to run. And as we live our lives, may we show our faith, love, and dependence on You.

Jennifer Barnett

23 ALL CREATURES GREAT AND SMALL

"...Inasmuch as ye have done it unto one of the least of these my brethren, ye have done it unto me" (Matthew 25:40).

Years ago, after having my third child, I sat in a Missions Conference listening to the speaker challenge us to use our "field of influence." That very phrase bothered me for several nights of the conference, because I was a stay-at-home mother and never really had great encounters with the outside world.

One night, as we drove home from the Missions Conference, I shared my thoughts with my husband. From the backseat, one of my children piped up, "Mommy, you share Jesus with me!" What an incredible statement about my field of influence! Right then the Lord showed me my position and great opportunities that I have in my home. My children are my greatest field of influence. If I cannot show them how to drink from the Living Waters or teach them how to clothe themselves with God's righteousness, then how can I look beyond to the rest of the field God has for me?

Valerie Lunsford
Missionary in Montana

24 I Don't Want To Be Like The Children Of Israel

"And the Lord said unto Moses, Is the Lord's hand waxed short? thou shalt see now whether my word shall come to pass unto thee or not" (Numbers 11:23).

Too many times, I find myself to be like the children of Israel when Moses was leading them. God showed them miracle after miracle and took care of them in ways unimaginable, yet they still complained about something. It seems like God would do something great for them, and they would turn around and quickly forget what God did or that it was God that delivered them. When I read about them, I get so aggravated. They are so foolish! You would think that they would catch a clue. And then God says, "Hey, sometimes you act the same way."

God shows me miracle after miracle, and yet I find something to complain about. When God helps with a problem or trial, before I have time to turn around, I have forgotten it was Him and not me. Sometimes I question how He will take care of a situation. How foolish I am! The Creator of the universe does not need my help, and anything good in my life is only because of Him! I really do know this, but I forget so often.

In Numbers 11, the children of Israel are tired of manna, and they begin to complain that they want some meat. Moses must have had all he could take because he starts to complain, too. In verses 18-20, God tells Moses to go and tell the people that He will supply them with meat for a whole month, until it comes out their nostrils. Guess what Moses does? He begins to question how God will supply the meat. God lets Moses know that He is very capable of handling the situation (Numbers 11:23).

I want to thank the Lord daily for the ways He takes care

of me and to give Him the praise that only He deserves. I hope this will help me realize that I have nothing to complain about and remember it is God that is working. He can handle any situation.

Debbie McKaig

25 My Cry... God's Ears

"In my distress I called upon the Lord, and cried to my God: and he did hear my voice out of his temple, and my cry did enter into his ears" (II Samuel 22:7).

Have you ever felt like you were getting lost in the black hole of "I just can't seem to get it all together?" This is where I found myself in the fall of 2002. At that time, I had a husband, a five-year-old son and an infant daughter. The life of having the house clean, the clothes washed, supper cooked, and having some quality time alone with God was one I now only dreamed of. To say the least, I felt very frustrated over my inability to get it all done.

My biggest frustration came from the fact that even when I had time alone with God, I just couldn't feel His presence. The more I tried to fix it, the more discouraged I became and the deeper into the black hole I fell. One day, as I was reading, the Lord gave me II Samuel 22:7. David cried out to the Lord, and the Bible says that God heard his cry in His temple and that the cry went into His ears.

As a mom, I am very familiar with the phrase, "In one ear and out the other." Seeing that David's cry entered God's ears and stayed there was a huge comfort to me. As I studied out "my cry" and "thine ear", the Lord showed me over and over how he hears the cry of the humble. In Lamentations 3:56, the Bible tells me that even when I can't put my cry into words, that God even hears my breathing. What a comfort to know that the God of my salvation, the great High Priest, is listening to my every cry and my every breath!

Amy Wright

26 The Search For Gloves

"Ask, and it shall be given you; seek, and ye shall find..." (Matthew 7:7).

Sonya was devastated. She had just received word that her mother had cancer. An operation was her only hope for prolonging life for a few more months. Their family doctor had recommended a capable surgeon who specialized in performing surgery on cancer patients, and a visit to him was the next step. "You must go to the pharmacies and buy all these necessary items to perform the surgery," the surgeon ordered as he handed her a list. "This must be done expediently if you expect me to help."

Since Sonya lived in Chisinau, the capital city of Moldova, she was elected by the family to begin collecting the supplies required. Sonya ran from pharmacy to pharmacy gathering the medicines, gauze bandages, scalpel, and everything else on the doctor's list. Although the process took the entire day, she was able to find every item except for the size 8 surgeon's gloves. Sonya hunted and hunted for the gloves. The pharmacies carried size 7, size 9, and all other sizes, but there was not one size 8 to be found. The surgery was scheduled for the following day, and Sonya had no gloves. She remembered the surgeon's emphatic warning: "Get every item on the list, or there will be no operation!"

In desperation, Sonya ran to the missionary's home. By now, she was teary-eyed. "What's the matter, Sonya?" the missionary anxiously asked as she opened the door. Bursting into tears, Sonya sobbed, "I need gloves, size 8, for the surgeon tomorrow. I've looked everywhere and cannot find them. Please pray with me." The missionary replied, "Of course we will pray. We will ask God to provide."

Sonya and the missionary bowed their heads. "Heavenly Father, please solve this problem for us," they pleaded.

"Please send some size 8 surgeon's gloves." Just as they were raising their heads, the missionary exclaimed, "Let's look in my medicine box under the bed. There might be something in there!" Sonya and the missionary dashed into the bedroom and pulled out the cardboard box. There were bottles of pills, bandages, sponges, and other medical items. While hurriedly pawing through the box, they spied some surgical gloves. "I wonder what size they are?" Sonya asked hopefully.

Yes, the gloves were the exact size needed: size 8! What praise and thanksgiving was offered to God! He had known of this need months before the operation. God had prompted a donation of surgical gloves from an American who had no idea how God would use them someday. What an awesome God we serve! How can anyone ever doubt Him?

Loreen Ittermann
Missionary to Moldova

27 HOW BIG IS YOUR LOVE?

"The Lord hath appeared of old unto me, saying, Yea, I have loved thee with an everlasting love: therefore with lovingkindness have I drawn thee" (Jeremiah 31:3).

When my youngest son was small, we had a little routine at bedtime of trying to outwit each other. I would say, "I love you, Jimmy," and he would reply, "I love you more." I would then respond, "No way."

One night, as I put him to bed, he said, "I love you-once," and of course, my response was, "I love you-twice." Then he would say all the numbers of the world. Finally he said, "I love you more than you love me, because I've loved you all of my life, and you've only loved me a part of your life." I couldn't think of a response, so for this particular night Jimmy won the contest.

This story helps me remember that God's love for us is

greater and longer than our love for Him. God has loved us all of our lives. How big is our love for Him and for others?

Carolyn Olive

28 HE IS MY FATHER

"O Lord, thou hast searched me, and known me" (Psalm 139:1).

One day I asked a friend to pray for me about a certain matter. She said she would. A few days later, she questioned me about why I needed her to pray for me. "Don't you know He's your Father, too?" she asked. Well, needless to say, that hit me right between the eyes. I had asked her to pray because: (a) I thought she was a better Christian than I was; (b) her prayers always seemed to get answered; (c) I thought she was more important to God than I was; and on and on. Anyway, her question got me on my knees.

As I prayed, I asked God to show me that He was my heavenly Father. I wanted to know that I was important to Him, and that He loved me personally, not just as part of the world. Each day as I studied His Word, the verses came alive in a way they never had before. As I read Psalm 139 one day, several verses stood out to me. In verses 1-12, we find that He knows everything about us, and we cannot flee from His presence. This Creator pursues each of us with His love. In verses 13-16, we find out just how special we are to God. We are "…fearfully and wonderfully made..." He fashioned our days "…when as yet there was none of them." It seems like God put a lot of time and effort into creating each one of us. And He wants to have a personal relationship with His creation. I find that amazing!

I discovered a loving, caring heavenly Father who daily tries to mold my life and change my heart. Don't you know He's your Father, too?

Danna Harbin

29 Talk To God

"And Jesus knew their thoughts..." (Matthew 12:25).

When my daughter, Olivia, was two years old, she was diagnosed with a rare disease and began chemotherapy. After 12 months, the doctors believed her tumor was gone, and she came off the treatments. When we went back to the doctors for a three-month check-up, they did exploratory surgery to determine if the cancer had returned. I was home alone with Olivia when the surgeon called and said the biopsy showed tumor cells. I was devastated! I sat and cried for two hours before I called anyone.

After the initial shock, I got angry. I just knew that after the original treatment Olivia would be cured. I was so mad at God and couldn't believe He would put us through this again! I talked to a good friend and told her my feelings and how disgusted I was with God. She called our pastor, Brother Doug Ripley, and later that afternoon, he called me. I thought, "Great, the big man calls, and now everyone knows how mad I am at God!" Brother Doug assured me that God was still in control. He told me that God already knew my thoughts, and the only way for me to get past it was to verbally tell Him my feelings.

When I got home that night, I went outside and sat on the swing and yelled out to God. I really gave Him a piece of my mind. After about an hour of crying out to God, it was as if He said, "Are you through?" He wrapped His loving arms around me and assured me everything was going to be okay. The anger was gone, and I could focus on helping my daughter through the coming days.

Our relationship with God is the greatest one we have, and I am so glad He allowed me to come to Him with my problems. He listened to me and healed my broken heart.

Pam Williams

30 GOD NEEDED A LOAN

"He that hath pity upon the poor lendeth unto the Lord; and that which he hath given will he pay him again" (Proverbs 19:17).

One afternoon, after my teaching hours in a Christian academy, I went home to my boarding house. All of the boarders there were not Christians. When I got inside, I saw one boarder who was crying and talking to another boarder. I sensed that there was a problem and I tried to ask about it. I learned that the crying boarder was a victim of theft. She was preparing for her nursing board exam and had gotten a job to make extra money. She received her salary that day, and it was stolen. She was heartbroken.

I really pitied her and tried to put myself in her place. I went up to my room and looked in my wallet to see if I had enough money to give her. I remembered that it was almost my payday, so I gave her P100 (one hundred pesos in Philippine currency) and told her to not pay me back. I could see the joy in her wet eyes. Later, I went to the market and bought some fruit to give her as well.

That happened on a Monday afternoon. On Tuesday, I was back in school when we received a visitor. She went to every classroom and observed students as well as teachers. When she came to my classroom, she asked me how long I had been teaching school, and I told her 12 years. She then exclaimed that I was the right person to proofread curriculum materials. She paid me P3000 to do the work. God paid me back abundantly.

Thelma A. Obid
Missionary to Cambodia

31 DON'T BE DEFEATED

"The thief cometh not, but for to steal, and to kill, and to destroy: I am come that they might have life, and that they might have it more abundantly" (John 10:10).

Is there something in your life that you are holding onto, robbing you of the joy of your salvation? Whether it is health, finances, failure of a relationship, or something else, let it go. God has a plan for your life. He does not want you to remain locked in your failure. He wants you to turn to Him and let Him use your situation for His glory.

In I Samuel 16:1, God asks Samuel, "...How long wilt thou mourn for Saul...fill thine horn with oil, and go, I will send thee to Jesse...for I have provided me a king...." God is telling him to get up, get ready, and take action, because He has a plan.

We let the circumstances of our life defeat us, but God sees beyond today. He knows our past, our present, and our future. Isaiah 43:18-19 says, "Remember ye not the former things...Behold I will do a new thing...." Don't be bogged down with your history. God has a plan to bring honor and glory to Himself through you.

Whatever your state is, wherever you are, God is ready, willing, and able to restore you to His perfect plan and bless you with an abundant life.

Dara Smith

1 I Saw That

"Let your light so shine before men, that they may see your good works, and glorify your Father which is in heaven" (Matthew 5:16).

While walking down the preschool hallway one Wednesday night, I bent to pick up a candy wrapper that someone had dropped. Assuming most everyone had gone home, I was startled to hear, "I saw that. Good for you." Someone had come around the corner, just in time to see me.

I have thought about this many times since then, wondering how many times someone had appeared just in time to see me react to something in a way that is inappropriate for a Christian witness. There are so few people that know us personally, compared to those who know us from a distance as we go through our daily activities. Are we leaving them with a Christ-like image that makes them want what we have?

I Peter 3:1 talks about your conversation (behavior) being able to win your husband to Christ. I Samuel 2:3 says God weighs our actions. In Matthew 5:16, we are told that our works should glorify God. In Philippians 1:27, we are reminded that our conversation (behavior) should be becoming to the Gospel of Christ. These principles can be applied to everything from our dress and our attitudes to our everyday reactions to simple situations. As you walk with God, are you living as though someone is always watching?

Pam Anderson

2 Through My Pain, I Can Help Others

"I will lift up mine eyes unto the hills, from whence cometh my help. My help cometh from the Lord, which made heaven and earth" (Psalm 121:1-2).

When I was living in Michigan, I met a young lady in my church named Jan. Jan and her husband had been trying to have a baby, but she always miscarried around her second month. She would call me to have a shoulder to cry on. My husband and I were expecting our first child, and I was in my third month of pregnancy when Jan called to tell me she was pregnant again. She asked me to pray that she would be able to carry this one to full term.

Once she reached the second month, Jan lost her baby. By now I was five months along, and she was tired of hearing me say that God had a reason for her miscarriages. To be honest, I was also tired of telling her that. I didn't understand why God was allowing this to happen to her. Although I tried, I was at a loss for words to comfort her. Shortly after Jan's miscarriage, I went to the doctor for my check-up, and everything was fine. Four days later, however, my baby stopped moving. After several tests, I learned my baby had died. I sat in the doctor's office and cried my eyes out. When I calmed down, he told me that Mother Nature takes over in situations like this, and we waited two weeks for me to go into labor. Those were the longest days of my life, knowing that the baby I carried inside of me was no longer alive.

During all of this, I never had the cleansing cry that God gives us to get to the recovery stage of grief. But one day while I was putting my baby's things away, the tears came. I must have cried for 30 minutes as I sat on my knees in my baby's room. I called out to God for help and strength, because I knew I couldn't do it by myself. He brought to mind Psalm 121. The Lord spoke to me that day and showed me how I could now help others who were going through the same kind of pain I had been through. With the Lord's help, I could now help my friend Jan.

Lord, thank You for reaching down to me with loving and comforting arms when I lifted my eyes up to the hills where You were waiting for me. Thank You for my pain and sorrow, for without it, I would have never experienced Your promise.

Vickie Copeland

3 God And Baseball

"Know ye not that they which run in a race run all, but one receiveth the prize? So run, that ye may obtain" (I Cor. 9:24).

Now that baseball season is in full swing, I would like to share some spiritual principles God has taught me by watching the game:

Catcher – A catcher catches the ball, like Christians should catch men. "And so was also James, and John, the sons of Zebedee, which were partners with Simon. And Jesus said unto Simon, Fear not; from henceforth thou shalt catch men" (Luke 5:10).

First Base – Life's not easy, but we must put God first like Matthew 6:33 says, "But seek ye first the kingdom of God, and his righteousness; and all these things shall be added unto you."

Second base – We turn a double play by first getting saved. "For whosoever shall call upon the name of the Lord shall be saved" (Romans 10:13). Then, we live the life God intended. "The thief cometh not, but for to steal, and to kill, and to destroy: I am come that they might have life, and that they might have it more abundantly" (John 10:10).

Third base – Christ gave us victory over death when He rose from the grave on the third day. Luke 24:7 says, "Saying, The Son of man must be delivered into the hands of sinful men, and be crucified, and the third day rise again."

Pitcher – A successful pitcher aims high to throw strikes, just like a successful Christian looks to God. Colossians 3:2 says, "Set your affection on things above, not on things on the earth."

Right field – We as Christians should follow that which is right. "He is the Rock, his work is perfect: for all his ways are judgment: a God of truth and without iniquity, just and right is he" (Deuteronomy 32:4).

Center field – This position protects mid-field, like Jesus Christ serves as an intercessor for us with God. Ephesians

2:14 says, "For he is our peace, who hath made both one, and hath broken down the middle wall of partition between us."

Left field – Be wise in judging the ball. "Length of days is in her right hand and in her left hand riches and honour" (Proverbs 3:16).

Short stop – Cut off the opposition's hit. Psalm 37:9 says, "For evildoers shall be cut off: but those that wait upon the Lord, they shall inherit the earth."

Lisa Pensworth

4 FIXING HEARTS

"And I will give them one heart, and I will put a new spirit within you; and I will take the stony heart out of their flesh, and will give them an heart of flesh: That they may walk in my statutes, and keep mine ordinances, and do them: and they shall be my people, and I will be their God" (Ezekiel 11:19-20).

My husband, Wayne, suffered a heart attack on what seemed like an ordinary Sunday morning, August 1, 1999. He was taken to Huntsville Hospital where that evening he had a more severe attack. On the following Thursday, he had open-heart surgery to repair three blocked arteries. Three weeks later, he survived complete respiratory failure. He was hospitalized for weeks and endured hours of physical therapy. Finally, on September 24, he came home. And what a homecoming it was! He made it through the first weeks of recovery at home, and after a month, we were anxious to visit his heart doctor so he could assess Wayne's "fixed" heart.

Dr. Riley walked into the room where we had been waiting for a few minutes. He looked at Wayne and checked him over, and then he sat down. For as long as I live, I will never forget what happened next. Wayne was sitting on the examination table, and he looked at Dr. Riley and asked in a very quiet voice, "You're the one who fixed my heart?" Dr. Riley looked up at him and nodded yes. Tears welled up in Wayne's eyes. He asked again, "You're the one who held my heart in your hands and fixed it?" Dr. Riley smiled a little smile and nodded again. I know Wayne wanted to say something. I know he wanted to say "Thank you," but he couldn't. He had no voice. He couldn't speak a word. There was a long but not uncomfortable silence in the room as these two men looked into each other's eyes and souls. It seemed to me that they connected in a way no one else would ever understand. Dr. Riley knew Wayne was thankful, and I know he understood his speechlessness. And Wayne realized this man had worked for weeks to save his life, and that he didn't really need any thanks. He was in the business of fixing hearts. It was what he did every day for folks.

We lost Wayne to heart disease in 2002 after a two and a half year battle. In reflective moments, I still remember that day in Dr. Riley's office. Sometimes, when my heart overflows with thanks to my Savior for all He has done for me, I too can scarcely speak. When I stop to think of it, God too has held my heart in His hands many times, but especially on that cold January afternoon when Wayne died. He took my broken heart in His big hands and began the work of fixing it. Sometimes the lump in my throat is too big to express aloud to my Jesus what I want to say to Him. But He knows me, and He understands. He is in the business of fixing hearts, whatever the problem. It's what He does every day for folks.

Give Him your heart, whatever the problem. He wants to fix it.

Carolyn Hogan

5 SOMETIMES WE ARE NOT AS HAPPY AS WE THINK WE ARE

"Looking diligently lest any man fail of the grace of God; lest any root of bitterness springing up trouble you, and thereby many be defiled" (Hebrews 12:15).

When we look at a tree, we see its leaves, bark, and precious fruits, but we never see the roots that are underground. This reminds me of my life. Although I felt very happy serving the Lord in my local church and the people around me could see my smile, but there was a root deep in my heart that was making my life bitter. My family started to notice it when I would snap at them, or when they would find me crying at night.

I didn't realize the bitterness I had in my heart until one night while I was at Bible College, and the Lord spoke to me. He told me that I had to get rid of my root of bitterness. I argued with Him, saying that I was happy. I was serving Him and doing what He expected of me, but the Lord told me I had to forgive. I said, "Forgive who?" He said, "Your parents." Then I understood that I never forgave my parents for divorcing and leaving me at my grandparents' house when I was a child. After forgiving them, the Lord showed me that the reason He let this happen in my life was so that I could be saved and raised in a Christian home.

This was God's way of preparing me to be a missionary's wife. Now I can teach the Venezuelan children that are going through the same things I went through as a child: to forgive and to ask forgiveness, which is the key to serving the Lord with true happiness.

Patricia Arce
Missionary to Venezuela

6 MAN OF GOD'S CHOOSING

"Call unto me, and I will answer thee, and shew thee great and mighty things, which thou knowest not" (Jeremiah 33:3).

I have a typical melancholy personality, and decision-making is not where I shine. Too many choices only add to my confusion. I had been divorced about three years when I began to petition God about the possibility of a husband in my future. I was finally getting past the hurt and pain of my divorce and realized that I still very much believed in marriage and wanted the opportunity again.

When I married at 18 years old, I did not seek the Lord's

guidance in my choice. I wasn't even saved at the time, and the thought of asking the Lord for direction would never have occurred to me. This time was going to be different. I presented a list of qualifications to the Lord that I considered to be of the utmost importance in a husband. After praying that way for a while, I began to realize that I could meet a man with all of these qualifications, and he still wouldn't be the "right" one if he was not the one the Lord wanted for me. So I began to pray in a new way. I simply asked the Lord to do something very special for me in answering this prayer. I wanted this man to utter a certain phrase to me that was known only to me and the Lord. I never breathed this prayer to a soul, and no one ever knew what the special phrase was.

During the next two years in my personal devotions, God began to impress certain Scriptures upon my heart. In January 2000, I was asked to serve on the administration team of the Capital Funds Campaign as Les Collier's assistant. I had served with him on the previous campaign in 1996, and we had become good friends. In the meantime, some dear friends had met a missionary whose wife had left him, and they really believed that he and I needed to meet. I had even been to his field of service at one time. But as Les and I spent time working together on the campaign and in the Singles ministry, I began to realize that God was changing my heart towards him. Those sisterly feelings I had were changing. In early March of that same year, I was earnestly praying for guidance, because the missionary was supposed to be coming to Decatur. God began to remind me of the Scriptures He had given me over the past two years and the way I had been praying. One day, a group of us were shooting the breeze, and Les looked over at me and said my special phrase. As soon as I got to my car, the Lord and I began to talk. I kept reminding Him of the missionary and the fact that I was four years older than Les and that he would never be interested in me that way. The Lord reminded me that I had told Him that He could choose, and He had answered my prayer exactly as I asked.

Les and I had our first date on April 7, 2000, and no, I did not tell him that we would be getting married one day. But we did marry the following year on May 18, 2001.

It is not hard to make a decision between what is right and what is wrong. That is an easy decision to make. But what about when the decision is between which is good and which is better? Only God can help us make the right choice then. By the way, the missionary never did make it to Decatur, which is further proof that I married the man of God's choosing. Thank You, Lord!

Sharon Collier

7 NOT MY STRENGTH, BUT HIS

"I can do all things through Christ which strengtheneth me" (Philippians 4:13).

Have you ever felt less than adequate? I have. Many times I have tried to do good things for God, yet fail miserably. I wonder, "I am doing this for God. Why doesn't it work?" God finally showed me. We are not to do things in our own strength but in His strength.

As a mother, there is always something to be done, especially if you work outside the home. There is never enough time or strength to get everything done. That is where God and His strength step in. He wants us to rely on Him, and through His strength accomplish the task before us.

Growing up, I was very shy. My Sunday School teacher introduced me to Philippians 4:13, and it has stuck with me all these years. Every time I think I cannot do something, I repeat the verse over and over, and God gives me strength. I know that I am the person I am today because of God's strength. He has always provided strength at just the right time. As I go through life's changes, His strength holds firm. Thank You, God, for being my Strength and my Rock.

Gayle Krohe

8 Jesus, Savior, Pilot Me

"But he knoweth the way that I take: when he hath tried me, I shall come forth as gold" (Job 23:10).

One morning at about 3 a.m., I woke and started singing to myself an old hymn called "Jesus, Savior, Pilot Me." As I lay there trying to remember all the words, I reflected back on just how much these words meant to me.

When our daughter, Kelly, died, I felt that I was unable to function on my own. But my Jesus put His loving arms around me and gently let me know in so many ways that He was there. Never before had I experienced such a complete trust in Him. Never before had I had such reassurance in my relationship with Him. Never before had I been tried and tested to this degree.

The words He spoke in so many Scriptures all became real and true. I had been taught to believe Him and never doubt Him, but only now did I know firsthand that it was true. What an awesome experience! The first verse of the song says:

"Jesus, Savior, pilot me,
Over life's tempestuous sea;
Unknown waves before me roll,
Hiding rock and treacherous shoal;
Chart and compass came from Thee:
Jesus, Savior, pilot me."

These words are so true in the lives of each Christian. To feel the loving arms of Jesus hold you and pilot you, you must have your faith tested and tried. What a comfort to be able to lean on Him so completely! Through the days, weeks, and now years since Kelly's death, my faith and my Jesus are more real and dear to me than ever.

Donna Haraway

9 CONFRONTING CONFLICT

"From whence come wars and fightings among you? come they not hence, even of your lusts that war in your members? Ye lust, and have not: ye kill, and desire to have, and cannot obtain: ye fight and war, yet ye have not, because ye ask not. Ye ask, and receive not, because ye ask amiss, that ye may consume it upon your lusts. Ye adulterers and adulteresses, know ye not that the friendship of the world is enmity with God? whosoever therefore will be a friend of the world is the enemy of God" (James 4:1-3).

If there is one thing that is true in life, it is the fact that conflict is a part of all human relationships. Conflict in and of itself is not a problem; it is in the unmanaged and unresolved conflicts where we find our greatest challenges. There have been volumes of books written on conflict management and conflict resolution, yet with all of this information at our disposal, we still have more murders, more violence, and more divorces than ever before. It is very important that we understand how to handle conflict, not from the failed approaches of a carnal society, but from a biblical perspective found in the greatest book of all time, the Word of God.

What are the sources of conflict? James paints a vivid picture of the source of conflict and the tragic consequences that result from it when we fail to bring it under the authority of the Word of God. First of all, conflict begins with lust. Lust is the passion for pleasure that rages within the body and its members. The picture is that of constant warfare, of our bodies craving, yearning, and grasping after whatever will gratify our pleasure. The progression is obvious. Lust turns into desire, desire turns into fighting, fighting turns into war, war turns into death, yet in the end we still "have not."

Secondly, conflict arises out of prayer offered with the wrong motive. The reason our prayers are so often not answered is that we ask for things that will gratify our lust and pleasure. We seek God's blessings so that we can have more comfort, better clothes, and extra recognition. Again, the results are the same: we "have not." Lastly, conflict arises out of friendship with the world. The point is this: our bond with Christ is to be so close that when we turn away from Him to the world, it is like committing spiritual adultery. Spiritual adultery means that we turn away from God to the world. We follow after the things of the world, instead of following after God.

So how are we to handle the conflicts that war within our members, the conflicts that cause us to want to control and hurt others because of our selfish desires? We must first understand that man's deepest and most restless craving is a spiritual one. Man's desire is never satisfied apart from God. A person must trust and call upon God to have his desires fulfilled.

Can you truly say today that Christ is all you need? Is there a conflict of lust and selfish desires warring within your members, causing you to lie, cheat, and steal the things that you could easily get from God if you had the right relationship with Him?

Sylvia Miller

10 BEFORE THEY WILL CALL, I WILL ANSWER

"And it shall come to pass, that before they call, I will answer; and while they are yet speaking, I will hear" (Isaiah 65:24).

It was our 24th year in Korea, and God was leading us to start a new church. We were living in Seoul, where we had "inherited" an old mission house that we were fixing up. We felt the Lord leading us to Kangnung, a city on the East Coast about three hours away. We thought we would just get a small room for sleeping in Kangnung and keep our house in Seoul. We would spend three days a week in Seoul and four in Kangnung. However, God had a different plan.

A Christian professor and his wife in Kangnung invited us to lunch. They were leaving for America for a year and needed someone to live in their apartment rent-free and take care of their things. Would we be interested? Of course, we agreed! This was the perfect solution for us. We thought God was really working out our plan!

A few weeks later, we received a call from another missionary, who told us we would have to move out of the old mission house in Seoul. He thought we would be devastated. We just said, "No problem! God already gave us an apartment in Kangnung!" He was more shocked than we were! How it warmed our hearts to know that God provided a home for us long before we knew we would need it!

Reba Dutton
Missionary to Korea

11 WHAT TO GET MY HUSBAND

"Wives, submit yourselves unto your own husbands, as unto the Lord. For the husband is the head of the wife, even as Christ is the head of the church: and he is the saviour of the body. Therefore as the church is subject unto Christ, so let the wives be to their own husbands in every thing" (Ephesians 5:22-24).

Today is the anniversary of the day we wed, me and you.
I wanted to get you something brand new.
Looking for the traditional gift for thirteen.
But in reality, I didn't have any green.
I could borrow from Peter just to pay Bob.
Lord Jesus, please, I need a job.
I said to myself, "The gift doesn't have to be bought."
"I can make him a present, maybe," I thought.
What do you give a man who is so sweet?
I can fix him a dinner, give him something to eat.
What do you give to a man who works hard every day?
Just to give his wife and children his pay.
What do you give a man who is so dear?
Who to your heart you hold so near.
I asked God in Heaven for an idea to suffice.

And God answered and said, "Heed my advice.
Things on earth surely will crumble and rust
But storing treasures in Heaven is a must.
Give a gift to him each and every day.
And all you have to do is pray.
Pray for his wife that she can behave.
Pray for his work that he can be brave.
Pray for his finances that he can survive.
Pray that he is faithful and gives Me his tithe.
Pray for his sexuality, too
For this is the thing that a good wife must do.
Pray for his affection, temptation of his mind.
Pray for his fears and things of this kind.
Pray for his purpose that his choices are good.
His protection, his trials, his integrity, you should.
His reputation is important, priorities are set
His relationship, fatherhood, his past to forget
His attitude and marriage, emotions and talk
And also just as important is that you pray for his walk.
Pray he is repentant and pray for his deliverance.
And one that is hard to pray for is his obedience.
Pray for his self-image that he is strong.
Pray for his faith so he can't go wrong.
The last thing to pray for is his future days.
You can pray for him in so many ways.
You look for a gift to give Gary your love.
The best gift you can give him is from above.
Give him a gift that is invisible yet one he can see.
Give him a gift and that gift is me."

Georgeanne Hept

12 Who Do You Love The Most?

"We love him, because he first loved us" (I John 4:19).

God recently used my four-year-old daughter to remind me of the place I give Him in my life. We were driving down the road on an ordinary day, and Kyleigh asked, "Mommy, who do you love the most?" Of course I said, "You, baby." Then she said, "What about Dusty?" I proceeded to say that I loved her and Dusty, my boyfriend, in two different ways. Then, Kyleigh said, "What about God and the trees?" Thinking she wanted me to reassure her of my love for her, I didn't say I loved God first. I continued the conversation with how much I loved God and how thankful I was for her and Dusty and that I wouldn't have either of them if it weren't for God.

Later on, I began to think about that conversation and whether I really do put Kyleigh and Dusty before God. In Kyleigh's little mind, she needed to know who I loved the most. I believe that God used her to stop me and help me get a check on my priorities. Who do I love the most? I had to be stopped and reminded on just an ordinary day that God needs to be first and foremost over everyone. Even when I give Him all the glory for the blessings of Dusty and Kyleigh, He still needs to know every day by my faithfulness Who I love the most!

Jessica Hancey

13 God's Special Plan

"Trust in the Lord with all thine heart; and lean not unto thine own understanding. In all thy ways acknowledge him, and he shall direct thy paths" (Proverbs 3:5-6).

It is amazing how God can take a simple children's story and use it to show us something that He has done or is going to do in our lives. Sometime ago, my younger sisters read me a children's story, "The Tale of Three Trees." The story begins in a forest where three trees are talking to each other, discussing what they want to do with their lives. The first tree wanted to become a treasure chest that held beautiful jewels and gold. The second tree longed to be at sea as a large sailing vessel that carried kings and nobles. And the third tree wanted to stay grounded where he was, so that when people looked at him they would see the heavens, to which he was pointing.

Have you ever been in a situation where you made a major or minor decision in your life that you believed was what the Lord wanted, only to find out that you were going in the wrong direction from where He was trying to lead you? That was the situation in these three trees' lives. The first tree did not become the treasure chest that he had dreamed of becoming. God had something different in mind for Him. He became a manger that animals ate from. However, he was not just any manger. The first tree became the manger that Jesus was placed in as a new baby – a treasure greater than any gold or jewels. The second tree did not become a huge sailing vessel, but he did hold a King. God used the second tree as a fishing boat that held Jesus – the King of kings and the Lord of lords. The third tree that wanted to grow tall so that he could point to the heavens was cut down and placed together in the shape of a cross. Later, that tree was used to hold Jesus Christ up during his crucifixion. Even though the third tree was cut down, God still used him to help point others to Jesus.

Although the trees never became exactly what they longed to become, God still used them for His glory, and look at the treasures they were able to hold. Sometimes we believe that we are on God's track, when in reality we are on our own track – going in the wrong direction. Only through prayer and daily Bible reading will we know God's direction for our lives. God will do the same for you and me as He did for the trees. He will use us for His glory as long as we place our trust in Him. Can you imagine the treasure that the Lord may place in your life if you just trust Him?

Lord, I pray that Your will be done and not my own. Direct me in Your paths and use me for Your glory.

Calista Blankenship

14 TERROR BY NIGHT

"He shall cover thee with his feathers, and under his wings shalt thou trust: his truth shall be thy shield and buckler. Thou shalt not be afraid for the terror by night; nor for the arrow that flieth by day; Nor for the pestilence that walketh in darkness; nor for the destruction that wasteth at noonday. He shall call upon me, and I will answer him: I will be with him in trouble; I will deliver him, and honour him" (Psalm 91:4-6, 15).

Starting out for a walk on a brisk morning, I could smell the newness of the day. I was completely alone, and dawn's light had not peeped through the clouds. Being alone was giving me time to listen to music and meditate with the Lord. Grabbing my Walkman, flashlight, and a wooden pole, I set out down the street. I was excited about the solitude, because I was going use it to talk to Him.

I started down the hill at a brisk pace. Settling into the music and my thoughts, my eyes searched the road in the dim light of my flashlight. Wait! Did I see a pair of eyes staring at me, or was it my imagination? There! This time they were coming toward me. I stopped quickly, debating what to do. My heart was beating so fast, and my stomach filled with panic. The eyes were large, and we stared at each other in the darkness. I turned and ran back the way I came, looking over my shoulder to see if the eyes followed me.

Once inside the safety of my home, I could not stop shaking. The fear was overwhelming. My heart and stomach would not leave my throat. I began to pray, and God reminded me that my fear was not from Him. He led me to verses in Psalm 91, and as I read this chapter over and over, I felt God's calming presence within me. He gave me this passage in the midst of my fears. When fear arises again, I recall this Psalm and run under His wings, allowing Him to cover me with His feathers.

Jane Whitt

15 THE FACES OF KENYA

"...Lift up your eyes, and look on the fields; for they are white already to harvest" (John 4:35).

I have always been fascinated by facial expressions. When I returned from a mission trip to Africa in October 2000, I saw a variety of expressions. Some people were intrigued, wondering about the cultural differences I experienced in a Third World country. Others were excited and asked about wild animals and scenery. Some looked fearful. Maybe they thought I brought home an infectious disease as a souvenir. But those faces did not compare to the faces I saw in Africa.

I traveled with a team from our church to Kenya to visit missionaries Randall and Phyllis Stirewalt. For more than 25 years, the Stirewalts have served the Lord in Kenya, and their ministry has grown to include hundreds of churches where tens of thousands of nationals worship each Sunday. All of the churches have congregations of committed people, most of whom walk to church each Sunday. They pack into the pews to a point most Americans would call uncomfortable, but the Kenyans don't mind. When the pews are full, they line chairs along the aisles. After that, they stand in the back of the church or outside around the windows just to hear the message. As we drove across the country seeing churches, the images that stayed with me were the faces.

I saw wet faces. At a church in Eldoret, where the

Stirewalts live, 44 people were baptized on the Sunday we visited. As they emerged from the chilly water, I saw bright smiles on the faces of these young Christians.

I saw young faces. Many of the churches we visited are in rural villages, and children ran out to greet us. Their wide eyes indicated they were unsure of this strange group of white visitors. But when we waved at them and pulled out a bag of candy, they were our instant friends. You don't see many old faces in Kenya. A national epidemic of AIDS has cut short life expectancy. At that time, about half of the country's population was younger than 15 years old, while only about two percent was older than 65.

Sometimes I saw confused faces as our interpreters tried to come up with appropriate Swahili words. And then there were the faces and gestures of universal understanding. A handshake, hug, and smile mean the same thing in any language. The faces of the 285 pastors and wives who attended the discipleship conference led by our team are the ones I'll remember best. They listened closely to our words, determined to learn how to biblically train other members of their congregations. Many of them have endured experiences that Americans could never fathom. Some have dealt with violent tribal clashes, and others have defied tribal customs to be a part of a Bible-believing church. Most of them live in conditions that Americans would consider poverty, but they don't know any other way of life. They seem content and intent on learning more about God.

I saw faces of wonder, but that was when I looked in a mirror. I was amazed at the outward beauty of the country, where zebras graze along the roadside like cows graze in Alabama. But I was also amazed at the inward beauty of these people, so dedicated to God and their churches that I started asking myself, "What can I possibly teach them?" I heard all the stories. One of our interpreters walks ten miles to church each Sunday. Another pastor rode his bicycle 80 miles to come to the conference. There are more stories like that, too many to tell, but all the stories and the faces create a picture of a country hungry to hear the Word of God. I saw a mission field, and I will never forget the faces.

Dawn Kent

16 ZACHARY'S WHISTLE

"Be careful for nothing; but in every thing by prayer and supplication with thanksgiving let your requests be made known unto God" (Philippians 4:6).

When my oldest son, Zachary, was three years old, his greatest desire was to learn how to whistle. He tried day after day. Then one afternoon he came running to me and said, "Mommy, I can whistle!" I asked him how he learned to whistle. He replied, "I asked Jesus to send me a whistle. I opened my mouth, and He just dropped it in!

Dear Lord, help me to always make my requests known to You, even for things as simple as a whistle. I know that none of my desires are insignificant in Your eyes. When I pray, help me to trust You for the answer with the anticipation of an innocent child.

Anita Blunier

17 KEEP WATCHING THE GAS GAUGE

"He giveth power to the faint; and to them that have no might he increaseth strength. Even the youths shall faint and be weary, and the young men shall utterly fall: But they that wait upon the Lord shall renew their strength; they shall mount up with wings as eagles; they shall run, and not be weary; and they shall walk, and not faint" (Isaiah 40:29-31).

When I was a child, my family and I took many trips. Each time we would begin a trip, my younger sister would always ask if we had enough gas for our journey. If she saw the gas needle getting near the "E," she would begin to cry. She had a fear of running out of gas. How about us? Do we constantly watch to see that we have enough fuel to keep us going? As women, we stay so busy trying to be superwomen that we sometimes forget when to stop, step back from our hurried lives, and take time to refuel with God's Word.

Wouldn't it be great if we had a warning light to let us know when we were taking on too many tasks and were in danger of burning out? It is important for us to take a little time with God's Word each day, so that we may truly know Him and refuel our tanks.

In the story of Mary and Martha in Luke 10:38-42, we see a drastic difference between these two sisters. While Martha was busy taking care of the meal, we see that Mary stopped to have personal time with Jesus. Although working for God is important, we need our personal time at Jesus' feet. It is only through Him that we can seek rest, strength, and clear guidance for the day ahead. If we can learn to do this, I believe we will have less stress, worry, and fear. God promises that He will take care of our needs. If we really believe Him, we have no reason to worry. As you start your day today, give all your troubles and cares to Him. As our verse for today tells us, "...they that wait upon the Lord shall renew their strength...they shall walk, and not faint" (Isaiah 40:31).

No one of us wants to be in a situation where we look to draw upon our reserved energy, just to find that there is none there. If we let our tanks run empty, we will not be equipped for what God has in store for our day.

Barbara Hays

18 All Things Work Together For Good

"And we know that all things work together for good to them that love God, to them who are the called according to his purpose" (Romans 8:28).

Just before we started deputation, God supplied us with a very nice conversion van for traveling. He used a Christian friend to give it to us, and it was just what we needed. While we were on deputation, we went to Grove City, Pennsylvania, for a Sunday meeting. After the meeting, the pastor invited my husband, Paulo, to a pastors' fellowship on Monday. We woke up early that Monday and arrived in time to tour the town. It was a beautiful day, and Paulo had his window down. All of a sudden, a bee flew into the van. As Paulo tried to swat it out of his face, he lost control of the van and ran into a tree. Since we were going about 40 miles per hour, our van was totaled, but we only had a few scratches. Then our oldest daughter, Kayla, started crying and told Paulo, "Look what happened to our van. How will we get back home and continue deputation?" Paulo replied that God knows what He is doing. We prayed and asked God to show us what He wanted us to learn.

A man came by with a phone, and Paulo called the police and a tow truck. Just imagine the impression we gave the pastors when we arrived at the fellowship in a police car! One of the pastors took us back to Delaware, where we were staying during deputation, and we rented a car. We did not have full insurance coverage on the van, so we did not have enough money to buy another van. When Paulo told our pastor what happened, he asked for a list of the churches that were supporting us. In just a few days, there was an overwhelming response, and we had enough money to buy another van. As we searched for another van, we were always open to what God would do through this situation.

One Sunday as we drove back from church, Paulo saw a nice van, and he went back the next day to see how much it cost. Paulo told the salesman that we were missionaries and why we needed a van. The salesman asked him what a missionary was, and Paulo began witnessing to him. An hour later, the salesman asked Jesus to be his Savior. Paulo gave him a Bible, and the salesman said, "You did not come here to buy a van. You came here because I had an appointment with God!" Today, that salesman attends a Bible-believing church. I have no doubt that God works in mysterious ways.

In the end, we got a better conversion van with less mileage than the first one. Through it all, we learned that God uses difficult situations to teach us that He has the power to change something bad for our own good and for the good of others. Praise the Lord! God is always in control!

Marilza Tavares
Missionary to Brazil

19 DARK VS. LIGHT

"Ye are the light of the world. A city that is set on a hill cannot be hid. Neither do men light a candle, and put it under a bushel, but on a candlestick; and it giveth light unto all that are in the house. Let your light so shine before men, that they may see your good works, and glorify your Father which is in heaven" (Matthew 5:14-16).

It's amazing how darkness cannot put out anything but darkness. The dark cannot add to itself. If a room is dark, then there is nothing you can do to make it darker. On the other hand, if a room is bright and you add more light to it, then it becomes brighter. Have you ever noticed that when you enter a dark place after just being in the light, you can't see anything at first? Once your body adjusts, you become more comfortable with your surroundings and start to make out images. The same goes with leaving a dark room and entering a bright one. Your eyes eventually adjust to the light and begin preparing your body for what's about to happen.

This is how our spiritual life works. Before we are saved, our lives are in darkness. Once the Lord becomes our Savior, we step into the light. At first, it's hard to adjust to the new surroundings, because the light that comes into our life completely overrules the darkness of sin. Light and dark can be contrasted in many ways, but comparing them is a little harder. After all, light is light, and dark is dark, and few things relate the two. In light we see everything; darkness hides what it contains. Which do you most resemble: the light that can't be put out, or the darkness that hides what it knows? Remember one small flame can increase the brightness, but it can also light up the darkness.

Cassie Belbey

20 THE EYES HAVE IT

"And the Lord turned, and looked upon Peter..." (Luke 22:61).

A lot is said about eyes. People recalling features of a person will many times comment about their eyes. How many women have talked about gazing longingly into their husband's eyes? Many adults also remember that during their childhood, one quick glance from Mom or Dad squelched any further thoughts of misbehaving.

God has blessed my husband and me with two beautiful, blue-eyed boys. The older one's eyes are always deep in thought, while the younger one's eyes brim with mischief. One thing that humbles me most is the fact that their eyes are watching me. What do they see? Do they see a godly mother and wife? Do they see me serving the Lord? Are my eyes fixed on the Lord?

In Matthew 26:33-35, Peter promises to never deny Jesus,

but in Luke 22:54-62, we see a story unfold that shows Peter breaking that promise. When Peter denied Jesus the third time, and the cock crowed, Jesus looked at Peter. Can you imagine what those eyes said to Peter? When Peter realized what he did, he wept bitterly.

If today I could look into Jesus' eyes, what would they say to me? My prayer is that they would be eyes of approval for my service for Him and that I, for the sake of my children, will always have my eyes on Him.

TINY EYES

When I gaze into those tiny eyes
Shining clear and bright,
I wonder what the future holds
What will be his life?

Wherever he may wander,
Whatever he may see,
I pray he'll always see, Dear Lord,
My eyes fixed on Thee.

Terri Gilliam

21 GOD DRAWS US TO HIMSELF

"Ye have not chosen me, but I have chosen you..." (John 15:16).

At times God allows difficult circumstances and trying times to come into our lives, so that we will see our need for Him. I was raised in a Catholic family, and although we went to church on Sundays and did all the church required of us, we were lost.

I was saved after I married, and we moved hundreds of miles away. I told my family about my salvation and about Jesus dying to save us. I told them that they needed to be saved, too, but I got nowhere with them.

In the late 1970s, my mom retired and moved to Alabama. She continued attending the Catholic church, living what she thought was the right kind of life. Then God allowed a difficult circumstance to come into my mom's life – breast cancer. We went to doctors and surgeons, who decided she needed surgery. It was a very emotional time, and the more I tried to talk to my mom about the Lord, the more she cried. She was so afraid of dying. I tried to relieve her fears but wasn't doing a very good job.

I asked Brother Bob Cyphers, who was then on our church pastoral staff, to talk to my mom, and he agreed. On the morning of her surgery, we arrived at Crestwood Hospital, and Brother Bob was waiting for us in the lobby. After I introduced him to my mom, I went to check her in. Brother Bob led my mom to the Lord, and we all were comforted. I knew that no matter what happened in surgery, my mom would be fine.

The surgery was successful. My mom was cancer-free, and more importantly, she was saved! God knows what it takes to turn our hearts to Him. If my mom had not had cancer, I don't believe she would have ever turned to the Lord.

My mom died in July 1998, and I am so thankful to know that she is at home with the Lord.

Denny Lane

22 THE GOOD LIFE

"Trust in the Lord, and do good; so shalt thou dwell in the land, and verily thou shalt be fed. Delight thyself also in the Lord; and he shall give thee the desires of thine heart" (Psalm 37:3-4).

Life was good in Auburn. For the first time in my life, I was surrounded by godly friends and was actively growing in my faith in Christ. It seemed that God had something new to tell me every day, and I was eager to hear what He had to say. Yes, life was good, but I wanted more.

Apart from learning God's truths and hanging out with my friends, my heart yearned for my lifelong dream — marriage. Just the thought of spending the rest of my life alone horrified me. I went to God with my fears and only days later did he answer me through His Word in Psalms 37:3-4. I took God at His Word. I was convinced that He had placed these desires in my heart, and He was big enough to fulfill them. My part was to be patient and wait on Him.

Soon after, I felt led to spend the summer doing mission work in New Orleans, Louisiana. Far from my family and friends, only then was God able to get me "alone enough" to see his promises fleshed out. I realized my fears of singleness were completely unfounded. I would never be alone with God! Furthermore, God couldn't trust me with another life to care for (a husband) until I could trust Him with my own future. Was God's plan working? I was trusting Him, doing His work and actually enjoying time alone with Him. But what about the "desires of my heart" part? In His perfect time, he did it. Much like God brought Isaac his camel-riding bride, Mike came into my life in a two-seater Ford Escort. This part was truly worth waiting for!

Melissa Whitt, wife of Michael Whitt
Pastor of Calvary Baptist Church, Cottonwood, Alabama

23 GOD HEARD MY HEART

"Likewise the Spirit also helpeth our infirmities: for we know not what we should pray for as we ought: but the Spirit itself maketh intercession for us with groanings which cannot be uttered" (Romans 8:26).

Everyone has days where everything seems to go wrong. I remember one day in particular that was going all wrong. Even though I had my daily Bible reading and prayer time, something just did not feel right. I had been thinking about what it could be, and I realized that even though I had followed my morning routine of reading and praying, it was just that — a routine. I had not spent quality time with God. I had sat down and read, then prayed a quick prayer to ask God to bless my day. I had not talked to God.

I had lunch with a friend that day, and we discussed my day. She told me that she had been trying to change her prayer life and that she had asked God to help her. She spent the first 30 minutes of her prayer time not asking God for anything. She just simply praised and thanked Him. "What a difference it makes in my day!" she told me. When I got home that evening, I could not wait until the next day to start changing my prayer time, so I started then. I decided to try the 30 minutes, but I thought I couldn't pray that long without asking for something. I was so wrong! I began praying, and the more I praised God and thanked Him for what He was doing in my life, the more I didn't want to stop. Half an hour turned into an hour, and by the time I was done, I was sobbing. I was elated from being reminded of what God was doing for me, but I was so ashamed that I wasn't doing more for Him.

That night when I went to bed, I was still thinking about my earlier prayer. I sat down on my bed and began to pray. I got to a place where I couldn't pray; all I could do was cry. Then God reminded me of a verse I learned during discipleship — Romans 8:26. I just laid there and cried. Although all I could hear was my crying, I knew God heard my heart. After a little while, I felt so renewed. It felt great just to crawl up in God's lap and let Him hold me. That night God brought me to a place where I knew that I could never again just go through the motions of my daily routine. I had a desire like never before to talk with Him every day and to thank and praise Him. I admit that I don't always do it, but I try to spend time every day, just thanking God for everything in my life. When I start my day like that, I never really stop. My attitude is so different, and my heart is blessed all day long from praising God.

Amanda McKeehan

24 For God So Loved The World

"For God so loved the world, that he gave his only begotten Son, that whosoever believeth in him should not perish, but have everlasting life" (John 3:16).

Since the day of my salvation, the Lord has changed my life by changing my way of thinking and acting. He has given me an unconditional love for people that I never had before. He has continuously provided peace and hope in all areas of my life at just the right time. It is good and comforting to know that I have someone to lean on and that I am never alone, even when I do wrong. At my lowest points, I look up to Him, and He alone provides the comfort, mercy, and grace I need.

My heart's desire is that people I come in contact with daily will know that I love God and that He loves me and them. It is not always easy to present a complete plan of salvation on the job, in the store, and other places we find ourselves. However, if I can't present the entire plan, I want everyone to see Christ in my life through my attitudes and actions. I have a tract taped to my computer at work, and my screen saver is John 3:16. I don't want anyone to be 40 years old, like I was, before someone tells them about Jesus. It was only by the grace of God that I survived those 40 years, because many times I wanted to take the easy way out and end it all. I did not want to face another day without hope in my life.

Even as a child, I knew the Bible verse, John 3:16. But I did not have a clue what it meant or that it was written for me until God sent someone to me to explain His love and Jesus' sacrifice. It has helped me to know that God has a plan for my life, and He will walk with me every step of the way. If you truly want a solid foundation for your life, marriage, and family, let me recommend and introduce you to my Lord and Savior Jesus Christ.

Sherry McAdams

25 CEUs For Christians

"But continue thou in the things which thou hast learned and hast been assured of, knowing of whom thou hast learned them; And that from a child thou hast known the holy scriptures, which are able to make thee wise unto salvation through faith which is in Christ Jesus. All Scripture is given by inspiration of God, and is profitable for doctrine, for reproof, for correction, for instruction in righteousness: That the man of God may be perfect, throughly furnished unto all good works" (II Timothy 3:14-17).

Thank God I am a member of a church that believes in continuing education for its members. As a registered nurse, I was required to get CEU's (Continuing Education Units) to maintain a license to practice. Many professionals, such as attorneys and doctors, have the same obligation. As Christians, we also have the same obligation. I once heard a preacher on TV refer to the Bible as God's "Basic Instructions Before Leaving Earth." Our God gave us His only Son to pay for our sins, and in return I am to love, honor, and serve God. What's remarkable is that He gave us written instructions, and most of us never bother to open the Book. When we accept Jesus into our lives as the only Son of God, we not only receive the precious gift of salvation, but we also receive the ability to profit from God's Word – which requires studying and opening the Book! Sometimes I wonder if God will look at our CEUs when we get to Heaven.

Dear Lord, I love You with all my very being, and I praise You for Your love and care for me. I pray that with Your help I will stay in Your precious Word and use it in my daily life. I especially pray for young parents to bathe their children in love and fill them with Your Word, being a Christ-like example to them. I pray that all mothers will protect their young and treat them like the precious gifts that only You can give to them. Thank You, Lord, that I can freely read and study my Bible.

Janet Gilliland

26 I Want My Money!

"Bring ye all the tithes into the storehouse, that there may be meat in mine house, and prove me now herewith, saith the Lord of hosts, if I will not open you the windows of heaven, and pour you out a blessing, that there shall not be room enough to receive it" (Malachi 3:10).

Mrs. Lawson is my three year old's favorite Sunday School teacher — partly because she is a terrific teacher, but mostly because Benjamin had her six times during our four-month furlough to 30 churches in 11 states. Near the end of our time in the States, she and the class presented Benjamin with $40 to spend on toys, books, or whatever he needed to take to Albania.

The next Sunday, I laid out $40 on the table and explained to Benjamin about tithing. "Four of these dollars go to God," I said. "You can keep the rest for your toys." Perplexed, the greedy little pagan objected and demanded to know why. "Because God will bless you if you honor Him first," I replied. Begrudgingly, he agreed to put four of the dollars in his shirt pocket for the offering basket. A few minutes after the service began, I went to check on Benjamin and his tithe. As I suspected, it was still a bulge in his pocket. I said, "Benjamin, you need to give your tithe to the Lord." Immediately, he clenched his hands tight over his pocket and cried, "I don't want God to bless me! I want my money!"

I wonder how many of us say the same thing deep down in our hearts. We are well taught in our "churchianity," so we know we should never say anything like that during the offeratory! But we sense that our flesh would rather have our well-decorated dream homes than the blessing of God communicated to us when we give and serve. Our houses can so easily become personal museums filled with knick-knack displays and Sharper Image comforts, while millions around the world earn less each month than we spend in one night at the Outback Steakhouse. Worse, many of them will die without having heard a clear proclamation of the Gospel.

Perhaps it would actually help us to clench our wallets and scream, "God, I want my money!" during the offeratory. It might help us understand the true folly of the way we make silly excuses to soothe our consciences for doing less than we ought!

Kristi Hosaflook
Missionary to Albania

27 A Thank You Note

"Enter into his gates with thanksgiving, and into his courts with praise: be thankful unto him and bless his name" (Psalm 100:4).

Don't you enjoy getting a thank you note, knowing that the person enjoyed your gift or service? As I hear prayers, many times I hear, "Lord give me good health, give me a new job, give me this, give me that, gimme, gimme, gimme..."

I use time in my car to thank God. The older I get, the more I reflect back and see the hand of God guiding me, even though I didn't realize it at the time. I am so thankful for my grandparents and great-grandparents, who lived in the hills of East Tennessee. Their lives were full of hard work and praising God. Living without electricity, phones, and heat when I was a child taught me to be thankful for those things now. I am also thankful that a lady from the city visited my one-room schoolhouse each week to pass out prizes for memorizing Scripture. Although I didn't know it at the time, I was hiding God's Word in my heart, and that would help me for the rest of my life.

I am thankful for my family, a husband, four children, and eight grandchildren. I'm also thankful for my friends. One very special friend never gave up on praying for me and inviting me to a home Bible study, and that eventually led to my salvation. For that, I will be eternally grateful. I have even learned to be thankful for the bad things that happened in my life. My parents' divorce has allowed me to relate to other children in the same situation, and it also helped me to adjust to new situations easily. My husband was sent to Vietnam, but that situation led to his salvation.

I am thankful for my job in a preschool and a great love for children that the Lord has given to me. I am thankful for my church and a pastor that lives God's Word. Most of all, I am thankful for my Lord Jesus Christ. Despite all the blunders and mistakes I have made, He keeps teaching me and will never stop working on me.

Sally Pieper

28 KATIE BETH SAVES THE CAMP

"The steps of a good man are ordered by the Lord: and he delighteth in his way" (Psalm 37:23).

It was summer in Moldova, and the weather was hot; nevertheless, there was a great deal of excitement in the town of Telenesti. A group of Americans had come to assist local missionaries in conducting a day camp for the boys, girls, and teenagers in the town. Among the American visitors was seven-year-old Katie Beth, her older brother, Jonathan, and close friend, Shannon. The children had come with their parents and other adults to assist with the crafts, sports, and any other activities that would make this camp a wonderful experience for the nationals. The local missionaries were responsible for teaching the Bible lessons.

All was going well for the first few days. The townspeople heard about the camp, and every day more campers came. Although space was limited, it was difficult to send anyone away. Everyone was having a grand time, and God was beginning His work in the lives of the campers. Then it happened! An inspector came by to look over the facilities and to make certain that the children were being cared for properly. Of course, he saw the tasty rolls and juices served upon the campers' arrival and the delicious, nutritious meal provided for them at noon. What could he say?

The inspector was not sympathetic to Christianity, so he started looking for an excuse to close down the camp. Soon it was announced that the camp must close. "For what reason?" the nationals and visitors asked. "You are serving the campers their noon meals in bowls made in Turkey instead of Moldova," the inspector emphatically stated. "The bowls may contain substances that could harm the people." After this announcement was made, most of the local missionaries hurried to the auditorium to give the plan of salvation to the campers before they were forced to leave. We wanted to be certain that they knew their way to Heaven.

Meanwhile, our director, John, was in the dining hall pleading with the inspector to change his mind. John argued that the hungry campers were being fed better meals at camp than they could ever hope to eat in their own homes, and the inspector knew it. Just then, Katie Beth happened to walk through the dining hall. "Who is she?" the inspector asked. "Oh, that's Katie Beth, one of our American visitors...and by the way, she's eating her meals out of these bowls," John said.

"Well," replied the inspector. "If the Americans are eating from the bowls, and no one is getting ill, I guess I can give you permission to continue with the camp. This is simply amazing that the Americans are coming here to help us and live as we live." Still shaking his head in disbelief, the inspector arose from his chair, shook hands with John, and walked out. The camp continued on full force, and as a result, many campers accepted Jesus Christ as their Savior that week. God took care of the situation!

We never know how God will use us. He truly directs our steps. We are all convinced that if Katie Beth had not walked through the dining hall at that moment, the camp would have closed. God had other plans, and He delighted in ordering the steps of a child to carry out His purpose. Let us all give ourselves completely to God for His use. Who knows what He might accomplish today in your life as He orders your steps!

Loreen Ittermann
Missionary to Moldova

29 THANK GOD FOR MY HUSBAND

"Husbands, love your wives, even as Christ also loved the church, and gave himself for it" (Ephesians 5:25).

This week, my husband sent me flowers. It wasn't Valentine's Day, my birthday, nor my anniversary. He sent them to me because someone had criticized me and hurt my feelings. He knew just how low I felt.

Sometimes you may think your husband doesn't understand you, or can't possibly know how you feel. Then he does something nice for you.

I call my husband a lot during the day, because I love to hear his voice just as much as I did 25 years ago. He's such a comfort to me, and I feel he can make everything okay. I love him very much.

Janice Cross

30 THE FEAST

"For I know the thoughts that I think toward you, saith the Lord, thoughts of peace, and not of evil, to give you an expected end. Then shall ye call upon me, and ye shall go and pray unto me, and I will hearken unto you. And ye shall seek me, and find me, when ye shall search for me with all your heart" (Jeremiah 29:11-13).

What if your best friend invited you over for dinner one evening at 6 p.m.? The meal was to include green salad, with dressing of your choice; steak, cooked to your taste; baked potato, with all the trimmings; green beans au gratin; homemade rolls with butter; and fresh corn on the cob. There were three desserts offered: New York cheesecake, pecan pie, and brownie ala mode. Now, these were not ordinary culinary treats. They were, in fact, low calorie and highly nutritious. Your friend promised that this food would be nothing but beneficial. You arrived at 6 p.m. The table was decorated with beautiful linens, candles, and flowers, all in your favorite colors. The food was displayed attractively and smelled divine. You suddenly turned away from the table and walked out the door without even tasting a morsel.

Each day of our lives, God has something to give us, or better yet, feed us. Our spiritual meal is our daily prayer time and Bible study. If we do not participate, we go spiritually hungry all day. If we go for weeks without any spiritual food, we become spiritually emaciated.

Perhaps the best way for us to remember to come to His spiritual feast is to sit back and reflect on what we are going to miss out on. He provides us with everything we need to be complete, while giving us joy and peace for dessert. There are no unneeded calories or high cholesterol levels in His food, and it's really satisfying! He offers us the best of the best. All we have to do is partake. However, if we choose to reject the feast and go our own way, He does not stop us.

Marcia Sheffield

June ________________________________

"Her children arise up, and call her blessed; her husband also, and he praiseth her. Many daughters have done virtuously, but thou excellest them all. Favor is deceitful, and beauty is vain: but a woman that feareth the Lord, she shall be praised. Give her the fruit of her hands; and let her own works praise her in the gates."

Proverbs 31:28-31

1 CHANCE?

"But he knoweth the way that I take: when he hath tried me, I shall come forth as gold" (Job 23:10).

Nothing is by chance occurred
In our lives and plans
For everything that comes to pass
Is molded by God's own hands.

Our lives are never led by fate
And accidents we do not have;
Nothing is ever early or late
For with God, it's all been planned.

We have come to think of life
As a game of chance or skill,
But each step we take is not our own,
But rather, planned by Him.

The Lord controls the universe
And all that is within;
He plans what we call better or worse,
He turns the hearts of men.

Everything that happens
He knows will come to pass,
For nothing is by chance occurred
When our lots with him are cast.

Margaret Hoskins Dellinger

2 RONNIE

"And of some have compassion, making a difference" (Jude 1:22).

Ronnie was only eight years old when Miss Nina entered his life. His parents were divorced, and Ronnie lived with his mother. His parents fought over many issues involving Ronnie's well-being. Out of anger, fear, bitterness, and rage, his mother slapped the boy around whenever he did something she didn't like. Ronnie's dad wasn't much of a role model, either, and he administered severe punishments to the boy as well.

Miss Nina was Ronnie's new stepmom. She and Ronnie's dad were married after a brief courtship, not really knowing the temperament and personality of one another very well. Miss Nina loved Ronnie in spite of his disruptive behavior. He was a big boy for his age and was constantly in trouble with anyone in authority. Miss Nina was soft-spoken and patient. She had had a good father figure in her childhood and was taught solid core values. She saw the good in Ronnie and tried to focus on the positive. She wanted desperately to make a difference in his life.

One evening while Ronnie was visiting his dad, Miss Nina put him to bed. She kissed him and told him she loved him. She then retired to her own bedroom. Ronnie's dad was already asleep, but Miss Nina lay in the dark contemplating how she might be a better influence in Ronnie's life. After lying there for what seemed a long time, she heard a noise in the room. She quietly opened her eyes and could see Ronnie's silhouette. He was rifling through her purse. She decided not to stir or let on that she knew he was stealing money from her purse. She knew if she disturbed her husband, he would administer punishment that would be much worse than the crime. She watched as Ronnie carefully made his way back out of the bedroom and closed the door. As she lay there in silence, she lifted Ronnie up to the Lord and asked for godly wisdom in how to deal with his behavior.

The weekend visit ended, and Ronnie returned home to his mother. A few days later, Miss Nina called Ronnie's mother and arranged to pick him up at a certain time. All she told his mother was that she had a surprise for him. When she arrived, Ronnie eagerly followed her to the car. Before they got into the car, she hugged Ronnie and told him what a good boy he was. She told him that she loved him and that she wanted to help him, but she needed his help, too. He eagerly asked what she needed from him, and she replied,

"Well, first I want you to return the five dollars you took from my purse a few nights ago." He looked at her in shock through scared eyes. He began to beg her not to tell his dad, and Miss Nina told him not to worry about that.

Miss Nina was a school crossing guard and had made several friends in the police department. She arranged to have Ronnie go through the jail and the juvenile detention center so that he might have a good look at how a life of crime could ruin his life. He wasn't very responsive that day, and Miss Nina was not sure if that little tour had given him enough of a glimpse inside a jail to make a difference in his life. Miss Nina began to see little changes in Ronnie's life, although he still had many problems. Not long after that, Ronnie's dad asked for a divorce, and Miss Nina moved out. She and Ronnie tried to maintain a close relationship, but his dad made that almost impossible. She lost contact with Ronnie and thought she would never see him again.

One afternoon several years later, Miss Nina was busy in the shop where she worked and looked up to see a handsome young man standing before her. She asked if she could help him find anything, and he said, "You don't know who I am, do you?" She looked at him for a few moments and replied that she did not recognize him. He said, "I am the little towheaded boy you took through the jail and the detention center when I was eight years old." Miss Nina couldn't believe her eyes. She began to cry and hug Ronnie. He had grown into a fine young man and had come to thank Miss Nina for the difference she had made in his life. God had called Ronnie to preach. He had gone through seminary and was the pastor of a church in Tennessee. Miss Nina is a great-grandmother now. She has seen many "Ronnies" in her lifetime. Only God knows how many of them she has helped through her love and compassion. I know this personally because of the great impact she has had on my life.

Dianne Stewart

3 TRUSTING HIM

"And the prayer of faith shall save the sick, and the Lord shall raise him up; and if he have committed sins, they shall be forgiven him" (James 5:15).

I believe God puts things into our lives to show us Who He is! He wants us to realize that we need Him in every situation, and we shouldn't turn to Him only as a last resort.

When I was 34 years old, I had just given birth to my third child, Alec. What a gift from God he was, just as my two other children, Ashton and Austin! At Alec's one month doctor's appointment, we were faced with the fact that he would need open-heart surgery unless the hole in his heart became smaller. Wow! This was a little more than I could swallow. My little one, so tiny and fragile, in surgery! But even then, as scared as I was, I knew God was in control.

On the morning of the surgery, I was trying to be strong as we walked down the hospital hall to surgery. I actually held it together until, out of nowhere, a nurse walked up to me and said, "The Lord just told me to stop and pray for you. May I?" She prayed the most tender prayer and when she was done, she said, "Honey, everything's going to be all right. He's in the Lord's hands."

I never saw that nurse again, but I believe she was put into my path to give me the extra encouragement I needed to trust God with my baby. Although we had one of the best physicians, he was only a tool that the Lord used!

Alec is four years old now and as healthy and precious as can be! God showed me that day, whether great or small the task, He is mighty!

Teresa Mabe

4 A Call To Obedience

"And while the children of Israel were in the wilderness, they found a man that gathered sticks upon the sabbath day. And they that found him gathering sticks brought him unto Moses and Aaron, and unto all the congregation. And they put him in ward, because it was not declared what should be done to him. And the Lord said unto Moses, The man shall surely be put to death: all the congregation shall stone him with stones without the camp. And all the congregation brought him without the camp, and stoned him with stones, and he died; as the Lord commanded Moses" (Numbers 15:32-36).

When I read this passage, my first reaction was, "God, why would you kill this guy just because he gathered some sticks on the Sabbath? It's such a little thing. What if it was freezing cold and he ran out of firewood and had to get some to survive?

Then God showed me how important my obedience is to Him. I always take it lightly whether or not I obey, as if I have a choice. I also seem to decide whether or not obedience is necessary based on the situation. God showed me that it's not a choice, but a commandment. If I don't obey, I get the consequences. No, I most likely won't be stoned outside the city, but I will face spiritual, emotional, and physical consequences, because God demands obedience from His children.

As I thought more about this passage, God also convicted me to appreciate the grace that I'm under. I'm not living under the Law, and God has given me a million second chances to obey Him. Although I can be very grateful for these second chances, I should never get used to them.

Anne DeKoker

5 God Is Right On Time

"Let us therefore come boldly unto the throne of grace, that we may obtain mercy, and find grace to help in time of need" (Hebrews 4:16).

In the summer of 2002, we were having some financial difficulties, and we learned that God teaches you things through difficult times. We were in need of a vehicle, and a friend let us borrow one for about two weeks. We had been looking and just couldn't seem to find anything we could afford. Then a very close friend of mine called me on a Wednesday and told me about a car, and we talked to the lady about seeing the vehicle on Thursday. That was also the day we had to return the borrowed vehicle.

We were having summer revival at the church at the time. That Wednesday night, Laura Vest, Teresa Mabe, and Melissa Kirby sang a song about God being right on time, even when we think He is late. God showed me through this that I can't fix the problems in my life. I have to give it all to the Lord, even though I think things are going to fall apart.

We were able to purchase the car the next day, and we returned the borrowed vehicle right on time. I learned, even though it is hard sometimes, to put my trust and faith in God. I know He will be right on time.

Wanda Kimbrough

6 My Desire

"If my people, which are called by my name, shall humble themselves, and pray, and seek my face, and turn from their wicked ways; then will I hear from heaven, and will forgive their sin, and will heal their land" (II Chronicles 7:14).

This verse of Scripture is what I obeyed as I fought the difficult battle of seeking my way back to God after years of sinning against Him. Sin had broken my relationship with God and had taken me so far from Him that I felt lost and alone in the midst of all my friends. I didn't get to this point overnight, and I knew it was going to take a time of proving myself before my relationship with God could be completely restored. Wretched and miserable could not begin to describe how ungodly and unworthy I felt at the time. Jesus Christ had shed His blood and died on the cross for me. He had filled me with His Spirit, given me power to overcome temptation and the world, blessed me beyond measure, and I had still failed Him.

I knew what David felt when he wrote in the Psalms, "My wounds stink and are corrupt because of my foolishness. I am troubled; I am bowed down greatly; I go mourning all the day long" (Psalm 38:5-6). This was part of the horrible guilt that I battled.

A friend of mine invited me to church, and I went. I didn't really know why I was going, because I felt God was through with me. Going to church only made the feeling of doom worse. Then somehow my God Who is rich in mercy broke my heart again, and I humbly wept before Him and prayed, "Dear Lord, please forgive me of my sin." The battle was still tough, but I began to seek God's face and turn from my wicked ways. To forgive myself was very hard, and to believe God could forgive me and love me was even harder. Though not sure of God's love for me, I still wanted to love and serve Him with all of my heart, mind, body, soul, and strength.

Once again, God had mercy on me and opened my eyes to the sins of David. David's dirty laundry was hung out for generation after generation to read about. Oh, how I praise the Lord for revealing this to me. As I began to see grace, I prayed and added to another prayer of David's. "Return, O Lord, deliver my soul: Oh save me for thy mercies' sake" (Psalm 6:4).

It was then that the last part of II Chronicles 7:14 took place in my life. God forgave me of my sin and brought healing to my heart. The battle was won, and the victory was mine! I owe the Lord so much for what He has done for me. My deepest desire is to truly be a woman after God's own heart.

Tamara Haden

7 I'M LOST!

"I have planted, Apollos watered; but God gave the increase" (I Corinthians 3:6).

Several years ago, I was concerned about my mother's salvation. I had tried in subtle ways to witness to her, but she was never receptive. Witnessing to relatives is always the hardest!

We were planning to meet in Huntsville and drive to Fayetteville, Tennessee, for decoration at the old cemetery where my grandmother is buried. I had prayed that God would give me an opportunity to talk to my mother about being saved. So as we wound along the back roads of Tennessee, I began to share with my mother about how I thought I was saved at one time, but I really wasn't. As I was about midway through my testimony, my mother looked at me with the strangest look and said, "Tammy, I'm lost." I said, "Oh, Mamma, you don't know how long I've waited to hear you say that." Then she smiled and said, "No, I'm lost! I don't know where I am!" I could have just died with embarrassment.

Needless to say, she did not get saved that day, but she did about two years later. On the way to the cemetery that day, my mother knew what I was doing, but she was just not ready. We laugh about that day now, but my mother has told me several times since, "Thank you for not giving up on me."

So never stop praying and looking for opportunities to share Christ, especially with your family members. God's Word clearly tells us that some of us plant the seeds and some of us water the seeds someone else has planted, but it is God who gives the increase!

Tammy Loyd

8 Drawing From The Well Of The Water Of Life

"Jesus answered and said unto her, Whosoever drinketh of this water shall thirst again: But whosoever drinketh of the water that I shall give him shall never thirst; but the water that I shall give him shall be in him a well of water springing up into everlasting life" (John 4:13-14).

Water is something we do not give much thought to. It is usually always there. We get water from the sink and the shower, and we flush the toilet without much thought. However, since my family moved to Nakuru, Kenya, we have had to think a lot about water. At times we have been without water for half a day, which is normal. Other times we have gone without the precious commodity for up to four months.

What do we do in these situations? We have to be prepared. We have a 150-gallon tank in the ceiling and a 500-gallon tank outside the house. These tanks are connected to the city water line. When there is no city water, we pump water from our outside tank to the upstairs tank, which serves all the sinks, toilets, and showers. Whenever our tank runs dry, we buy water from a private well. We have learned to adjust to this situation.

It is impossible to live without water, because we use it for everything. When it is not there, everything comes to a halt. Most of the time we are trying to conserve the water we do have. It reminds me of how a life without Christ is much like living without water. Man is dry, empty, and constantly searching to have his spiritual thirst quenched. As we have learned to adjust our lives here in Nakuru to obtain water, we must also make adjustments in our lives so we can draw from the well of water that springs up into everlasting life. Maybe we need to set aside other "important" activities, get up earlier or stay up later, and schedule it into our daily routine. We need to do whatever it takes to draw from the well of the water of life to satisfy our spiritual thirst. If we don't, we will find that our spiritual tank has run dry.

Karen Hainline
Missionary to Kenya

9 Living Each Day In God's Presence

"...in thy presence is fulness of joy..." (Psalm 16:11).

If you've ever experienced the joy of God's presence, you know that there is no greater joy than that. It truly is "fulness of joy," or a feeling of wholeness, in need of nothing but Him. Unfortunately, many Christians are disillusioned, thinking this is a mystical experience only a few "chosen" can enjoy, when in reality it is meant for every child of God.

The key to unlocking the manifestation of God's presence is not hard to find. God reveals it to us in His Word. He tells us in Psalm 22:3 that He inhabits the praise of His people. Since we know that inhabit means to dwell or reside in a place, that leads us to the conclusion that God dwells in the midst of our praises for Him.

As a busy wife, mom, or single woman, making time for intimate worship in God's presence is difficult, sometimes seemingly impossible. Even though we know this time alone with God is needful and that we can't survive without it, our intimacy with God doesn't have to exist only in our prayer closet. I Corinthians 10:31 says, "Whether therefore ye eat, or drink, or whatsoever ye do, do all to the glory of God." You may be conditioned to believe that you can only worship God at church or in your quiet time, but according to this passage, we can and should do all things to His glory in an act of worshipping Him.

So as you go through your day, whether you're in the workplace, doing laundry, changing a diaper, shopping for groceries, or cooking supper, offer up whatever "service" you're performing to God as a sacrifice of praise. That may not seem like much of an offering, but offer whatever God has given you. If it comes from a pure heart seeking to honor and bless Him, He will gladly receive it and surround you with His loving presence, bringing complete joy and fulfillment to your fast-paced life.

"The essence of worship is just being in love...a true woman of worship will allow her life to be an 'I Adore You' to her Lord." – Darlene Zschech

Suzanne Spiers

10 THE BEGINNING OF MY PRAYER LIFE

"Confess your faults one to another, and pray one for another, that ye may be healed. The effectual fervent prayer of a righteous man availeth much" (James 5:16).

My mom and dad were married September 14, 1940. My mom was a Christian. Although my dad was a good man, a hard worker, and an excellent provider, he was not saved.

We lived in a small community in Ohio, but there was no Bible-believing church in our area. My grandparents, along with a young man just out of seminary, started a church. As the church grew and several activities began, Dad never objected to our attending. He even gave us money for church camp.

When I was ten years old, I was led to the Lord by my grandmother, who was my Sunday School teacher. Then I began to pray for my dad to get saved. At 11 years old, I was still praying for my dad to get saved. Every Sunday, my sisters or I would go into my parents' bedroom and ask Dad if he was going to church with us. He never did. Our church had a prayer list and my dad's name was always on the list. At age 13, I was still praying for my dad to get saved. As I got older and church activities increased, my dad continued to never object to church attendance. By the time I was 15 years old, the house rules were a little more strict—no movies, no dances, and no boyfriends unless they were Christians – but I was still praying for Dad's salvation.

Dad started going to church some of the time and when a building program began, he was there to lend a hand. Finally one Saturday my mom, sisters, and I decided to go shopping. While we were gone my grandfather came for a visit. They were sitting on the porch, and my grandfather said, "LeRoy, don't you think it's time?" That day my dad gave his heart to Jesus. The next Sunday Dad went before the church and made a profession of his faith. At prayer meeting the following Wednesday, my dad's name was not on the prayer list, for his name was now written in the Lamb's Book of Life. For many years I prayed for Dad to be saved. As I look back I can see how this was the foundation of my prayer life. I praise the Lord I was led to begin praying for my dad, and I was able to see my prayer answered.

Darlene Heath

11 JESUS, THE AUTHOR AND FINISHER OF OUR FAITH

"Looking unto Jesus the author and finisher of our faith; who for the joy that was set before him endured the cross, despising the shame, and is set down at the right hand of the throne of God" (Hebrews 12:2).

At our annual women's conference in La Esperanza, Honduras, the theme was "A Woman of the Word." By reading and meditating on God's Word, we are strengthened and renewed. II Corinthians 4:16 says, "For which cause we faint not; but though our outward man perish, yet the inward man is renewed day by day."

Many times as we read familiar passages, the Lord shows us something we have not noticed before. The verses in Romans 8:15-18 were the ones that the Lord gave me. What a blessing it was to realize that when I received Christ as my personal Savior I had "received the Spirit of adoption" and could therefore cry, "Abba Father." Romans 8:17 then explains that as children of God we are His heirs and "joint-heirs with Christ."

Yes, we may be called on to suffer with Christ, but "...the sufferings of this present time are not worthy to be compared with the glory which shall be revealed in us" (Romans 8:18). May each of us keep our eyes on Jesus.

Provi Martin
Missionary to Honduras

12 God Led Us To The Best

"But my God shall supply all your need according to his riches in glory by Christ Jesus" (Philippians 4:19).

From the day he was born my son cried. For his first five months the only time he slept was when he was nursing. He wouldn't take a pacifier or a bottle. I loved my son, but this was getting old fast. I kept asking doctors and friends why he never slept. Their answers were that he had colic or that he would grow out of it.

When he was four and a half months old, we traveled to Oklahoma with some friends to attend a funeral. While we were there, I found blood in my son's diaper, and I took him to the emergency room. The doctors at that hospital could not diagnose the problem, so they sent me to another doctor who was 40 miles away. When we arrived, the doctor was waiting on us and did a test immediately. He told me that my son had intracaception, and he set up an ambulance to take my son to Children's Hospital in Little Rock, Arkansas. During the ride in the ambulance, my son was becoming lethargic. When we arrived in Little Rock, there was a slew of doctors, nurses, and surgeons waiting on us. As the nurses were trying to put in an IV, my son's lips turned blue, and he stopped crying. During a lower GI test, the doctors saw that his intestines were telescoping each other, and they immediately took him to surgery.

As I handed my son over to a nurse, I had a feeling of peace. After the surgery, the doctor came out and told me everything was fine. He also said he had found and corrected birth defects in my son's bowels. If those defects had not been corrected, my son would have died before he was five years old. We were thankful the intracaception happened, or we might have never known about the birth defects.

A week later, we went to a specialist for a check-up, and he told me that the surgeon who performed the surgery was the best in North America. My son is now a healthy 12 year old, and I am continually grateful that God led us to the best.

Cheryl Freeman

13 NO MAN CARED FOR MY SOUL

"I looked on my right hand, and beheld, but there was no man that would know me: refuge failed me; no man cared for my soul" (Psalm 142:4).

On January 19, 2001, Scott Vaughn Hancey died of melanoma cancer, leaving our 25-year-old daughter, Jessica, and their 23-month-old daughter, Kyleigh. It only took six months for Scott to go from a healthy young man to his death.

On July 31, 2000, when Jessica and Scott left the doctor's office after being told that cancer was in his brain, lungs, bones, and adrenal gland, Jessica told Scott, "You had better be sure that you know for certain that you are right with God, because you are very sick." On August 10, 2000, my husband, Doug, prayed with Scott in the living room of his home, completely assured that he gave his heart to Jesus. Scott followed the Lord in believer's baptism soon after that, something he would have never done before.

A few weeks after Scott died, Jessica, Doug and I went out for lunch together. Jessica asked our opinion of why God allowed her to meet Scott, when he was raised in Utah and was introduced to her through a Marine buddy? Such strange circumstances brought them together, and then they were married for only four years and four months. They were just getting used to each other, and their marriage was just getting over some rough spots.

From the moment we learned that cancer had taken over Scott's body, Psalm 142:4 continued to echo in my heart, "…no man cared for my soul." For almost an entire year before Scott got sick, Jessica began to question his salvation. Scott had little to no hunger for spiritual things. Jessica began to ask everyone that had a relationship with Scott to help him. "Make sure he is saved," she said. Scott had professed that he was saved when they first started dating, but the lack of fruit in his life bothered Jessica. She talked to her dad, her brother, Jeremy, Scott's Bible study teacher, his fishing buddy, me, and anyone she felt could reach Scott. We all took our turns speaking to him, but he would tell us all the same thing – he knew he was saved.

I believe with all my heart that God allowed Scott to come into Jessica's life so that he could be loved into Heaven. Scott did not have the privilege to be loved and cared for in a home like all children should be. He basically raised himself. He fished and hunted until he finished high school, and then he joined the Marines. Until he and Jessica met, he had very few plans and dreams for his future. So, for the last five years of his life he had someone that loved and cared for him, and he knew that beyond a shadow of a doubt. I believe Scott was allowed to have someone care for his soul.

God, thank You for trusting Jessica in the life of Scott. Now continue to heal her and make her what You want her to be.

Katy Ripley

14 The Influential Role Of My Stepmother

"The heart of her husband doth safely trust in her, so that he shall have no need of spoil. She will do him good and not evil all the days of her life" (Proverbs 31:11-12).

Although blending two families together can be difficult, my stepmother, Katie Tumlin, never hesitated to treat me like her very own daughter. She has helped me through tough trials in my life, and overall, helped make me the person I am today. Katie has always stood by my side and has given me advice in areas such as walking with God, dating, and friendships. She has been an inspiration and encouragement to me.

Katie is a Christ-like image and has a strong faith in the Lord. By watching Katie set a good example, I learned the biblical roles of a wife and mother. She is a very biblical, respectful, supportive, and honorable wife and mother to my family and me. Katie has a strong, passionate desire to be a biblical wife, mother and friend. She has been a wonderful blessing and will continue to be a wonderful blessing to my family and me.

The Bible says that a virtuous woman is a crown to her husband. I know she is a crown to my dad because she is a loyal and supportive wife. She holds a special place in my heart because of her unconditional love and compassion.

Amy Tumlin

15 RAISING CHILDREN WITH CHRIST

"Children, obey your parents in the Lord: for this is right. Honour thy father and mother; which is the first commandment with promise; That it may be well with thee, and thou mayest live long on the earth. And, ye fathers, provoke not your children to wrath: but bring them up in the nurture and admonition of the Lord" (Ephesians 6:1-4).

The moment we find out we are expecting a child, we begin preparing for this wonderful addition to our family. Many parents attempt to juggle the daily rigors of raising children in today's society without having the guidance of Christ in their lives. I have come to learn that to raise a well-rounded child, a parent needs Christ. With His guidance, parents also need time, patience, and understanding to raise children. Even with all these essential elements, parents will falter and stumble through the growth of their children.

Perhaps a parent's greatest dilemma is how to better handle time constraints. Parents are constantly moving from their homes to their jobs, appointments, church, and school. A daily weekday schedule might include transporting children to and from school, going to work, and then running to after-school activities. This might include soccer practice, band practice, or drama practice. In between all the running and shuttling, parents try to squeeze in quality time with their children. Busy parents often think 30 minutes of "family time" is wasted and unproductive, but to children, this time is priceless. Parents who allow their children to be a part of their prayer time teach the children that they depend on the Lord for guidance. Parents must be willing to give up their time to be with their children. In doing this simple, yet often difficult thing, children will see what an important part they have in their parents' lives.

Becoming a parent taught me that patience is extremely

important in rearing children. I have found that with Christ's help and patience, I have become a better parent. Adults tend to lose sight of this needed quality and often get frustrated with their children. Parents tend to grasp situations quickly, working problems through their minds to find the best answers. Children often procrastinate and repeat a problem multiple times before resolving it. Often, children will not go to their parent, because they are afraid of the parent's reaction.

Just as we took the time to prepare for our children's arrival as babies, we as parents must exercise that same patience and preparation as we lead them through their lives.

Jodie Glossick

16 Keepers At Home

"The aged women likewise, that they be in behaviour as becometh holiness, not false accusers, not given to much wine, teachers of good things; That they may teach the young women to be sober, to love their husbands, to love their children, To be discreet, chaste, keepers at home, good, obedient to their own husbands, that the word of God be not blasphemed" (Titus 2:3-5).

The picture of the perfect woman in Christ is clearly depicted in this Scripture. He expects us to be sober minded, and to love our husbands and children. This love, I'm sure, is the kind that has hands, feet, ears, and eyes. We can allow Him to love them through us. We are to be discreet and not be a blabber-mouth or boastful.

We are to be chaste, pure, and keepers at home. There is no place safer or more restful and restorative than the home. The home is the nucleus of society, and we are keepers there. What an awesome responsibility! God must have a lot of faith in us to assign us this task, and being the God He is, I believe He created us specially to have the necessary sensitivity, intelligence, and stamina to successfully fulfill this assignment!

We are also to be good and obedient to our husbands that the Word of God be not blasphemed. Maybe He wants us to be obedient to them so they can take care of us. Whatever His reason, we will be blessed for using His plan as a pattern for our lives.

Loretta Clark

17 My Protector

"When thou passest through the waters, I will be with thee; and through the rivers, they shall not overflow thee: when thou walkest through the fire, thou shalt not be burned; neither shall the flame kindle upon thee" (Isaiah 43:2).

When I was in high school, God allowed me to be touched by this verse. At the time, I was having physical problems, and my father had just had back surgery. A few years later, my parents went through a messy divorce. During this time, my mother, brother, and I were without a home, clothes, and food, but this was a most enlightening time.

Just as the verse says, God was there for us. He gave us shelter, clothing, and food. We didn't have need of anything. He even provided a needle, button, and thread to mend our worn clothes. It was during this time of need that God proved to be everything we needed. He never let the waters overtake us or the fire burn us.

What problems are you facing? There is nothing too great or too small for God to handle. Today, as you face the world, remember that He is there and He will be protecting you all the way.

Kimberly Hedden

18 God Answers Every Prayer

"And all things, whatsoever ye shall ask in prayer, believing, ye shall receive" (Matthew 21:22).

I remember well the day I got my little dog. It was in the summer of 1979, and she was only eight weeks old. A lady had brought in a litter of pups for me to choose from. My little dog picked me out by looking straight at me and doing something that she continued to do for the rest of her life; she sat up on her hind legs and put her front paws together and begged.

Because of her loving nature, I named her Snuggles. She was three-fourths Poodle and one-fourth Peek-a-Poo, and she grew to weigh six pounds and one-fourth ounce.

Snuggles was by my side for many years. Since I could not have children, I put my mothering into loving her, and she, in turn, loved me. She went through some very bad times with me and also some very good times. She was there when I asked Jesus to come into my life and when I met and married my husband.

When she started getting old, I asked three things of the Lord: that I would not have to put her to sleep, that she would not suffer and that I could be with her when she died. In His great mercy, He answered my prayer. On February 14, 1998, at 4:10 a.m., she died in my arms.

The reason I'm telling this story is to let people know that God cares about us, and there is no prayer He will not answer.

Dear Lord, help me to let people know there is no prayer too small for You, and there is nothing about us that doesn't concern You.

Sharon McCulloch

19 YOU ARE LOVED

"Behold, what manner of love the Father hath bestowed upon us, that we should be called the sons of God..." (I John 3:1).

When our son, Blake, was 19, he spent the summer in Albania serving on the mission field with a missionary from our church, Jeff Bartell. We kept in constant communication via the Internet. I printed out every letter we sent each other, even if it was only a couple of sentences. I put them in a book so that we would always have them and never forget his time in Albania. He did a great job of keeping us updated and telling us how much he loved and missed us. We were so grateful that he did. He said all the things every parent wants to hear.

During that time, Blake wrote a letter that God really used to speak to my heart. In it, Blake thanked me for praying for him, taking time to read his letters, and writing him back. He said he knew I was busy, and it took a lot of my time. Can you believe that? I just couldn't believe he said that. What on earth could be more important to me? I am his mother, and my heart longed to hear from him. Didn't he know that? I checked the computer ten times a day, hoping to hear from him. Everything that was going on in his life was important to me. Hadn't he been reading my love letters? Didn't he know how much I loved him? I would give my life for him. Surely he realized that, especially after the many times I told him and showed him.

Then God spoke to me: "Now you know how I feel. I can't believe you don't realize how much I love you either. Everything you just said can be said for Me, too, but to the gazillionth degree. I love you more than you could ever love Blake. I gave my Son's life for you. I love you more than your mind can comprehend. Haven't you been reading my love letters? I wrote 66 of them and put them into a book for you so that you could read them again and again. I don't want you to ever forget how much I love you, or Who I am and what I've done for you. I long to hear from you and want to answer you. Don't you realize that? How many times have I told you and showed you? Come and talk to Me. Tell Me all the things a parent loves to hear."

Boy, God had seared my heart. I forget at times how much He loves me, and that He is my Father, as well as my God. I feel so insignificant in His big world that it is hard for me to realize that He really cares about every aspect of my life. What an object lesson this was for me. Who am I that God would acknowledge me? The answer is so obvious. I am His child.

Oh, Father, forgive me. Thank You for loving me and for all that You have done and are doing for me. Please help me to love You more. My relationship with You means more to me than any here on earth. Please help me to show it.

Jennifer Barnett

20 A Woman Named Dorcas

"Now there was at Joppa a certain disciple named Tabitha, which by interpretation is called Dorcas: this woman was full of good works and almsdeeds which she did" (Acts 9:36).

Sometimes when I do my daily Bible reading, it's easy to skim through and try to get it done as quickly as possible. It's even easier when the reading is a story that you've heard many times before. How many times have we heard about Paul on the road to Damascus or Lazarus being raised from the dead? You'd think that a dead person coming back to life would be enough to catch my attention, but sometimes even that can be easy to overlook.

Acts 9:36 gives a good description of a woman named Dorcas. The next few verses tell how Dorcas died and was raised from the dead. Before, whenever I read the story, I always focused on the miracle itself, but the third or fourth time I looked at it, a light bulb went on over my head. I finally began to see what the passage said about Dorcas. Her life was full of good works and almsdeeds. Can you imagine having a testimony like that? It doesn't say that she did a few good deeds every once in a while. She was full of good works, demonstrating her love of God through her love of others. Dorcas must have sacrificed her time, her energy, and her comfort to earn such a testimony.

One simple verse that I overlooked so many times has challenged me to look at my own life in comparison with that of Dorcas. My life doesn't measure up to hers and it probably never will, but it will always give me something to think about. What sacrifices am I making?

Stephanie Gilliam

21 FEEDING HUNGRY CHILDREN

"He that hath pity upon the poor lendeth unto the Lord; and that which he hath given will he pay him again" (Proverbs 19:17).

As missionaries working in southern Honduras in 1983, we were surrounded by unbelievable poverty. A war was going on just a few miles away in northern Nicaragua, and refugees were pouring into Honduras trying to escape the war. My job, as a missionary wife and mother of two young sons, became very hard as I tried to teach hungry children about the love of Jesus.

In November of that year, God gave me an experience in the village of Azacaulpa that changed my life. After a morning service, where my husband preached and I taught a large group of children, the people asked us to stay for another service. The pastor proudly served us cold tortillas, pickled sardines, and hot Pepsi. As we tried to eat this meal seated on crude benches outside a small hut, my eyes caught sight of a little girl peeling a green grapefruit and never taking her eyes off me. That morning, the Lord used this little girls to speak to my heart. I was, treated to a feast, wore a pretty dress and shoes, and sat on a bench. She had nothing but a green grapefruit to eat, and she was wearing no clothes as she sat on the ground. Yet, I had taught her that morning that Jesus loved her, had died on the cross for her, and was building a beautiful home for her in Heaven. She could have asked, "But what about now? Doesn't Jesus love me now? Does Jesus love the missionary more than He loves me?" Those thoughts probably never entered the mind of that little girl that morning, but that day changed my life.

God began to deal with my heart about the hungry children – thousands of them. What could I do? I was just one person, and there were so many hungry children. I couldn't sleep at night, because so many thoughts crossed my mind. "I am just one person, and there are so many," I thought. Then a voice inside me would say, "But you can start with one." And that's what I did. We started with just one, and then another and another. By 2002, there were more than 3,000 children who receive a good, hot meal each day, all provided by our Lord Jesus. Yes, He loves them, and He doesn't want them to be hungry. He loves them just as much as He loves the missionaries. Since that day, thousands upon thousands have not only been fed, but they have been taught the Word of Jesus. Three pastors with Good Samaritan Baptist Missions were saved as young boys because of these kitchens now operating all over southern Honduras and northern Nicaragua.

Joan Tyson
Missionary to Honduras

22 MY MOTHER, MY COMFORT

"Her children arise up, and call her blessed; her husband also, and he praiseth her. Many daughters have done virtuously, but thou excellest them all. Favour is deceitful, and beauty is vain: but a woman that feareth the Lord, she shall be praised. Give her of the fruit of her hands; and let her own works praise her in the gates" (Proverbs 31:28-31).

Recently my daughter Brooklyn and I looked at some of her baby pictures. As we looked at these, I thought about the many responsibilities of motherhood and the examples, discipline, love, and sacrifices we make for our children. As I thought about these things, I thought about my mother and the relationship that I have with her. I hope my daughter and I have that same closeness that I have with my mother. Of course, it wasn't until I had children of my own that I realized how special my mother was.

In 1987, my life was shattered! My husband of ten years and my four-year-old son drowned in a boating accident. With the grace of God and the love of my mother, father, and other son, Brandon, I survived that tragedy in my life. My mother was there to comfort me, although she was also suffering the loss of her grandchild and son-in-law.

Philippians 4:13 says, "I can do all things through Christ which strengtheneth me." The Lord gave my mother the strength to comfort me even in her grief. My mother and father were married for 44 years. In 2001, my dad went to be with the Lord, and we have all missed him so much! The Lord has given me strength day by day to comfort my mother just as she comforted me.

Pam Morgenthaler

23 ETERNAL SAVIOR

"Wherefore he is able also to save them to the uttermost that come unto God by him, seeing he ever liveth to make intercession for them" (Hebrews 7:25).

In the summer of 2002, I went on a mission trip to France. God really opened my eyes while I was there, and I will never be the same. I saw many people whose religion is based on tradition — people who were searching for healing and forgiveness through dead idols.

During my daily reading in Hebrews 7, God began to show me that the people in France knew Who Jesus was, but they did not know that He was the Eternal Savior. God has used this mission trip to speak to my heart. I want to be willing to go anywhere He may call me, and I want to pray earnestly for laborers, specifically for France. Most of the people I know are saved, but only a handful of people in France are saved. All of the testimonies I heard while in France were from people who were disowned by their families after they received Jesus Christ as Savior. God has been so good to me, and I am so glad He allowed me to see His work in France.

Alisha Sherman

24 VICTOR'S SACRIFICE

"Give and it shall be given unto you; good measure…and running over…" (Luke 6:38).

The 50 full-time Christian nationals serving with a missionary in Moldova receive a monthly salary of approximately $100 a month. On this sum, the pastors take care of their families and conduct their ministries. Every lei is squeezed to its limit! Knowing the situation of the pastors, the missionary still felt led to challenge these young men to ask

God to send an additional $100 each during the next few months that they could donate to the new "Street Kids Shelter" the mission was in the process of building. Swallowing hard after hearing the idea, the pastors decided to at least pray about it. What could they lose? The missionary had emphatically stated that this $100 was not expected to be given from their usual monthly allotment. It was to be an extra amount that God would send in.

After the meeting, Victor, a young national pastor who had been a juvenile delinquent before he came to Christ, approached the missionary. "Here's my $100," offered Victor. The surprised missionary replied, "Oh Victor, you don't understand. You're not expected to give your monthly pay." "It's okay, please take it," Victor urged. "I believe God wants me to do this. I learned to trust Him with money two years ago. Don't you remember?" Confused, the missionary inquired, "What are you talking about? What happened two years ago that has you so sure that you can trust God by giving away your entire salary like this?" Victor recalled, "Two years ago I was a student in Bible College. I was in church one Sunday with five lei (about 50 cents) in my pocket. That's the total amount I had available to live on for the entire next week. However, when the offering bag was passed, I felt I should give an offering of one lei. My dilemma was attempting to figure out how to get four of the lei back as changed from a five lei bill. As I was pondering what action to take, the bag quickly arrived. I put the five lei in, but before I could retrieve the four lei in change, the offering bag was gone!" Intrigued, the missionary asked, "What did you do?" Victor replied, "Well, I prayed. I asked God what I was going to live on for the next week. Needless to say, I was worried."

"What happened?" asked the missionary. Victor smiled at the missionary and said, "You were the answer to my prayer!" he exclaimed. "After church, you came to me and said you were moving that week and needed someone to assist you. I said I would be happy to help. You paid me $20 for my work and gave me some clothes and other gifts. Then, before I left, you insisted I accept another $5. That day, I learned an important truth: God definitely can be trusted with money affairs!"

Now Victor is the most giving national on our team. In fact, he and his wife committed this summer to give God 20 percent of their monthly salary! Needless to say, God keeps rewarding Victor over and over again. He and his wife, Marina, are happy to share with anyone who will listen about their blessings from giving.

Do we have this kind of faith? Do we believe we can trust God with our finances? If you are not certain, why not prove Him as He asks you to do in His Word.

Loreen Ittermann
Missionary to Moldova

25 Where There Is Loss, There Is Grace

"And he said unto me, My grace is sufficient for thee; for my strength is made perfect in weakness. Most gladly therefore will I rather glory in my infirmities, that the power of Christ may rest upon me" (II Corinthians 12:9).

Another baby – I was thrilled! I longed to hold another baby in my arms, to smell its sweetness, and to feel the velvety softness of baby skin and hair. It would be another person to lead into God's family.

But it was not to be. I had a miscarriage, followed by several more. These were very difficult times, but God is always gracious and loving. When I asked, "Why?" God said, "For as the heavens are higher than the earth, so are my ways higher than your ways, and my thoughts than your thoughts" (Isaiah 55:9). God knows why, even when I don't. Hebrews 4:16 says, "Let us therefore come boldly unto the throne of grace, that we may obtain mercy, and find grace to help in the time of need."

God the Father allowed His own Son to die to save me. He loves me, I trust Him, and He gives me peace when I need it. I can cast all my care upon Him for He cares for me.

Lisa Watson

26 FAITH

"Now faith is the substance of things hoped for, the evidence of things not seen" (Hebrews 11:1).

What is faith? According to Hebrews 11:1, faith is believing without seeing. Many people have a hard time trying to grasp the concept of faith and how it really works. So many times when we have trials in our lives, we want to take matters into our own hands instead of letting go and letting God take care of things.

In my own life, I have seen God come through many times when everything seemed hopeless. God taught me a long time ago what faith really is. He showed me how He will take care of us just as He does the lilies of the field and the bird of the air.

But do we really know what faith is all about? It is when we take that step and trust that He won't let us fall. It is when we are at our lowest point in life and we have nowhere else to look but up. It is when our child is sick, and we pray for healing. It is when our finances are tight, and we still pay our tithe and faith promise offering. That is when God shows Himself faithful more than ever. He has never left us. He was there all the time. Times like these are when our faith begins to grow.

When we actually put our faith into practice and see God do a work in our lives is when we can see the hand of God.

We say that we have faith, but I don't think anyone can understand what faith is until you put it to the test and see God do a work in your own life.

Rebecca Kirby

27 Only What's Done For Christ Will Last

"Delight thyself also in the Lord; and he shall give thee the desires of thine heart" (Psalms 37:4).

I was saved at the age of seven, and from that moment my prayer was to serve the Lord. At a very young age, my interest was in playing the piano, and my heart's desire was for the Lord to use me as a church pianist. God began working in the lives of two people whose ultimate desire was to serve Him, and over time He brought us together through circumstances only God could control. God gave me the desire of my heart when I married my husband, a minister of music. We served Him together in the music ministry for 36 years.

After my husband and I had children, our prayer was for our children to serve the Lord. We can get so materialistic and work so hard for things here on earth. Our desire was to not emphasize on things of this world but to show our children that we are just passing through. Our lives are just a vapor. We wanted to instill in our children to lay their treasures up in Heaven. Don't work for this world. Our desire was for our children to realize that only what's done for Christ will last.

God gave my husband and me the desire of our hearts. Our children are each serving the Lord and are actively involved in church. Before my husband went home to be with the Lord, God enabled him to see his son, Chris, and his family surrender to go to the mission field. God allowed our family to go and see the work on the field He had called our son to. On December 3, 2002, we stood and watched the plane take my son and his family back to the mission field for the 11th year. God has given us the desire of our hearts by allowing our children to realize that only what's done for Christ will last.

Patty White

28 PIE VS. PRIDE

"Pride goeth before destruction, and an haughty spirit before a fall" (Proverbs 16:18).

There — into the oven it goes — this most-beautiful-pie-of-my-life pie crust. For once, I will have something tasty and beautiful to take to the family Thanksgiving dinner. So many of my foods seem to come out on the short side of gourmet beauty. I guess I always feel that if I can make it taste good, then that will suffice.

There goes the buzzer — so far, so good. Maybe I'd better slide it out and take a look to see if it is nice and brown on the bottom. No, it had better go back in for a few minutes. That's when it happened. The pie slid out of my mittened hands into the back of the oven, dangling halfway on the pie plate and halfway on the hot coil.

I am overcome, first with frustration and then with laughter. What else could I do? I realized the sense of humor my Lord has along with His teaching methods. To Him, my pie was not nearly as important as my pride. Thanks, Lord, for running that lesson by me again. I'm a slow learner.

Reba Cofield
Missionary to Canada

29 THE GRACE TO FLY

"Trust in the Lord with all thine heart; and lean not unto thine own understanding In all thy ways acknowledge him, and he shall direct thy paths" (Proverbs 3:5-6).

For most of my life, I have had acrophobia, the fear of heights. This fear can greatly handicap your life and rob you of much joy. I was afraid of being on mountains and bridges, riding boats in deep water and terrified at the thought of flying.

One day, I received a call that my dad had been hospitalized, and they were sure it was his heart. He lived more than 600 miles away, and the only way I could get there was to fly. As I got on the plane, I was terrified! The whole time I was there, I was shivering at the thought of having to fly back home.

A few years later, it was necessary for me to fly there again, twice within the year. The second time, as I was returning home, I thought, "This is not so bad—I don't feel so afraid this time."

Several months later, my husband and I were asked to go to Germany with a group in our church to teach biblical discipleship. My husband really wanted to go, but I told him I would have to pray about it. I really didn't think I could possibly fly all the way to Germany! But, after seriously praying about it, I could not say "no" in peace. When I told him, "Yes, I will go," the Holy Spirit spoke to my heart, and I knew that this was what God had been preparing me for. Little did I know that my next flight would be to fly across the ocean to serve Him!

Barbara Allred

30 Fruit For Our Labor

"...Suffer the little children to come unto me, and forbid them not: for of such is the kingdom of God" (Mark 10:14).

My mother led me to the Lord at a young age, but as a teenager I rebelled against what I thought were the restrictions of Christianity. In college, I became an agnostic and married an unbeliever.

I was blessed with a precious daughter whom I adored. One night after putting her to sleep, I lingered by her bed gazing at her angelic three-year-old face when a dreadful thought struck me. What if God was real…and Hell was real? What would be her fate? As the days passed I could not shake these forebodings and resolved that I would not risk her life. I began to include Bible stories and prayers in our nightly bedtime ritual. As simple as our nightly devotionals were, God used them to restore me to fellowship with Him, and in time bring both my daughter and a younger son to salvation.

My daughter is now in college, and although her own faith has wavered, one thing that has guided her through relationship choices is her determination to bring up her children, when she has any, in the faith of Jesus Christ. My mother's care for my soul is producing fruit into the third generation.

Joanna McAbee

31 He Never Leaves

"For the Lord knoweth the way of the righteous: but the way of the ungodly shall perish" (Psalm 1:6).

I have read the quote that says picking up toys with small children in the house is like shoveling snow in a snowstorm. Usually, I have a house full of children all the time. On one particular day, I was trying to pick up some toys when my little girl called out to me from upstairs.

After I went upstairs and took care of her, I started back downstairs with her trailing behind me. As I was going down the steps, picking up shoes and toys and all the other things children leave at the bottom of the steps, my daughter cried out, "Mother, don't leave me, don't leave me!" I said, "I'm not leaving you. I'm just clearing the way for you, so you don't stumble and fall."

At that moment, the Lord, our heavenly Father, spoke to me as if to say, "That is what I tell you a lot of times when you are saying, 'Father, don't leave me. I am having a problem!' I am not leaving you. I am just clearing the way for you, so you don't stumble and fall." I had to stop and thank the Lord for all the times I had not trusted Him and for being so good to me all the time and for all the lessons we learn from our children.

Mitzi Sims Oaks

1 God Keeps His Word

"Fear thou not; for I am with thee: be not dismayed; for I am thy God: I will strengthen thee; yea, I will help thee; yea, I will uphold thee with the right hand of my righteousness" (Isaiah 41:10).

While we were serving in Norway as missionaries, I went through the hardest trial of my whole life. My first thought was that it was just not fair, because I have desired to serve God all of my life. I struggled with God each day as I read my Bible and asked Him to help me through this, but I thought it would never end. As the months dragged on and I felt there was absolutely no one with whom I could talk, I felt as if I would die. I cried out to God for help, but it seemed that I only got more desperate as time went on. I had little appetite and began to lose weight. I felt powerless and cried often.

After my trial had gone on for almost a year, I decided that I could not go on this way anymore. Arriving home one evening in a desperate state of mind, I went into the small bathroom of our home and looked out the window and into the sky as if I could see God. Then I poured out my heart. I told God that if I kept on going in this desperate way, I was headed for a nervous breakdown. Then I told Him that I was willing to entrust my emotions and thoughts concerning this trial to Him if He would just take control of the situation and of me, my body, and my fears. At that moment, I faced the possibility of losing my family, my ministry, and my testimony. I told God that if that was part of His plan for me then He would have to help me through it, but I was relinquishing this battle to Him.

I reminded God that, as a missionary, I am often asked to speak when we are in the States. I told Him that the only way I could give a testimony, instead of ending up as a missionary's wife disaster statistic, is if His Word is true and He keeps His Word. Now the battle was His! The next day, I wrote

Isaiah 41:10 out on a 3x5 note card, since my mind was in such a desperate state that I could not memorize any verses. Every time after that, when I began to feel desperate, I would get that card and read it out loud. Then I would tell God that I believed those words and wanted to put them into practice, but I needed His help. I stopped thinking about the anxious things in my mind by not praying for the details that were causing my anxiety. My prayers always accelerated into anxious, desperate worry sessions.

There are times when we have to recognize our limitations and the completeness of God Almighty. Just be faithful in walking with the Lord — reading His Word and praying. Stop worrying and start committing every burden to the Father, because His yoke is easy and His burden is light. I am not repeating cliches. I have been there. I have done this, and it works. God is faithful to keep His Word as He promises.

Lori Brown
Missionary to Mexico

2 LIFTER OF MINE HEAD

"But thou, O Lord, art a shield for me; my glory, and the lifter up of mine head. I cried unto the Lord with my voice, and he heard me out of his holy hill. Selah. I laid me down and slept; I awaked; for the Lord sustained me" (Psalm 3:3-5).

I remember a time during my senior year in high school when we were asked to discuss our greatest fears. It was interesting to hear all the different things that were fearful to 17 year olds. I remember that my response was that my greatest fear was being alone.

More than 20 years have passed since that time, and it amazes me how the things that I expressed as my greatest fears have come to pass. It was almost as if God was saying, "Good, I will use this fear to show Sherrie how great I am and how much I love her." That is exactly what I learned. Those things that I was so fearful of have proven to be great times of growth and victory. I have learned that with God on my side, there is nothing that I need to fear. He will never leave me to go through things alone.

Whatever you are fearful of today, place your trust in the only One that will never leave you and will get you through those fearful times. We can walk boldly through life because God is the lifter of mine head.

Sherrie Britton

3 I Have a Cool Mom

"Her children arise up, and call her blessed; her husband also, and he praiseth her" (Proverbs 31:28).

My idea of a great day as a child was lining up my caterpillars on the porch and making them march, or going across the street to the vineyard and catching lizards and horned toads. If it ever bothered my mother, she never voiced it, unless I left the creatures in the hot sun and they baked. She explained that it was cruel to not take care of my special friends. Many times when I would come inside for lunch, she would say, "How are all your bugs today?" Then I could tell her about the neat ladybug I caught or the lizard that almost got away. My mom was so cool.

Because Momma and I shared this unusual love of bugs, I couldn't understand why it bothered other adults. My mother's sister lived in Missouri and we lived in California, so every summer we would travel 2,000 miles and visit for about two weeks. They lived on a farm, so they had chickens that roamed around in their yard. I would spend hours hiding in the bushes waiting for a chicken to walk by so I could catch it. When I would come inside, my aunt would shake her head and say, "Look at that dirty face, there is not a clean place on you." But Momma would pull me into her lap, wipe my face with the tail of her apron, and whisper in my ear, "How's your bugs?" I would jump down from her lap with a big smile. She would pat me on the rump and tell me to go back outside and play. I knew Momma was proud of me — dirty face and all. Momma knew what was important.

When I was a young mother, and now as a grandmother, my prayer has been that I would remember to let children be children. They get dirty, and they make messes. They are loud, rambunctious, talkative, and truthful (at the most inappropriate times!). But they are ours for such a short time. Let the children be children!

Dear God, thank You for our children. They are Your special gifts to us. Help us to not complain when they are acting like children, and help us to enjoy the brief time they are in our home.

Katy Ripley

4 THROUGH THE EYES OF AN ADULT CHILD

"When I was a child, I spake as a child, I understood as a child, I thought as a child: but when I became a man, I put away childish things" (I Corinthians 13:11).

We all have things that hurt us as a child. I guess you could call them issues. They are things that our parents or other people said or did to hurt us at one time. Looking back on my childhood, I must say that I had Christian parents who loved me, took me to church, and did their best to raise me with good values. They hugged me when I needed hugging and spanked me when I deserved it. Of course, as a child I thought I never deserved it.

There were also times when my parents made mistakes, and the Lord showed me as an adult that I was still holding onto those hurts. One day, as I prayed, God began to show me that I was still seeing my past through the eyes of the child I was then. He said, "Tammy, this has left you frustrated, bitter, and angry." Then He gave me I Corinthians 13:11, and I decided to put away my childish behavior.

II Corinthians 5:17 says that we are new creatures in Christ. If I truly want to be that new creature, I must put away old things, such as the hurts of my childhood. Then I can move forward with the new life I have in Christ. God has also showed me the importance of honoring my parents by forgiving them for their past mistakes.

Tammy Gordon

5 SUMMER CLASSES WITH BOYS

"So shall my word be that goeth forth out of my mouth: it shall not return unto me void, but it shall accomplish that which I please, and it shall prosper in the thing whereto I sent it" (Isaiah 55:11).

One summer, our school administrator asked me to handle a class of prospective new students, who were all boys and non-Christians. The ages of these boys, almost 30 of them, ranged from about fifth grade to high school. Since I taught in a Christian school, there was always a devotional before class starts. For me, it was an opportunity to share the Word of God. On the first day of summer classes, I tried to study the boys' faces and told myself that they were not interested in the Word of God. Their faces were hardened, and their minds were not focused.

However, during the second week of class, I attended a summer training class, and my assistant took over my class of boys. My assistant did not do a devotional. When I returned from my training class, she told me that one of the boys had asked about me. He had questioned why she did not do a devotional and said, "Are you not going to do what Teacher Thelma does?" Right then and there, I said, "Lord, Your Word is working. Your promise that Your Word will not return void is true."

Dear Lord, help me to never underestimate the power of Your Word. I believe You when You promise that Your Word will not return void. I will trust You in any situation, because I know You have a purpose that is beyond my understanding.

Thelma A. Obid
Missionary to Cambodia

6 FOLLOW HIS LEAD

"...I will follow thee whithersoever thou goest" (Luke 9:57).

My daughter, Olivia, was first diagnosed with Histiocytosis-x at the age of 22 months. We had been going to our local pediatrician and then to the local ear, nose, and throat specialist, because she was having problems with her ear. After the ENT treated her for ten days, he said he didn't know what it was and referred us to an ear specialist in Birmingham. At this point I was scared and thought, "Something is really wrong."

After speaking to my sister, we decided to forego the Birmingham doctor and make an appointment with Dr. Shea in Memphis, Tennessee. My sister had been to see him and highly recommended him. She got us an appointment the next day and off we went to Memphis. He looked at Olivia and said it would take a 15-minute outpatient surgery to correct the problem.

Well, that 15-minute surgery turned into a four-day stay after he found the mass in Olivia's ear. After going from doctor to doctor, we ended up with an oncologist who assured us that everything would be okay. He said that if at anytime he could not treat Olivia, he would transfer her to St. Jude Children's Hospital immediately. After two years of chemotherapy treatment, Oliva was transferred to St. Jude. They accept our insurance as payment in full on any services.

I can look back after seven years and see why God led us

to Memphis. If we had gone to Birmingham to see the doctor in the first place, we would not have been so close to St. Jude, and we would have been in deep debt with doctor bills. Thank God He knows what's best for us, even when we don't know why or how. I am thankful we were sensitive to His leading and can truly say God knows best.

Pam Williams

7 A Written Plan For Roadblocks

"But they that wait upon the Lord shall renew their strength; they shall mount up with wings as eagles; they shall run, and not be weary; and they shall walk, and not faint" (Isaiah 40:31).

A little over a month after our youngest child started school, we gradually came to face the fact that she had learning difficulties. The situation was complicated by the fact that she was learning everything in a language that was not her "mother tongue," and she had problems with her eyesight that could not be corrected with glasses or surgery. We hoped and prayed that things would improve and that maybe it was just a matter of adjustment to school.

Halfway through the year, it was obvious that things had improved very little, if any. Finally, we were faced with making some kind of decision for her and her schooling, and we were really questioning what the Lord would have us to do. There seemed to be no clear-cut answer, as there were multiple factors and opinions to be considered in the matter. It led to confusion and discouragement. One day in my desperation I sat down and wrote the following plan for dealing with this "roadblock" in my life:

Pray for wisdom and for God's guidance in the situation.

Be willing to change, adjust my schedule, and try new methods and ways to help my daughter.

Memorize Bible verses with her, especially at night before she goes to sleep.

Take one day at a time — make necessary plans and preparations, but don't look into the future to foresee difficulties and hardships that may not even come to pass.

Pray for God's protection on her and her mind.

Trust God to lead us in making the right decisions.

Believe that He has allowed this and has a purpose in it.

Encourage her — learn that all people desperately need encouragement and praise.

Treat her like a normal child. Do not spoil her or deprive discipline when needed.

Do not seek to get sympathy from others. Most will probably not understand anyway. Do not speak negatively about her or tell everyone about her problem. Respect her need for privacy and dignity.

Help her adjust to changes in her life. Prepare her for changes in her routine and schedule.

Expect great things from God. Do not rely upon yourself. Do not make plans and preparations for things that may not be in God's plan. Leave it in His hands.

O God, prepare me for the challenges that lie ahead. Give me wisdom and knowledge, as well as patience and understanding as I encounter disappointed hopes, discouraging experiences, and trying moments. Help me to be gentle and encouraging with my daughter when she needs motivation. Encourage me when situations loom and cause my faith to waver.

Tricia Dubbe
Missionary to Germany

8 FOR A MOMENT

"For a small moment have I forsaken thee..." (Isaiah 54:7).

One day while I was cleaning out a drawer, I found an index card with two verses on it. My mom had written out the verses and had given the card to me to encourage me during a difficult time. I tucked it away, and as things got better, I forgot about it.

The verses are Isaiah 54:7-8: "For a small moment have I forsaken thee; but with great mercies will I gather thee. In a little wrath I hid my face from thee for a moment; but with everlasting kindness will I have mercy on thee, saith the Lord thy Redeemer." As I read those verses, it brought to mind that in times of discouragement, it seems as though God has forsaken us. During the hard times, when we feel as though He's not around, that's when God is working great things in our lives. I also thought of the feeling of being gathered up into the arms of God and the security of knowing He is there with me.

The Bible is full of verses tucked away inside that God brings to us at different times to refresh and encourage us – at the moment we need it. So in times of discouragement, remember to turn to God's Word for encouragement and don't worry, it's only for a moment.

Terri Gilliam

9 YOU CANNOT OUT GIVE GOD

"Give, and it shall be given unto you; good measure, pressed down, and shaken together, and running over, shall men give into your bosom. For with the same measure that ye mete withal it shall be measured to you again" (Luke 6:38).

For more than 20 years, I worked in the banking business and managed to do quite well. But during 1997, the bank I was working for began to change, and those changes created a lot of frustration and anxiety for me and indirectly for my husband, Ron. We began to pray for God's guidance, and we firmly believe that He orchestrated the events that led to us starting our own mortgage business. We had joined Decatur Baptist Church and were already tithing and trying to serve the Lord in various capacities, but this move was indeed a leap of faith. I was going from a salaried position with great benefits to starting a company where nothing was guaranteed. In fact, we were faced with making a rather healthy investment just to open the doors. Ron and I have continued to give, even way beyond our tithe, and God has proven over and over again that you simply cannot out give God.

One instance that comes to mind is a Sunday, a couple of years ago, that had been designated as the First Fruits Offering for the building fund campaign at church. Ron and I had already decided to give a certain amount, but during Bible Study hour God impressed upon me to give more than we had previously discussed. I usually never bring my checkbook to church, but I had it with me that Sunday. I wrote a check for the increase God led me to give. I didn't have the opportunity to discuss what I had done with Ron, because he was busy with the Greeter/Usher Ministry.

After church, I attended a baby shower, and Ron had an appointment to show a building we own in Moulton to someone who was interested in renting it. Later Sunday night, we finally had time to talk and I asked him about his appointment. Ron told me that he had not only rented the commercial building, but he had also rented a house we own. He went on to say that the renter of the commercial building had amazingly paid six months of rent in advance, which is extremely rare. I asked how much he had paid and was absolutely shocked to find out that the amount was exactly the same amount of increase I had given to the building fund. We gave and God gave it back the same day.

Our mortgage business continues to prosper beyond our wildest dreams, and Ron and I are amazed every year at the amount we are able to give to God's work. We have truly found that you absolutely cannot out give God.

Darleen Hill

10 BEAUTIFUL FEET

"...How beautiful are the feet of them that preach the gospel of peace, and bring glad tidings of good things!" (Romans 10:15).

One day I needed a haircut, so I went to a salon owned by a woman named Hilda. Eventually, I became a regular. In the Dominican Republic, salons usually have a couch for women to sit on and talk, so I got to know Hilda and her two daughters well.

One evening, I went by to see Hilda, and she was free for a pedicure. She soaked my feet in cool water then began the ticklish process of filing and clipping my toenails. We were chitchatting when she paused and began asking me questions about my faith. I had already told her I was a missionary, and I began to tell her the story of Jesus. She began to cry, but she kept up with the pedicure! Finally, she said she had been looking for a way to come to God but didn't know how. There in a little salon, still holding my feet, she prayed and asked Christ to come into her heart. That's why Romans 10:15 is one of my favorite verses. Several weeks later, I went with Hilda to her new church, and she introduced me as the person who brought her to the feet of Jesus! What an introduction!

Dear Lord, please make my feet swift and beautiful for the Gospel so I may bring others to You!

Alli Hale
Missionary to the Dominican Republic

11 GOD HONORS THE CHILDREN

"Take heed that ye despise not one of these little ones..." (Matthew 18:10).

From time to time, large containers are shipped from the States, loaded with equipment and goods for missionaries in the economically deprived Republic of Moldova. In one particular instance, there were five missionaries who decided to share a container. They were expecting office furniture and boxes of blankets, clothes, and teaching supplies – all important items necessary to serve the needy nationals.

The ship carrying the container docked in Odessa, Ukraine. It sat there for weeks while missionaries worked with officials on getting the container released and on its way to Moldova. Experiencing nothing but failure, the missionaries finally hired an agent to work with the custom authorities. This agent was well experienced and devoted many long hours to the problem, but it was to no avail. Despite the prayers of many people, the container continued to sit on the dock. The mafia was asking for thousands of dollars in bribes and adamantly refused to surrender the container unless this demand was met. They even threatened to kill the agent if he did not cooperate with them.

Then one of the missionaries remembered how God had often honored the prayers of children through which He accomplished great things for His honor and glory. She quickly emailed her sister, Gwen, who had also served as a missionary in the past. Gwen was currently teaching a class of second-graders in a Christian school in Florida. Surely, she would understand.

Gwen immediately rose to the challenge, and explained the situation to her little students. They were eager to pray and had complete confidence that God would answer their prayers. Before leaving for home at the end of the day, Gwen gave each student a little shampoo sample with the instructions to take it home and place it somewhere where they would see it often and be reminded to pray. The children were happy to do this!

When Gwen wrote her sister to report what she had done, her sister confidently announced to all: "Now the container will be released!" Sure enough, a couple of days later, the missionaries received a telephone call with the good news. The container was on its way to Moldova. Needless to say, there was not only great rejoicing in Moldova, but there was also great rejoicing in that little Florida classroom of faithful second-graders.

When you've prayed and prayed, and there is no answer, try asking children to pray. Over and over again, many have witnessed how God honors the expectant faith of a child!

Loreen Ittermann
Missionary to Moldova

12 MY MOTHER

"Who can find a virtuous woman? for her price is far above rubies" (Proverbs 31:10).

My mother is the most wonderful woman in my life. I know that without her I would not be where I am today. When I was a teenager, she was always there for me. She corrected me when I did wrong but loved me at the same time. Proverbs talks about the virtuous woman, and my mother is just that. I cannot pick out one verse over the others that best describes her. To me, all of them apply to her.

She has faced many trials, and they have made her a very strong woman. She has made decisions that I did not understand at the time. But now I understand them, after watching her and her actions. She has handled situations in a totally different way than I would have, but after seeing the outcome I know that I would want to handle things the same way. Mother always has advice when you ask for it, but at the same time, she does not push her opinions on you.

When I got married and moved out of my parents' home, I did not rely on her as much as I used to. Now that I have children, I see that she is just as important in my life. My children love their Gran, and I know that she will be as important in their lives as she is in mine.

Tonya Dotson

13 CRIPPLING PRIDE

"...Most gladly therefore will I rather glory in my infirmities, that the power of Christ may rest upon me...for when I am weak, then am I strong" (II Corinthians 12:9,10).

I was brought up in a loving Christian home and recognized my need for Christ at a young age. I was present at every church service, went to VBS every summer, and sang in youth choir. I attended Christian school for 12 years and was, for the most part, a good Christian girl. But at the age of 12, a cancer began to grow inside my heart that would cost me more than I ever fathomed it would. This wasn't a physical cancer, but a spiritual one. I had the cancer of pride.

I was 12 years old when I sang my first solo, and more than anything else, I loved the attention it brought me. From that time and on through the next 10 years of my life, I craved the spotlight. Centerstage was where I wanted to be, not because I was praying "God, please use me to touch a hurting soul" but because I loved the prestige of being a singer. I tried to take the glory that belonged to the Lord. Little did I know how dangerous it was to try to steal God's glory away from Him, even if it was an inward mindset that no one could see. God tells us in Isaiah 42:8 that He will not give His glory to anyone else! The Bible repeats over and over again how God rejects the proud but is near to the humble. Pride says, "I can do all things myself without any help." Humility says, "I can't do anything without God's help." If God gives grace to and draws near to those who realize they are nothing without Him, then what is His response to those who think they've got it all together? He takes whatever they're doing (even if it's supposedly done "in His name") and causes it to crumble into dust.

God took my singing ministry when I was 22 and broke it down to ground zero. He finally said, "No more!" I began to experience what I later discovered to be panic attacks. And the strange thing was that I had them only when I was in the "spotlight." Every time I'd get onstage to sing, unbelievable fear would come over me. It was something I couldn't explain, but something I begged God to take from me. Surely this couldn't be of God! I've now spent the last five years of my life crippled by these fears. God definitely opened my eyes to see that it's His ministry and not mine. But the nagging questions of why God would let this happen to me have continued to linger through those years. Then a message I recently heard preached by Dr. David Shepherd answered my question of "Why, Lord?" The message addressed the sin of sowing to the flesh, taken from Galatians 6:8: "For he that soweth to his flesh shall of the flesh reap corruption...." The sin I committed wasn't an outward physical sin, but it was a fleshly sin. Pride is a sin of the flesh. One of the points stressed in this enlightening sermon was that even if you sow to the flesh with sins of the heart, you will still reap physical corruption.

God revealed to me that night the results and consequences of trying to share His glory. I was reaping physical corruption for years of having a pride-filled heart. He did whatever it took to bring me down, and it worked! The reaping of corruption is still ongoing for me. Fear continues to grip me every time I sing. I'm crippled and walking with a limp, so to speak. I don't know if God will ever take my limp away. But if He doesn't, I'm still going to keep singing for His glory, realizing the awesome privilege He's given me to minister through song and asking Him to bless others through me. Even though I'm wounded, I will join with Paul in saying, "...Most gladly therefore will I rather glory in my infirmities, that the power of Christ may rest upon me...for when I am weak, then am I strong" (II Corinthians 12:9,10).

Suzanne Spiers

14 THE BLESSING OF A HUSBAND

"Wives, submit yourselves unto your own husbands, as unto the Lord" (Ephesians 5:22).

The Lord has blessed me with a wonderful husband, and I have struggled for a long while to let him take care of me. I have a strong will to take care of myself. The Lord had to humble me and break my spirit to show me that His love is sufficient for me. When I came to a place in my walk with God that I let my husband lead our family, it was a burden off of me. I have heard my husband give spiritual advice to both of our children, and he has made the hard decisions that I was thankful I didn't have to make. I have praised God every day for loving me enough to give me a godly husband.

Judy Knight

15 DOES YOUR LIGHT SHINE?

"Let your light so shine before men, that they may see your good works, and glorify your Father which is in heaven" (Matthew 5:16).

"It's one thing to know what's right and another thing entirely to do it." This statement was proved entirely to me by a co-worker. As an unsaved young adult, I observed this lady who boasted her dedication to her church, yet the life she lived did not reflect her "good works." We did not relate very well to each other for two reasons. I was living a life of sin, and I looked down on her "Christianity." That brought her conviction, and she sorely disliked me for it.

We worked side by side for weeks, trying to avoid one another. I sneered at her every time she would share with other co-workers about singing in the church choir or teaching a children's Sunday School class, because I understood how a Christian was to live, and she was not living it.

Unbeknownst to both of us at the time, God had a plan for our lives. He had been convicting me of my life of sin as He was dealing with my co-worker's "double life" as a Christian. She rededicated her life at her church, and I received salvation at a revival. All this happened within a week's time, without our knowing of each other's encounter with the Almighty. At work, we slowly began to recognize differences in each other, and we quickly became best of friends because of the common thread that bonded us together.

Fortunately, this story has a happy ending and should bring us all to a realization of how our lives should be lived before others. Does your life around others reflect Him or does it keep others from knowing Him? Be honest with yourself, but most of all, be honest with Him.

Dear Lord, help me to be a light to those I am around. Let my light shine brightly that it may bring others to Your saving grace. Thank you for giving me the opportunity to be a light in a dark world.

Denise Phillips

16 To Our Graduates

"Train up a child in the way he should go: and when he is old, he will not depart from it" (Proverbs 22:6).

Our children graduated one year after the other, and I wrote them a poem as a graduation gift. As I read it, I realized that this was something that every parent would want to say to their kids before they left for college, so I decided to share it.

To say that we are proud of you
Could only be a start,
For the joy and blessings you have brought,
Just overwhelms our heart.
Through every stage and every phrase,
We wouldn't trade a minute,
We can't even begin to imagine
Our lives without you in it!

Now we can't believe the time has come
For you to graduate!
We feel a hint of sadness,
Although we celebrate.

You are truly something special,
We love you more than words can say.
We're so grateful to have had this time with you,
And for you we will always pray.

That you'd keep your mind on what's eternal,
Your eyes be fixed on Christ,
Don't labor only for the temporal,
As you journey through this life.

Our citizenship's in Heaven,
Down here, we're just passing through.
Keep God first in everything,
And to His Word stay true.

We did our best to train you,
In obedience to the faith,
And now then, kids, it's up to you,
So be good — for Heaven's sake!

Jennifer Barnett

17 Prayer And God's Timing

"Likewise the Spirit also helpeth our infirmities: for we know not what we should pray for as we ought: but the Spirit itself maketh intercession for us with groanings which cannot be uttered. And he that searcheth the hearts knoweth what is the mind of the Spirit, because he maketh intercession for the saints according to the will of God" (Romans 8:26-27).

It is important to know how to pray specifically, but it is also important to realize that the Holy Spirit intercedes for us, even when we do not know what to pray for. Many times we pray and demand God to answer our prayers the way we want and when we want. That is what happened to me.

My husband and I were newlyweds, and I wanted more than anything in the world to start a family. I prayed every day that God would give me a baby, even to the point that I became demanding, questioning why God had not given me one yet. I was serving Him. I was faithful to church. I thought, "What else do I have to do?" It got to the point that I was obsessed with having a baby.

Then I read the story of Hannah in I Samuel. Her story really impacted my life, because she, too, wanted more than anything to have a child. Her passion to become a mother touched my life. I realized that I was wrong in the way that I was praying, so I first asked the Lord to forgive me. Then I asked Him to help me accept His will. I knew that if I were going to have a child, it would be in His timing. I felt as if a load had been taken off of my shoulders. God gave me peace, because I was willing to accept His will over my own. My life was changed from that point on, and now when I pray, I have a very different attitude.

That all happened when my husband and I were traveling on deputation. When we arrived back in Mexico City to start the First Baptist Church of Texcoco, we found out that we were expecting our daughter, Nayeli. That was the happiest day of my life. Although I was very sick for the first three months of my pregnancy, I didn't mind. God also taught me a valuable lesson. If I had been pregnant while we were on deputation, it would have been unbearable while traveling around the country in my condition. God knew what He was doing, and He did not give me my child until I was in a place where I could rest and rely on my family to help me.

Xochitl Canada
Missionary to Mexico

18 MARY'S LITTLE LAMB

"And when he putteth forth his own sheep, he goeth before them, and the sheep follow him: for they know his voice" (John 10:4).

While I was growing up, I was continually teased about my name. I loved having the same name as Jesus' mother, but there were also jokes, such as "Hey, Mary Quite Contrary!" or "How's your little lamb doing?" Sometimes it was annoying, but I learned to live with it.

I started to see these jokes in a different light after I took a precepts class. In the class, we studied Jesus' statement to Peter: "If you love me, then feed my sheep." I have learned a lot about shepherds and their sheep. Shepherds brought their flocks together and corralled them for the night. In the morning, each shepherd retrieved their respective sheep by calling them. As each shepherd called, only his sheep came, because sheep know their shepherd's voice, and they follow it.

I have started a collection of sheep figurines, which remind me of the children I teach in Children's Church. I am so thankful that God has entrusted me to play a special role in their lives, and I take that duty very seriously. I am helping to feed these children the Word of God, and I am doing it because I love my shepherd, the Lord Jesus Christ. Just as sheep know their shepherd's voice, and my children know mine, I know my Father's voice and will follow when He calls.

Mary Raths

19 Over The River And Through The Woods

"But speaking the truth in love, may grow up into him in all things, which is the head, even Christ" (Ephesians 4:15).

"Over the river and through the woods..." We are all familiar with these lyrics, which eventually lead us to Grandma's house. However, God's destination for us is His image, although we sometimes have to travel the same path that takes us to Grandma's.

In my journey through life, I have often found myself going over the river and through the woods of diverse circumstances toward a destination that seemed obscure or uncertain. There have been times when I could not figure out how the deep water and dark woods I was going through could yield anything positive.

I recently marked 25 years of being a Christian, and I have spent time looking back and reflecting on God's faithfulness to me. There have been times of grief and sorrow, shame and stagnation, and times when I simply lacked faith. There have also been times of great victory, when God has used me to teach, to convert, and to rescue. The same God whose hand was upon me during those times of victory did not let go in times of trial (Matthew 28:20). Every bump in the road, every mountaintop of victory, and every valley of defeat have been either initiated or allowed by God to shape me into His image. It does not matter how many times I fall down, and it does not matter how many times I am knocked down. What matters is that I keep getting up and running the way of His commandments (Philippians 3:14). I have learned to trust the refiner's fire. He knows the good and the right way for me; He knows those lessons that I will learn with ease and those which will take more wrestling and more times in the wilderness to prove me (Deuteronomy 8:2).

I would encourage each woman who is reading this book

to examine the goodness of God and to trust His heart toward you. No matter how black it may seem at times, He is working all things for your good and His glory.

Julie Moline, wife of Dale Moline
Pastor of Wellspring Bible Church
Denver, Colorado

20 BE BOLD AND ANGRY, BUT SIN NOT

"The wicked flee when no man pursueth: but the righteous are bold as a lion" (Proverbs 28:1).

God has so richly blessed me with two children that have such a love for things of Christ. We have the privilege of visiting them at our neighborhood school on occasion. One time, as we were about to enter our son's classroom for a Valentine's Day party, his teacher pulled us aside. She told us that she had seen Whitaker behave in an unusual way, and he ended up crying. After the party, my husband, Barry, suggested that we take him home for the remainder of the day to see if he would tell us what happened. We got home, and he was more than ready to tell us.

As Whitaker began to tell the story, big tears formed in his eyes and rolled down his face. He said a boy next to him was using God's name in vain and swearing repeatedly. Whitaker began raising his hand to get the teacher's attention. After several minutes, during which the boy continued to swear, Whitaker threw his pencil down in frustration. By that point, our son was so upset over hearing those piercing words that he began to cry. He had finally gotten the teacher's attention because he threw his pencil, and he got in trouble for that.

After hearing the story, I began to cry with Whitaker. We should all be literally sick inside when we hear our Lord's name used in vain. Whitaker was most definitely bold and angry, and he probably went too far to get the teacher's attention. But my son taught me a valuable lesson that afternoon. I wonder if we, as adults, are as bold and angry when it comes to defending our Lord and Savior. Wouldn't we be better Christians if we were?

Sabrina Boshell

21 MY POWER OR HIS POWER?

"Likewise, ye wives, be in subjection to your own husbands; that, if any obey not the word, they also may without the word be won by the conversation of the wives; While they behold your chaste conversation coupled with fear" (I Peter 3:1-2).

When I became a believer, my marriage was falling apart. My husband had a drinking habit that was about to destroy our family. Continual arguments, nagging, and crying were the order of the day. Although I had been saved by the grace of God, I continued doing what I had always done. I fought to fix what was wrong and rebelled against the things that hurt me. Everything I did in my own power to fix what was wrong didn't work.

One day, God showed me I Peter 3:1-2, and it was a hard pill to swallow. Can you imagine? How could I be in subjection to a man who was often drunk and who showed me no respect or love? How could I keep a chaste conversation or a meek and quiet spirit when all I wanted was the opposite?

Well, I had trusted God to save me from condemnation, I had placed my eternal destiny in His hands, so how could I not give in to this request? I decided then to do as He was instructing me to do. It was not easy, but I prayed for God to give me the strength. He did. I prayed more than I have ever prayed and felt that the Lord was keeping me company. I was not alone, and although I felt unloved by my husband, I felt God's love all around me. My heart was at peace, although I didn't understand why.

There were many miracles in our lives, but it was a long and painful process of transformation. Just as silver has to be put through fire seven times to remove the dross that dulls its beauty, we had to go through difficult times to remove all that was interfering with our becoming all that God intended for us to be. It was a time of great struggle, but I trusted by the Word of God that it would be the best in the end. My husband once said to me, "When you shut up, I started hearing the Holy Spirit." When I obeyed God and was in subjection to my husband, he was changed, but I had to change first.

Praise the Lord, we have been redeemed! This redemption that Jesus Christ accomplished for us took us out of the world of death and sin. Although we are living in the world, we no longer belong to the world. When we trust in our flesh and in our own power, we deny the power of the Spirit given to us. Daily we must make a conscious decision to allow the Holy Spirit of God to work in our lives. We must let the power of God transform us.

Thank You, God, for allowing me to see the Holy Spirit work in me and bring my husband to the saving knowledge of Jesus Christ. Thank You that the truth of Your Word works.

Elena Moore

22 SLEEPING IN PEACE

"I will both lay me down in peace, and sleep: for thou, Lord, only makest me dwell in safety" (Psalm 4:8).

Moving into my own apartment after graduating from college was a big change for me. I lived in the dorms at school and had never lived alone. To top it off, I moved to a city where I had no friends or family!

Although I have never been particularly skittish, the first few nights of independence frightened me. I lived in an apartment on the second floor of an old house that creaked with every wind gust. Every thud and every bump sent me into a panic, because I was sure someone was trying to open my windows or break down my door. I taped the phone number of the local police station next to my phone on the night stand, and I kept a hammer propped up beside the bed, ready to use at a moment's notice.

Nevertheless, I slept fitfully, until one night the Lord led me to Psalm 4:8. The words jumped off the page of my Bible as I realized my heavenly Father was speaking to me. From that night on, I never got scared, because I placed my trust in the only One Who can ensure my safety.

Dear Lord, thank You for taking care of me every day and night of my life. Thank You for Your Word and the way You use it to comfort Your frightened children.

Dawn Kent

23 TRUSTING IN THE LORD

"Trust in the Lord with all thine heart; and lean not unto thine own understanding. In all thy ways acknowledge him, and he shall direct thy paths" (Proverbs 3:5-6).

Many people are having a tough time. Many people are shut in because of weather or illness in the family. Some feel lonely and forgotten, while others face financial problems. The days and the nights become long and sad, as memories plague minds and affect emotions. Maybe you find yourself in one of these situations.

Let me encourage you with Proverbs 3:5-6, verses which have been beneficial to me. If we trust and obey our Lord, we can always be sure everything will turn out right, although sometimes it does not seem like that is what the outcome will be. My Bible tells me about the might, power, riches, holiness, and love of God. He is all that we need. Many times, we may not understand why something happens, but we should keep on going and obeying His commands. Just trust Him, for He is trustworthy. He has promised to guide our lives if we trust Him and obey. He will do it! If we believe He died on the cross, can He not care for our everyday needs?

Srichand Horn
Missionary to Thailand

24 HALFWAY OBEDIENCE

"And Samuel said, Hath the Lord as great delight in burnt offerings and sacrifices, as in obeying the voice of the Lord? Behold, to obey is better than sacrifice, and to hearken than the fat of rams" (I Samuel 15:22).

Have you ever been halfway obedient to God, only to realize that partial obedience is really disobedience? Has Satan ever tried to take your victory in an area that God had promised victory, if you were obedient to His Word? If so, you can relate to my testimony.

For 50 years I suffered from clinical depression and never sought medical attention, until almost three years ago. At that time I felt my life was too overwhelming to function. I had prayed for years for God to heal me and at times I felt as if He had, but it would not take long for that darkness, that emptiness, that hopelessness to resurface.

At last, I decided I had to have help and went to my doctor. After trying me out on several anti-depressants, he decided to send me to a psychologist. In a couple of months, I was healed, but it was not because of the doctor or the drugs. It was God – plain and simple. I will never understand why God waited so long to answer my prayer, but I know He did. You see, God told me as plainly as if He knocked on my door to do a few simple things. He told me to get rid of all the true crime books I collected and also to stop watching true crime stories on T.V. So I packed them up and put them in the trunk of my car. Immediately I felt God's peace on my life, a peace I had never felt before.

I rode around with those books in my trunk for about a day, trying to convince God that I had invested too much to just throw them away. He didn't care. I had learned years ago while doing a Bible study on knowing and doing the will of God that partial obedience is disobedience. Reading in Genesis 32-34 about Jacob's disobedience confirms that. So I took all of my books to the dumpster.

In about three weeks, I felt this overwhelming darkness come over my life again. I was angry and told God so! I couldn't figure out why God would give me victory and a testimony only to take it back. He didn't. He revealed to me then that anger was the problem, not depression. After repenting of that, He healed all the anger too!

Any time the Devil tries to tell me different, I just claim my previous victories. Now I have true joy and peace that only God can give. Praise Him, for He is worthy!

Mary Turner

25 EMBOLDENED THROUGH CHRIST

"Ye are of God, little children, and have overcome them: because greater is he that is in you, than he that is in the world" (I John 4:4).

I recently celebrated my second spiritual birthday. As I thought back to that wonderful, life-changing day, I realized how much I had grown as a Christian and how much I had been blessed in such a short period of time. You see, in the beginning I wondered if receiving Jesus Christ as my Lord and Savior relatively late in life would allow me much time to grow. After all, most of the people I met seemed to have been in church all their lives and had all this "religious" stuff down pat. After attending classes and reading the Bible and listening to my pastor, I finally figured something out. It's all about having a personal relationship with Jesus and not about all this "religious" stuff. That's very simply what He keeps telling us all through His Word: love Me, know Me, and live according to My instructions – the Bible. That is the most important thing in this messed up, crazy, carnal world.

Heavenly Father, I am so very thankful that You gave us instructions to guide us in our lives through the Bible. You know that we are sinful in nature and we need Your reassurance, guidance, and love in order to live in this carnal world. Forgive us where we fail and help us to stay on the correct path. Give us the wisdom and discernment we need in our Christian walk as we study and learn Your will for us. We love You and adore You, Father, and we praise Your Holy name.

Janet Gilliland

26 TEMPTATION AND DISCOURAGEMENT

"Behold, the Lord thy God hath set the land before thee: go up and possess it, as the Lord God of thy fathers hath said unto thee; fear not, neither be discouraged" (Deuteronomy 1:21).

Have you ever been tempted or discouraged in your walk with God? This is my story about being tempted and discouraged at the same time.

God was really blessing my life. My job and my social life were going great, and I thought, "Man, it can't get any better!" That's when doubts began to plague me: "You don't have the same testimony as most people," a little voice said. "How do you even know God is there?" "Because," I would say, "it's something I feel and believe. It's just pure faith!"

"That's just what you were taught," the voice would reply. "Those who believe in Buddha were brought up to believe in him, too. What makes your God so special?"

On and on it would go. I felt like Jesus in the wilderness! The voice began to ask me all those hard questions, such as where did God come from? I was now being discouraged. I prayed constantly about this, but it kept getting harder.

Then I got a cold. I felt miserable! I was flat on my back

and had nothing to do but stare at the ceiling and talk to God. In doing that, I realized that I had not been spending time with Him like I should; I had been too busy with all of the blessings He had given me. I had lost my joy. It took God stopping me in my tracks with a bad cold to remind me that true joy comes from walking with Him, not from the blessings He gives me.

That night, I thanked God for showing me where I went wrong. I looked at how God had blessed me with the job of my dreams and a wonderful husband, and I realized that neither of those blessings would be a reality if it were not for my relationship with God. That night, lying in bed, sick as a dog, I was so happy! I had rediscovered my joy!

Dear Lord, thank You for the joy You have given me. Besides salvation after death, You have allowed me to live on earth. Please help me to remember daily that I have Your mercy.

Sandy Smith

27 TOTALLY DEPENDING ON GOD'S CHOICE

"Behold, the Lord's hand is not shortened, that it cannot save; neither his ear heavy, that it cannot hear" (Isaiah 59:1).

In 1989, my husband, David, was rushed to the emergency room in Nashville for a bleeding ulcer. Through his emergency surgery and God's intervention, he was diagnosed with chronic myelogenous leukemia. Test results alerted us to act quickly before the disease became acute, and our choices of treatment were taken away. The doctors advised us that without a bone marrow transplant, David's life expectancy was less than two years. This transplant could prolong his life. However, if his body rejected the bone marrow, it could kill him within the first six weeks of treatment. Our decision could end his life within weeks, or he could immediately begin a series of chemotherapy and radiation treatments just to prolong the inevitable. We were up against the most traumatic decision of our lives, and we desperately needed to hear from God. We knew we did not want to live with regrets and feelings of guilt over having made the wrong choice.

We had never faced a situation that required total dependence on God, but we both knew that we could not trust our wisdom for the right answer. In fact, we were really afraid that we would not know how to hear from God. How could we really know beyond a shadow of a doubt that the life-changing choice we were about to make was the right one? The hospital shared all the negative effects of both choices. The transplant would put him in isolation and kill his immune system, thus exposing him to every bacteria and every virus. Something as minor as a fever blister could kill him. The seriousness of the whole situation overwhelmed us daily as we struggled with time limits put on both choices.

Before the bone marrow transplant could take place, David and potential donors had to go through blood typing. He had five brothers and sisters, who were all willing to go through the treatment for him. But the match had to be perfect, and we were told that only 20 percent of families find a compatible sibling donor. I was more afraid of the transplant because it meant the decision would be made quickly, happen quickly, and might be over too quickly.

We talked to trusted, godly men in our church about the effective way to pray. We told many people that we were praying, asking God to supply that brother or sister donor, which could give a cure. If the donor was not found, we knew that God, not man, gave the gift of life, and whatever time He gave, we would try to live it to the fullest as a family. When the results of the tests came back, we were thrilled to learn that David had not just one, but three compatible donors. This had never happened before in the history of the transplant unit at Vanderbilt.

God did not just open doors for us; He kicked them wide

open. We had no doubt as to which direction the Lord wanted us to take. Through it all, God blessed in every medical situation that followed. David was a model patient, and none of the horror stories about complications applied to him. The doctors were amazed at his recovery, but we weren't, because we knew our Source and Strength. This cancer changed our lives and affected everyone that knew us. David's recovery was a living testimony to the hundreds of people he came in contact with at work. I know this is true, because upon his death 11 years later, many people told me what an encouragement he was to them. It was comforting to know that his life counted for God. David's illness was the most difficult trial our family ever faced, but experiencing God's overwhelming movement in our lives was something we would never want to change.

Cheryl Gibson

28 WHERE WAS I PUTTING MY TRUST?

"The rich ruleth over the poor, and the borrower is servant to the lender" (Proverbs 22:7).

We struggled a lot this past year. My husband didn't have a lot of work at times, so instead of putting my faith in our Lord, I borrowed money against each paycheck. I would not always tell my husband, and I made a mess of our finances. Through a series of sermons on the family, I learned that my problem was a basic lack of faith in God to meet my family's needs. Wow! I always thought I trusted God, but my actions were telling a different story. I prayed for strength to not borrow, and God gave me that strength. He has blessed us so much.

Mildred Eldridge

29 A Woman Named Gill

"Howbeit certain men clave unto him, and believed: among the which was Dionysius the Areopagite, and a woman named Damaris, and others with them" (Acts 17:34).

On the foreign field in which we were serving, we had been going through a bit of a dry spell as far as people coming to Christ. We had been having visitors in the services, and our witnessing ministries were continuing, but there were no visible eternal results.

A young missionary family working with us at the time invited a young mother named Gill to bring her ten-year-old son along to our after-school Bible club. He really enjoyed the club and was soon attending Sunday School. His mother would sit in Sunday School with him and not attend the morning service. One Sunday, their lesson was about Jesus telling Peter to get the tax money needed by going fishing and looking in the fishes' mouths for a coin. Gill's son, Matthew, spoke up and indignantly said, "That's not in the Bible. You are making that up." It really embarrassed his mother, but she was impressed when the teacher kindly turned her Bible around and let Matthew read it for himself.

Gill and her friend, Allison, began to attend the morning services regularly. For more than six weeks, they both sat there and wept every Sunday but would not respond to the message. Finally, one Sunday morning as my husband and I said goodbye to the people at the back door, Gill and Allison asked to speak to us in private. What a thrill it was to see that dry spell end with both Gill and Allison receiving Christ. The next Sunday, they both sat there with glowing faces and no tears. They both said it was so good to be in church without the Lord breaking their hearts over their spiritual needs.

These two ladies are now in discipleship and growing in the Lord. What a joy to receive a card recently with this note:

"People never forget their first love, and I will never forget you for introducing me to the most important love, God's love. Gill" What a thrill! Folks, this is what missions is really all about!

Christine Schrimshire
Missionary to Great Britain

30 SEEING MY MOTHER IN HEAVEN

"Lord, thou hast been our dwelling place in all generations" (Psalm 90:1).

In 1990, my mother was diagnosed with dementia and later had two strokes, one of which left her partially paralyzed. I brought her to live with my family so I could take care of her. Until her death in 1996, I watched as she suffered the effects of her illness and medication.

My mother was a Christian, a beautiful person who loved everyone. She wanted to make certain the whole family would go to Heaven with her. Even while she was ill, she prayed faithfully for all her family to receive Christ, and before her death, God answered her prayers. My youngest brother and sister were saved, and my mother was able to see it.

Thank You, Lord, for answering my mother's prayers and thank You that my siblings and I will see her again in Heaven.

Helen Helms

31 MY LIGHT AND SALVATION

"The Lord is my light and my salvation..." (Psalm 27:1).

This morning as I look out my window, the sky is covered with dark clouds. I feel cold and prefer to stay inside where it's warm, safe, and dry. But as I look again, I realize the clouds are moving, and that they will not always be there. This storm will pass. I am also reminded that there is light above the clouds. The sun is still shining, although I cannot see it. It is still there, bringing light and warming the land. But right now, the clouds are obscuring the light.

I am about to enter the storm. The rain will fall, and the wind will blow. What will I do? Will I focus on the storm? Will I let it drench me, frighten me, and send me scurrying for shelter? Or will I remember the light? It is still there, waiting its turn to shine on me, warm me, and fill my day with brightness. Will I cower in a corner and wait for the storm to pass? Or will I go about my day doing my tasks one at a time, looking for God's presence and purpose in all that I do? Will I praise Him or will I whine and pout and fear the troubles of the storm? I awoke looking for sunshine, but God has sent me a storm. If I focus on the storm, I will forget the light. If I focus on the light, it is still hard to ignore the storm, but I can endure it with hope and peace. The light is coming.

In my life, I experience many storms, but I do not always focus on the light. I am too busy being wet, cold, uncomfortable, frightened, overwhelmed, nervous, frustrated, worried, or angry. Why are there so many storms in my life? Why doesn't the sun always shine in my life? Doesn't God want to bless me? Yes, but He must continue to send the storms until I have learned to concentrate on the light. If I am going to please God with my life, I must choose to find the light in every storm.

Jesus said, "...I am the light of the world: he that followeth me shall not walk in darkness, but shall have the light of life" (John 8:12). Can I not remember His presence and His light in the midst of my storms? Will I, one day, have a life free of storms? Probably not. My hope is that I will have learned this lesson well and though the storms continue to blow, my faith will not fail. I will keep my eye on Him.

Lord, help me to see Your light in every storm, and let Your light shine in me to a lost world whose only hope is in You.

Suzanne Taglialatela
Missionary to Spain

1 My Rock And My Fortress

"...The Lord is my rock, and my fortress, and my deliverer...in him will I trust... (II Samuel 22:2-3).

In September 2002, my husband and I went on a mission trip to Merida, Mexico, along with our pastor, his wife, and 18 church members. Little did we know that we would go through a hurricane named Isidore. Powerful wind blew pieces of tin through the air, walls were blown over, houses were blown down, trees uprooted, and limbs were broken off trees. God gave me a peace that we would be safe. During the storm, we had great fellowship, praying, singing, playing guitars, preparing food, eating, and giving testimonies. I remember the calmness we all felt. At one point during the storm, two pieces of straw landed on the window in the form of a cross. I felt that God had His hand of protection over us.

Through this experience, God showed me His power, mercy and grace. Our pastor, Brother Doug Ripley, reminded us that God gives us the grace to handle whatever adversity we are dealing with. After we returned home, our five-year-old granddaughter, Carly, asked me if I had been afraid. I told her that I felt that God had protected us, that we had prayed for God to protect us, and that people in our church had prayed for us. She said, "We were praying for you too."

Dear Lord, help me to follow You wherever You lead me and to remember that if I am in Your will, You will protect me and You will hold me in the palm of Your hand.

Margaret Bond Marble

2 Determination, In Spite Of Our Fears

"I can do all things through Christ which strengtheneth me" (Philippians 4:13).

Every Saturday, it is a custom in our church to go passing out flyers. I was not going, because I had planned to stay home to watch my three-year-old son, Erik, and a two-month-old baby whose mother wanted to participate in the event. William, my six-year-old son, went along with his father to pass out the flyers with the rest of the people. He was very excited, and since they were gone and the baby and Erik were doing fine, I was able to get some work done.

About an hour and a half later, my husband showed up with William and a member of our church. I was wondering why they had returned so soon. As they were walking in the door, they told me the news. William was bitten by a dog that came running out of a house when a boy opened the door to receive the flyer. The dog bit him twice. One bite was on his back on the lower right side and the other was on his right inner thigh. I was shocked. I checked him right away to see how bad the bites were. They had already taken him to the doctor, and fortunately, no stitches were required. My son was going to be okay. I just hugged him and was happy to see him whole. His daddy asked him if he still wanted to go pass out flyers the next Saturday, and William said yes.

The next Saturday came along, and they were passing out flyers again. William and his dad approached a house that had a dog. My husband said, "Here, let me put the flyer underneath the door." But William said, "I'll do it." After he put the flyer underneath the door, he said, "You see, I did it even when there was a dog."

When they came home, they told me the exciting story, and I was very proud of him. I was very proud to see such a brave Christian soldier in a six-year-old boy who was determined to pass out a flyer in spite of what had already happened to him. In spite of our fears and what has happened to us, we can still have determination to do things for God.

Gloria Brown
Missionary to Mexico

3 Our Mother

"She openeth her mouth with wisdom; and in her tongue is the law of kindness" (Proverbs 31:26).

My mother-in-law was not an easy person to speak to when I was trying to share my heart. While searching for a new cross-stitch pattern, I discovered this poem and gave it to her for Christmas. Each stitch was stitched in love, hoping that she would sense the love that was there:

"To 'His' Mother"
'Mother-in-law' they say, and yet,
Somehow I simply can't forget
'Twas you who watched his baby ways
Who taught him his first hymn of praise,
Who smiled on him with loving pride
When he first toddled by your side.
'Mother-in-law' but, oh, 'twas you
Who taught him to be kind and true;
When he was tired, almost asleep,
'Twas to your arms he used to creep;
And when he bruised his tiny knee,
'Twas you who kissed it tenderly.
'Mother-in-law' they say, and yet,
Somehow I never shall forget
How very much I owe
To you, who taught him how to grow.
You trained your son to look above,
You made of him the man I love;
And so I think of that today,
Ah! Then with thankful heart I'll say
'Our Mother.'

Author Unknown

My mother-in-law has gone to be with the Lord. Before she passed away, she returned this cross-stitched poem to me, the treasure from my heart that I gave to her. She will always be with me as I read this poem, "Our Mother," Nameless Whitt.

Jane Whitt

4 A USEFUL LIGHT

"Let your light so shine before men, that they may see your good works, and glorify your Father which is in heaven" (Matthew 5:16).

In our Sunday Bible study, we did a series of lessons in Matthew from the Sermon on the Mount. During the week of our third lesson, our Bible study teacher called each of us ladies and asked us to bring either a special salt shaker or a special light with us to Bible study the next Sunday. We were to be prepared to tell what made our selection special. Because I carry a small flashlight in my purse, my choice was easy.

There are plenty of times a flashlight comes in handy, but it must meet certain criteria to be useful. First of all, it needs to be readily accessible. My purse flashlight is convenient, because it is small. If I had only a big, bulky flashlight, then I would do without and find myself in darkness. Secondly, my flashlight must have fresh batteries in it, or it will go dead and leave me stumbling around where I could get hurt.

Our Christianity truly parallels the use of the flashlight. We are a light to the world, but we must use our light wisely. If we act like obnoxious Christians, saying "Look at me, I'm so important," many people will turn from Christianity and say it is not for them. Just like the big bulky flashlight, that obnoxious attitude is useless. Instead, we should have a humble attitude that makes us easily accessible to lost people, so they know they can ask us about the hope we have in Christ. We must also keep our light charged by spending time with God, reading His Word, and praying. Just like a flashlight that has dead batteries, our Christian light is useless if we do not pay attention to our spiritual batteries.

Dear Lord, help me to use my Christian light as wisely as I use the small flashlight I carry in my purse. I want to be a witness to my lost friends, showing them what You have done for me and what You can do for them.

Anita Voss

5 Let God Do The Worrying

"Which of you by taking thought can add one cubit unto his stature?" (Matthew 6:27).

When my sisters and I were growing up, my dad always tried to find ways to keep us happy. When I was about seven years old, my ten-year-old sister and her friends wouldn't play with me. I ran in crying to my daddy. He sent me back out with an empty paper sack and told me to not let other children see what was inside. Of course, that game only lasted about ten minutes, when they talked me into letting them see inside the bag. But I was happy, because they finally wanted to play with me. When I was married with my own children, I tended to worry about everything under the sun. My dad would tell me, "Just let me do the worrying for you. I can worry for both of us." I would laugh, of course, really wishing he could, and wishing I hadn't a care in the world.

Even though my dad wanted to help me, there was not a lot he could do for me and my family through one particular trial. Everyone kept telling me to "give it to God." That's a hard thing to do, when you don't really want to give up that control. I tried to give it to God, but I kept getting in the way, manipulating the situation and the people around me. God, in His grace and patience, gave me the chance to learn again. It was the same trial, just a year later. This time, I finally learned that when you give up control and ask God to control, life is so much better. The problem did not go away and there was still heartache, but I knew God had it in His hands. I no longer had to try to fix everything. I didn't even try.

Just as my dad always wanted to make me happy and wanted to do my worrying for me, my heavenly Father wants the same thing. Jesus tells us in Matthew 6:27, "Which of you by taking thought can add one cubit unto his stature?" Giving control to God is pretty scary, but once you do, you'll never want to go back, because knowing that God is in charge gives you the peace and freedom to really live.

Susan Holladay

6 OPEN HANDS

"For whether we live, we live unto the Lord; and whether we die, we die unto the Lord: whether we live therefore, or die, we are the Lord's" (Romans 14:8).

When my oldest son, Marcos, was five months old, he became very ill, and the doctor put him on a special diet. As his condition worsened, he lost weight and never cried. He only moaned. During this time, one of my unsaved family members suggested that I take him to see a witch, because doctors cannot cure everything.

One afternoon, I was very anguished and fell on my knees to pray to God. "My son is Yours," I cried. "I place him in Your hands. I would rather see him die than involve him in the things of the Devil. I give him to You for Your glory." The next day, one of my uncles visited me and recommended a new doctor. That doctor was able to diagnose my son's illness, and he began to get better. Marcos is now 26 years old, and he recently married a woman who loves God. They are serving the Lord in the ministry that we have had in Argentina for the past 30 years.

When my baby was so sick, I had to ask myself whether I was really placing his life in God's hands. I had to recognize that Marcos was not mine; he was something precious that God placed in my hands to enjoy. God has placed us as administrators over all that He in His grace has given us, such as our lives, our loved ones, material possessions, and time. But being a good administrator is not only about protecting those things. It is also about surrendering them to God's control.

That afternoon, when I fell on my knees before God, He did not want my baby's life. He wanted my heart – a heart that puts Him first and trusts in His sovereign control of my life and the lives of my loved ones. Open hands before God will never be empty.

Griselda Gimenez
Missionary to Argentina

7 TRUST IN JESUS

"Trust in the Lord with all thine heart; and lean not unto thine own understanding" (Proverbs 3:5).

"Through it all, through it all, I've learned to trust in Jesus, I've learned to trust in God. Through it all, through it all, I've learned to depend upon His Word."

This song has become so real to me in the last 20 years. I trusted Jesus as my Savior when I was ten years old, serving God through my high school years. I married an unsaved man, and we had two children. He was abusive physically and mentally, and we divorced after seven years of marriage. I trusted in Jesus to protect and to provide for me and my children, but I was giving Him very little of me. I learned many things from the mistakes I made.

I married again nine years later, trusting him to be the spiritual leader of our home. It was another mistake. He wanted a divorce after one year. I experienced distrust and insecurity. In 1991, I had a thyroidectomy, and the doctors didn't know if I would make it through the night. Until then, I had never really surrendered my all to God. I realized I almost died, and I told God I knew He had something more for me to do. I wanted to share with others what God had done for me.

I had a precious prayer warrior, who was my Sunday School teacher. She and I visited others and prayed with each other. I finally began tithing and shortly after that, Jim Vaughn came into my life. I asked him on our first date if he went to church. He said he didn't. I told him I'd pray for him. Eight months later, he was saved. I never pressured him. God got a hold of him. I watched him love the Lord with all his heart, mind, and soul. After two years of observing this, I then trusted him and believed him when he told me he loved me and would always be good to me. Brother Doug Ripley married us in 1993. We have a wonderful marriage, but along with it comes tests.

In 1995, I was diagnosed with cornea dystrophy, and in

1998, I had a cornea transplant. As I was recovering, I learned that I had breast cancer, and I had a lumpectomy and radiation therapy. In addition to more surgeries, my eyes have also suffered the adverse effects of the cancer treatment. The radiation dried up the fluids in both eyes, and now I battle dry, painful eyes every day. In 2001, I learned that my breast cancer was back, and I had a mastectomy. Thankfully, no cancer was found in the lymph nodes, so no other treatments were needed.

Through it all, I am overwhelmed at how God's wonderful grace and strength have been with me. I have learned to totally trust in God whatever comes my way. I know He still has a purpose for me, and I want to serve Him, love Him, and give Him all that I can until my time on earth is done.

Peggy Vaughn

8 My Loving Mother

"This is the day which the Lord hath made; we will rejoice and be glad in it" (Psalm 118:24).

God couldn't be everywhere, so He created mothers. Isn't that the way the saying goes? God gave me a wonderful mother. She has been such an example: she's loving, she's strong, and she trusts God. I was born and raised in Memphis, Tennessee. Mother and Daddy had many friends there but gave that up to be close to me and my family. They moved to Scottsboro and became babysitters for their granddaughter. Later, our daughter married and moved to Decatur, and soon after, my husband, Don, and I transferred to Decatur. As Daddy's health began to fail, my parents once again moved to be closer to us. It was easier this time, as they had two precious great-grandchildren to tend to. Church family has always been their lifestyle, and they fit right in at Decatur Baptist Church.

When my parents joined our church, it was as if our family was coming home. Mother's faith and strength were put to the test when Daddy suddenly passed away, and then months later, she faced major surgery. As she recovered, she never complained about how she felt and was eager to return to her normal activities, which included attending church and taking care of family and pets.

She looks forward to Tuesdays when she helps put together pages of the Bible to send overseas. She recently lost two siblings but has never failed to keep a good outlook. She always tells me that God will never put more on a person than they can bear, and she lives that promise. The Lord truly blessed me with the sweetest, most loving mother of all, Sarah Faulk McCullough.

Juanita Smith

9 God Sent Ola

"Pray ye therefore the Lord of the harvest, that he will send forth labourers into his harvest" (Matthew 9:38).

The local missionaries had written a curriculum of 50 Bible lessons for children and teenagers in the Russian language, and 50 songs had been composed and taped in Russian, in addition to the many Sunday School papers and puppet/drama scripts for programs. People were receiving the materials with great enthusiasm and continued to express their deep gratitude for a project well done. Meanwhile, the Romanian segment of our ministry did not have any materials available for them in their own language, and they were not happy. They pleaded with us to translate the Russian language materials into their Romanian language. We definitely needed a Romanian translator!

We began searching for a translator, but we were not satisfied with anyone who was available. We continued to pray for this need as we opened our Teacher Training Institute program where many Sunday School teachers would be trained and adequately equipped with materials...in Russian. It did not take us long to realize that 30 adults in a small four-room apartment meant it was necessary to keep cleaning all day long. Now we had to find a competent, honest person for this task. We had already had an unhappy experience with a lady who had stolen items several times, so we had to dismiss her and look for someone else. Kola, one of our team members, suggested Ola. She attended his church, and he assured us she was a good, honest worker who was praying to find a job. We thought we would give Ola a try, and are we ever glad we did!

Ola came to us and quickly completed all the cleaning tasks given to her, from the hand-brushing of the carpets to the scrubbing of the floors. She displayed a quiet, calm spirit, and we all found her to be a joyful, pleasant person. One day, when we were praying again about the need for a Romanian translator, specifically in the area of music, someone suggested that we ask Ola. She sang in the small praise group in her church and had a reputation there of being a capable musician. I approached Ola the next day and asked, "Ola, do you think it would be possible to take the 50 Russian songs we wrote and translate them into Romanian?" Ola said, "I can always try, with God's help." Ola took the Russian tape and in a few days came to me with the announcement that she had already translated 17 songs! This was amazing as it is not easy to keep the message of the song intact and coordinate the new words and music. However, Ola did just that.

Since then, Ola has translated all the music, curriculum, scripts, and activity papers. Now all the materials are written in both languages. Now, both the Russian and Romanian people are pleased. Jesus told us what to do when we need workers in God's harvest field, and He certainly is capable of answering that prayer. Let us remember to pray that many laborers be sent out into all the world to carry out the plan God has for bringing many precious souls into His Kingdom.

Loreen Ittermann
Missionary to Moldova

10 SEEK YE FIRST THE KINGDOM OF GOD

"But seek ye first the kingdom of God, and His righteousness; and all these things shall be added unto you" (Matthew 6:33).

A group from our church had been invited to teach discipleship at a church in Tennessee. My husband and I signed up to be on the team, and my husband was taking the only vacation time he had for the year. We had not had a vacation for several years, and I was a little disappointed that we were not going to have one again this year.

While we were in Tennessee, we would be staying in the homes of the church members. When we arrived at the church, the pastor met us with directions to where we would be staying. As he came to my husband and me, he said, "And since this is the only married couple on the team, we are giving them the vacant house on the lake." It belonged to a couple in the church who only used it on weekends. They called it their "Garden of Eden."

The lake was beautiful, and pretty flowers were everywhere. God blessed us with the most wonderful week! It was better than any vacation we could have ever planned.

Barbara Allred

11 THE POWER BEHIND THE THRONE

"She will do him good and not evil all the days of her life" (Proverbs 31:12).

One day, clarity came to all my questioning of my role as a godly woman and future wife. As a pastor introduced a couple to the church, he referred to the wife as "the power behind the throne." My mind paused. "Is that what I am?" I thought. "The power behind the throne?" I immediately thought about where power comes from, and prayer, of course, was the first thing on my mind. Then, thinking about the characteristics of prayer warriors in my own life, I noticed a quality of sensitivity and awareness in their lives. What does it take to be a woman that is sensitive to needs that require prayer? Emotion was the only thing I could come up with.

Slowly my thoughts came together, and I concluded that the ancient struggle between male and female, with men being "too logical" and women being "too emotional," was not meant to be a struggle at all. Although 99.9% of females go overboard with their emotional kick, emotion is the very tool that we were given to be sensitive prayer warriors. A true woman of virtue trusts her husband and is confident in him. She comforts and encourages him all the days of her life. God designed the two to complement one another: the husband to serve and lead, and the wife to trust and support. The Word says, "Husbands, love your wives, even as Christ also loved the church and gave himself for it" (Ephesians 5:25). As I considered a woman's role of being a prayer warrior for her husband, I began to see myself in the symbolism of the Church. Christians petition God for their needs and are called to humble themselves and pray and turn from their wicked ways (II Chronicles 7:14). If the Church and her relationship with Christ are symbols of me and my relationship with my husband, then my greatest role is to petition and intercede for my husband.

So, women, our emotion is a tool to enable us to be all that God created us to be. Whether it is being in prayer for our husbands or for others around us, let's use that tool wisely and view it as a gift and not a curse so we may be that power behind the throne.

Claire Roberson

12 MY GRANDMOTHER'S FAITHFULNESS

"O love the Lord, all ye his saints: for the Lord preserveth the faithful, and plentifully rewardeth the proud doer" (Psalm 31:23).

My grandmother was an ordinary person who lived in the country all of her life. I can remember when we went to visit her, we would collect chicken eggs, milk cows, watch her churn butter, and fish in the pond. She always had a Christmas present for everyone: children, grandchildren, great-grandchildren, and even the great-great-grandchildren. We would always gather at her house sometime during the Christmas holiday and also at Easter. We would have some huge Easter egg hunts.

There are so many good memories. Yet the one memory that stands out in my mind more than the others is that no matter what, my grandmother was in church, Sunday after Sunday. All of the family get-togethers were scheduled with this in mind. The Easter egg hunts were always after the Sunday morning service. Going to church was not as important to the rest of the family as it was to her, but everyone knew not to ask her to miss church. She did not use any of these events as an excuse to skip church.

My grandmother passed away in October 2002 at the age of 91, and I will miss her not being there when I come home for visits. She did not express her feelings openly often, but just before I left for China, she told me that she was very proud of my family and me because we were going there as missionaries. I will always remember that. I will also remember how her actions taught a lesson in faithfulness.

So many times we try to find a legitimate reason to not be in church. She could have, but didn't. She never drove a car and my grandfather had nothing to do with church until very late in life, but that didn't stop her from going. The church had a bus that picked her up on Sunday mornings and Sunday nights. She rode it and taught Sunday school for many years. Not until her health began to worsen several years ago did she stop attending.

My call to China might have some root in my grandmother and her faithfulness. Maybe God rewarded her by giving her a grandchild who is serving on a foreign field. I know she was proud of me and I am so proud of her. I can only pray that when I am gone from this world, that the loved ones I leave behind can say the same about me.

Cindy Mills
Missionary to China

13 What Could Have Been

"...and though I give my body to be burned, and have not charity, it profiteth me nothing" (I Corinthians 13:3).

I did not know my stepgrandfather very well, and that was my fault. We did not have a lot in common. He was not as clean a person as I preferred, and his apartment smelled. Although I went by to cut his hair every time he called and was respectful and kind, I went out of obligation, not love. He always greeted me with a smile and talked of God's goodness, but I was always too busy to take the time to sit down and talk to him.

When he died, I went to his funeral, which included a presentation of the Gospel and kind words that brought comfort to the family. I began to consider the value he could have added to my life, as well as the value I could have added to his, if I had only slowed down long enough to see the inward man. Reflecting on his life and his character made me realize that I had experienced a great loss. I asked God for forgiveness and help to see people through His eyes and love them through His heart.

Lorrie Austin

14 The Valley of the Shadow of Death

"Yea, though I walk through the valley of the shadow of death, I will fear no evil: for thou art with me; thy rod and thy staff they comfort me" (Psalm 23:4).

When I was nine years old, my newborn sister died. Because it was my first experience with death, I remember the details vividly. She was born at my grandmother's house, and she cried once and died. Momma let me name her Annie Marie and choose her coffin. I continued to deal with death after I was married. I had a miscarriage, and then we had a daughter, Julie Anne, who died of pneumonia when she was three months old. Two weeks later, my ten-year-old sister died from a kidney defect. Cancer later took my father's life, and eventually, death claimed my brother and my mother. In April 2000, I had a more personal experience with death. Heart disease caused my heart to stop beating, but the doctors were able to resuscitate me.

Despite my experiences with the valley of the shadow of death, I know that God has been with me every step of the way. Since I was saved, I know that I will never have to experience eternal separation from family members and friends who knew the Lord. He has promised to never leave us or forsake us, and if they are with Him and He is with us, they cannot be far away.

Heavenly Father, thank You for Your promise to never leave us, even in death. Thank You for Your Son Who suffered and died for us because You loved us so. It is because of Him that we are able to spend eternity with You and our loved ones who knew You. Thank You that nothing touches us that has not been filtered through Your fingers first. Even though we may walk through the valley of the shadow of death, we are never alone because You are with us. Lord, draw our unsaved loved ones to You, so they can live for You and have endless joy, instead of a hopeless end.

Pat Porter

15 OVERCOMING FEARS

"I will love thee, O Lord, my strength. The Lord is my rock, and my fortress, and my deliverer; my God, my strength, in whom I will trust; my buckler, and the horn of my salvation, and my high tower. I will call upon the Lord, who is worthy to be praised: so shall I be saved from mine enemies" (Psalm 18:1-3).

My oldest daughter went through a difficult time with fears when she was about eight years old. Her fears became so real to her that she was afraid to go to sleep at night. We talked to her and prayed with her to try to calm her fears, but she couldn't seem to let it go. The more sleep she lost, the larger her fears became.

We asked God how to help her overcome this. His

answer was simple: allow her faith to grow and in turn, her trust in Him would grow also. My very wise neighbor told me once that to teach a child to pray is a wonderful thing, but to nurture their faith as a child is just as important. She told me that when a child asks God something in a prayer and God answers it, parents should always let the child know that it was God Who answered that prayer and He will always be there in their lives. Over time, the child will rely on God with prayers, and their faith will grow.

I searched the Scriptures and found many verses dealing with fears and how to trust in God. I listed the verses on a card that my daughter could tuck under her pillow or keep on her night stand. We continued to pray with her, and when she got scared, she would read those verses over and over. In time, her faith did grow, and those verses became comforting words that proved to her that God heard her prayers and was there to protect her and love her. I am very thankful for those verses and promises in His Word that will never change.

Myra Bazzel

16 CODY

"And Jesus looking upon them saith, With men it is impossible, but not with God: for with God all things are possible" (Mark 10:27).

One summer, my grandson Cody went to day camp for a month. He was involved in many activities such as basketball, baseball, bowling, and skating, as well as Bible-based activities. Whatever was going on, Cody participated just like the other kids. The teachers and kids noticed how determined he was, and he made quite an impression on several people there. One of Cody's friends even told her parents about him, how he would always try and never give up.

Cody has a mild case of cerebral palsy, and his left side is weaker than his right side. He walks with a limp, but that doesn't slow him down or make him think he can't do something. He was scheduled to have corrective leg surgery later that summer, so his class had a goodbye party for him. They made him a big card and gave him a large stuffed animal. Two friends gave him a card just from them with $1.63 in it, and they said they would pray for him. Cody had the surgery on both legs, and he was in a wheelchair for six weeks. On the last day of camp, the kids had a party and a food fight. Cody didn't want to miss it. Although he was still in a wheelchair, he went and had a good time. One of his teachers said she had never seen a child with such determination.

Sometimes I think back to Cody's birth and realize how far he has come. Back then, he was tiny, only 1 lb. and 12 oz. I am amazed, because to me, he's a miracle. God has a reason and a purpose in everything. When I look at Cody, I see someone who is very special. He is living proof that with God, all things are possible.

Denny Lane

17 WOULD THERE BE A DIFFERENCE?

"And of some have compassion, making a difference" (Jude 22).

A number of years ago, while raising support to go to Brazil, our deputation trails led us to North Dakota. We were scheduled to present our work in a church in the Sunday morning and evening services. Unfortunately, the evening service was canceled due to a threatening blizzard. The thought of actually being caught in a blizzard excited this Texas girl! Our lodging was in the church building, so we stayed put.

The blizzard worsened, and we received word from no one, including the pastor. A single man requested to spend the remaining day with us, and the three of us decided to have an evening service. I planned to sing a special, and my husband planned to preach, but neither of us had any idea what God had planned.

As we started the service, we noticed a commotion at the church entrance — a human being! He stomped his boots, shook off the snow, and found a place amongst our trio. We soon discovered that he was a Christian truck driver seeking a place to worship. Before the service ended, our visitor suggested that a missionary offering be taken. We received a $200 offering, given by him alone. From the parking lot, we waved a huddled goodbye to our new friend as he maneuvered his diesel truck back into the storm. God provided that night, and a truck driver made a difference.

How many times have I been tempted to skip "just this time?" Volunteer? Surely there's someone else. Had a truck driver not chosen to be present in the Lord's house, despite circumstances, would there have been a difference? Would there have been a difference in the life of that wounded soul, had the Good Samaritan not stopped? Would there be a difference should I choose to be different?

Stephanie Lunday
Missionary to Brazil

18 JUST TAKE THE MEDICINE, YOU'LL FEEL BETTER SOON

"...and a little child shall lead them" (Isaiah 11:6).

During a recent trip to Alabama to visit with my sister Katy Ripley and her family, the Scripture, "and a little child shall lead them" became true to me. After a few days of "too much fun," eight-year-old Devin, my great-nephew, awakened in the wee hours of the morning with the stomach flu. Since we had plans for the upcoming day, he was disappointed in addition to being ill. His granddad and I attempted to offer support in the form of flavored Tums and other types of stomach medication. Devin wouldn't have any part of it. Disliking the taste of medicine, he seemed to prefer suffering. I felt he was saying that he would rather be sick than take his medicine. The only thing he said was, "This is just not fair, and it's not my fault." Finally, after persuasion from us all, he reconsidered, accepted the medicine, and recovered nicely.

Shortly thereafter, I returned home and back to work at my job as a public relations officer for the Department of Veterans Affairs. During an intense business meeting, a co-worker known for being aggressive and mean-spirited began to verbally attack me and my ideas, asserting lies to support her opinions. To keep from adding fuel to what might become a raging fire, I excused myself from the meeting in order to regain my composure. I needed to go for a walk and do some serious praying. But my prayer was little more than a pity party. "Why me, Lord? You know how hard I try. How can I recover from this embarrassment? This is just not fair and no fault of mine."

Isn't it just like God to let us rant and rave, for a little while at least? Fortunately, my anger quickly turned to hurt. I then had a heart and mind prepared to listen. As I again asked for help, the answer came almost immediately – forgive her and pray for her. My first response was, "No way!" The Lord continued to deal with me, reminding me that this was the medicine I needed. It was not going to taste that good going down, and I could refuse it, continue to be ill, and potentially cause an epidemic. My mind quickly went to the episode with Devin. I was reminded how I felt. I kept thinking, "Why won't he take the medicine? It will make him feel better." Then I sensed God asking me, "Are you going to be like Devin, or are you going to take the medicine that I have prescribed for you from My Word in Romans 12:17: 'Recompense to no man evil for evil...?" I had to stop and think, "Do I want to be better?" I asked God for help, and this was the medicine He prescribed. I, like Devin, reconsidered and took the medicine, and God was able to heal my broken heart and allow me to forgive my co-worker.

Thank You, God, for allowing Devin's attitude to teach me to willingly take the medicine You supply to make me well.

Sandi Davenport
St. Louis, Missouri
Sister of Katy Ripley

19 THE BIRDS DON'T WORRY, WHY SHOULD I?

"Behold the fowls of the air: for they sow not, neither do they reap, nor gather into barns; yet your heavenly Father feedeth them. Are ye not much better than they?" (Matthew 6:26).

My second daughter was born early Friday morning, March 8, 1996. She was a beautiful baby, and my family had just grown from one child to two children. For a young family, it was a big change, not only physically but also financially.

Shortly after her birth, I was by myself and began thinking about our new joy and the extra responsibility that came with it. How were we going to afford milk, diapers, and all the other necessities? At that moment, I began to hear a lot of little chirping right outside my window. I got out of my hospital bed and went to the window, and there was a bird's nest filled with baby birds and a mother feeding them worms.

I wondered why the Lord put those birds outside my window and not the other windows in the hospital. I watched in awe of how our Creator takes care of even the smallest bird. My mind went back to Matthew 6:26 and how the Lord takes care of the birds. They don't worry about food and clothing, so why should I? I then looked down at our new bundle of joy, and I knew that the Lord would take care of us just as He was taking care of those tiny baby birds outside my window.

Mitzi Sims Oaks

20 PROMPTED TO PRAY

"Blessed be God, which hath not turned away my prayer, nor his mercy from me" (Psalm 66:20).

As I was driving home after a long day of teaching high school students, I was prompted to pray for my teenage son, Jake, who would also be driving home from school at the same time. I prayed for his safety and that God would protect him in any situation that might occur. When I arrived home,

I immediately knew something was wrong, because neither my son's car nor my husband's truck was in the driveway. I told myself to not panic and to continue praying for Jake. After trying both of them on their cell phones with no luck, I decided to wait for them on the front porch, hoping they would return soon.

While I was waiting, I prayed that "no news was good news." An hour later, Jim's truck turned into the driveway with both of them in it. I ran through the yard to meet them, relieved that Jake was safely home. I asked Jake, "Where is your car?" He explained that an elderly lady had pulled out in front of him and that he could not keep from hitting her car. He was traveling at 55 miles per hour when she darted from a side road to cross the road he was traveling. The elderly lady was transported to a hospital, where she was treated and released. Jake was relieved that she had only minor injuries.

After I heard about the accident, I began to look over my son for injuries. He said, "I am fine, just shook up." I asked him to lift up his shirt so I could look for bruises, and I expected to see a mark from the seat belt. He did, and there was no bruise, redness, or any evidence of injury. I then explained to Jake and Jim how I was prompted to pray for Jake's safety. Jake truly believed that God had intervened, because his car was totaled, and he and a friend who was riding with him walked away with no injuries. When the news of the accident trickled to fellow students at Jake's high school, they would ask, "What happened?" He would respond by saying, "My mom prayed for me."

Dear Lord, thank You for prompting me to pray for Jake when You knew he needed it. Thank You for using this accident to show a teenage boy Who You are! Forgive me for all of the times that I did not follow through on Your promptings to pray. Help me to be forever faithful in future promptings and realize the urgency to always stop and take the time for what is important to You!!

Denise Phillips

21 EXCUSES, EXCUSES

"Teach me good judgment and knowledge: for I have believed thy commandments" (Psalm 119:66).

"Excuses, Excuses" was the title of one of our homework assignments in my "First Place" Bible study class. When I first read the heading, I thought it was going to be a humorous lesson. Boy, was I wrong! The teacher said: "Excuses. We all make them. So what is an excuse? An excuse is a lie disguised as a reason. Take away our excuses, and we're forced to assume personal responsibility for our actions. Take away our excuses, and we have no place to hide. We can only stand and stare in the mirror, knowing we must deal with ourselves."

Oh my, those were pretty strong words. I knew right then that I didn't want to do that week's homework! I didn't want to have to face myself. It is so much easier to make excuses than to admit the truth. But she was right. We have to get honest with ourselves and with God if we want to be victorious. We have the freedom to make choices – either good or bad. The key to making good decisions and right choices is to keep our eyes focused on Christ and His Word and to walk in obedience. It is our responsibility to study God's Word so that we can make the right choices. It will also help us in giving support to others who have choices to make. We must commit ourselves to learning more about His Word so that we can live according to it. Is there anything in your life that you have been making excuses for rather than dealing with it?

O Father, I guess I have made excuses for every area of my life. I try to rationalize every failure I have made. O Father, I am truly without excuse. Forgive me, O God, and guide me into all truth.

Jennifer Barnett

22 Complete And Daily Surrender

"And he said to them all, If any man will come after me, let him deny himself, and take up his cross daily, and follow me. For whosoever will save his life shall lose it: but whosoever will lose his life for my sake, the same shall save it" (Luke 9:23-24).

"Lord, whatever You want me to do, I'll do it." I prayed this before surrendering to full-time Christian service and missions, but I never imagined God would call me into either. However, in December 2002, I found myself in a foreign country crying out to God to show me His plan. I had felt the Holy Spirit leading me to France for some time, but I didn't have confirmation from God's Word that that was His plan for me.

As I bowed and cried to God for direction, He reminded me as only He can, that surrender is not something that happens once, but daily. It is not something that happens in part, but completely. As God broke me that night and showed me areas I had not surrendered and the pride in my life, He gently said to me, "Now you can hear me because you have lost yourself in Me!" The next Sunday morning in the service at Central Baptist Church in Paris, France, God gave me the confirmation I needed from I Corinthians 2:9-12.

I have surrendered to God and committed to going to France to serve, but it doesn't end there. Luke reminds us that we must die daily. Every day I must remember to give God control over every area of my life. I must say yes to Him immediately when He gives me direction for my life. God doesn't want just part of us! He wants all of us! Complete and daily surrender! Lord, I pray that You will rule over every area of my life. I surrender completely my relationships, my finances, my decisions, my time, my future, and my desires. Enable me to die daily to myself and follow You. In all I do, may it be for Your glory.

Becky Baxter

23 JOY

"...the joy of the Lord is your strength" (Nehemiah 8:10).

Joy is a result of dwelling, not briefly visiting, in God's presence. All of us know someone who consistently demonstrates this in their life. If we allow Satan to evict us so that we no longer fellowship in God's presence, the joy is gone. Being filled with joy is a genuine manifestation of the Spirit's work.

WEBSTER'S DICTIONARY gives the definition of joy as a feeling of gladness, happiness, and peace. Since happiness is dictated by "happenings" we might expect to lose that feeling of exhilaration with change of circumstances. Therefore, we will not rely on those things that cause us temporary feelings of well being. Joy and peace, I believe, are the direct result of a life stabilized in the person of Jesus Christ. When we know the Lord and the Holy Spirit control our lives, we use Galatians 5:22-23 as an inventory to determine if we are on the mark: "But the fruit of the Spirit is love, joy, peace, longsuffering, gentleness, goodness, faith, meekness, temperance: against such there is no law."

As you know, whenever we girls find a housekeeping product that is both economical and successfully meets our needs, we are compelled to share this information with other women. Also, Paul, in his writing to Titus, admonishes us older women to pass on spiritual and practical experiences to our younger sisters. With this directive, I'd like to share a valuable lesson I learned in 1978. My oncologist told us that if treatment proved ineffective, two years would be a long life for me. Since I had a family, a professional career, responsibilities as a pastor's wife, and a few other social obligations, I often stayed up into the wee hours of the morning doing routine housework, food preparation, and hobbies. It took this frightening experience to make me realize that those mundane domestic tasks can be pleasant and joyful. In the years since my recovery, I can now say I enjoy cooking and cleaning. I say, "Thank You, God, that I have a family to use all these dirty dishes. Thank You, God, that we have food to cook and a dishwasher to help me clean up. Thank You that I'm physically able to do these dishes." It is much easier to find joy in these menial tasks now. After all, whether I enjoy them or not, they must be done.

Dear Lord, fill our hearts with joy and peace. Give us sweet communication with You and those around us. Help us fill our days with labors of love You have ordained for us and help us sleep calmly and sweetly. Protect our loved ones and our homes from the one who disturbs and destroys. Show us that praising You is the lifter of depressing days and situations we cannot change. Help us be aware that songs of praise change lonely hearts and exhausted bodies. We know that You told us in Psalm 98:4 to "Make a joyful noise unto the Lord all the earth: make a loud noise, and rejoice, and sing praise." And finally, Father, You told us in Psalm 5:11, "But let all those that put their trust in thee rejoice; let them ever shout for joy, because thou defendest them: let them also that love thy name be joyful in thee." Lord, we love you; we will be joyful.

Colleeon Dozier

24 THIS TOO WILL PASS

"And the world passeth away, and the lust thereof: but he that doeth the will of God abideth forever" (I John 2:17).

When my beautiful daughter was born, I was overwhelmed at the handiwork of the Lord. I gave her back to the Lord for His guidance. He has guided daily, but every parent knows how problems come and go as time passes.

I love to walk. It's my time to myself to pray, cry, sing, and enjoy things. As I walked this one particular day, my heart was heavy. My daughter was making a decision I felt was not in God's will. I was thinking about how problems come and go in our lives. As the houses passed, I sang and talked to the Lord. It seemed as if the Lord said, "You see all of this? It is all temporal, and it will pass away." My mind went back to the burden on my heart, and the Lord spoke in His still, small voice: "This too will pass." My heart sang out with renewed peace and joy.

The Lord is in control. He loves us so much. As Christian moms and wives, we should remember the Lord truly is in control and nothing gets to us without His knowledge. If we allow Him to, He will carry our burdens and take care of all our needs. Praise God from Whom all blessings flow!

Sandra McKeehan

25 A VIRTUOUS WOMAN

"Who can find a virtuous woman? for her price is far above rubies" (Proverbs 31:10).

In 1979, my father walked out of the house for the last time, leaving my mother to raise four children alone. It was this devastating event in my life that brought me to my salvation. However, it was not until much later that I learned to be thankful for that occurrence.

Life was in many ways a financial struggle for us. My mother made countless sacrifices to make sure our needs were met. Often her feet were swollen, and she would continue working and making time for our school activities. She doubled as father and mother. She did without new clothing or shoes to see that we had our needs met. She would stay up nights sewing clothes for us. She never faltered, having an eternal perspective. She viewed the situation as temporary, knowing that this too would pass. I still am amazed at her integrity and self-sacrifice. She never gave up. She always told me and my siblings that we could do anything we set our minds to. Her faith has made that more real to me.

Having to be thankful no matter the circumstance is difficult. I once read a book about Corrie ten Boom, who was in a Nazi concentration camp in Germany. Corrie's sister had asked her to thank God for the lice, but Corrie was reluctant and rebellious because lice are parasitic pests. Eventually, she did thank God for the lice. Later she discovered that the soldiers had left them alone, allowing them to share the Gospel and hide their Bibles, because Corrie and her sister had lice.

I have had to learn to be thankful for the "lice" in my life.

I am so very thankful that my mother was a virtuous woman. What she has done for me over the course of my life is more costly than gold or jewels. She was my first example of what the love of Christ is really like.

Jan Reid

26 LIFE LESSONS

"And it shall come to pass, that before they call, I will answer and while they are yet speaking, I will hear" (Isaiah 65:24).

"You want to help me write a book?" asked my co-teacher. We had just spent another fun-filled Sunday School time in class with the three-year-old children. Some of them had lost their smiles in their cereal at breakfast, and some just needed to give Mommy and Daddy one more kiss and hug before they let go. However, it did not take long for them to join in and begin having fun with the others. We spent some time on the floor playing with the blocks and animals. We did puzzles and colored pictures. Sometimes we cooked food in our little kitchen for our baby dolls. All morning, we talked about their week, their families, and the things they did through the week. As teachers, we blended in the simple truths of God's love for them.

After we cleaned up the toys and spent some time learning a Bible verse, we were ready for the Bible story. They had learned that the Bible is God's Word, a special Book, and they were ready to listen and learn. As we studied the unit on creation, I began to notice that these children were teaching me a lesson. I asked questions as I told them how God made the world, all the animals, the trees, and flowers. They knew that God had made the sky, clouds, and nighttime for us. As I asked them to respond to questions, I noticed that for almost every question I asked, one of the children would reply "God" or "Jesus." It didn't seem to matter to them what the questions were. They had the answer.

What a life lesson for all of us to learn! I began to think about the questions that we as adults often ask. We don't know all the answers, but we should know where to look to find the answers to our questions. May we all have the simple faith of these three-year-old children and believe that no matter what the question, God and Jesus are always the right answer.

Maybe we should title that book we're going to write "Everything I Need to Know, I Learned in Three-Year-Old Sunday School."

Beth Bennett
Missionary to Jews

27 GOD'S POWER AND ANSWERED PRAYER

"But verily God hath heard me; he hath attended to the voice of my prayer" (Psalm 66:19).

I would like to share how the Lord showed His power to my husband, our families, and me by answering prayer. On July 27, 1999, my son, Eric, and I were in a serious car accident that left me in traction for three and a half months and him in a coma for four months.

Our helicopter ride to the hospital was only the beginning of a long journey. All we could do was leave it in God's hands, since the doctors couldn't determine the extent of Eric's brain injury. He had to learn all over again, since even the most basic function such as chewing, was no easy task. At this point, a newborn baby was more capable than he was. He was fed through a stomach tube for months until the doctors determined that he could swallow. Walking, talking, hygiene, and dressing were words that didn't exist in his vocabulary. His speech didn't resume until five weeks into the recovery. Meanwhile, I was in traction from destroyed ankles, a broken hip, and a badly burned right foot. We both had extensive rehabilitation, and without the power of prayer, our recovery wouldn't have been as swift.

Through church, school, work, family, and friends, there were literally people all over the world praying on our behalf. With family and friends in Europe and South America, as well as an extensive network here in the States, God showed Himself true by answering our prayers. Eric learned to talk again, and he defied the doctors' expectations.

After missing 12 weeks of school, he made the honor roll and was hitting baseballs on the ball field. The doctors had said neither would be possible, given the nature of his injury. To God be the glory, great things He has done! This has been shown in our lives and will never be forgotten. To this day, I am thankful. Praise God for the power of prayer!

Debbie Frank

28 Excuse Me, But I Am Here To Speak To Elisha

"Run now, I pray thee, to meet her, and say unto her, Is it well with thee? is it well with thy husband? is it well with the child? And she answered, It is well" (II Kings 4:26).

In II Kings 4:8-37, we are told of the great woman of Shunem and her reward. She and her husband noticed that Elisha, a holy man, passed by their place continually. They decided to build him a chamber where he could find a place of shelter during his traveling. Elisha was so very thankful for the place that the Shunammite lady had supplied for him that he asked her what he could do for her. She answered him by saying "I dwell among mine own people." In other words, "I have everything I need, I am at home!" Elisha then spoke to his servant, Gehazi, about what he could do for her. Gehazi said, "Verily she hath no child, and her husband is old." Elisha went to the woman and told her, "About this season, according to the time of life, thou shalt embrace a son." And she said, "Nay, my lord, thou man of God, do not lie unto thine handmaid." Just as Elisha said, the woman conceived and bare a son.

One day, the child went to work with his dad and became sick. Dad sent him home to see his mother. She held him in her lap all day and at the end of the day, the child died. The Shunammite woman laid him on the bed and went to see the man of God. Before leaving, she went to see her husband and told him that she was off to see the man of God. Her husband asked her why, "...it is neither new moon, nor sabbath." She responded, "It shall be well."

As she arrived in Mt. Carmel, the man of God saw her coming and sent Gehazi to meet her. Verse 26 reads, "Run now, I pray thee, to meet her, and say unto her, Is it well with thee? Is it well with thy husband? Is it well with the child? And she answered, It is well." Then verses 27 and 28 say, "And when she came to the man of God to the hill, she caught him by the feet: but Gehazi came near to thrust her away. And the man of God said, Let her alone; for her soul is vexed within her: and the Lord hath hid it from me, and hath not told me. Then she said, Did I desire a son of my lord? did I not say, Do not deceive me?"

The Shunammite woman did not speak to her husband about the problem. She did not speak to Elisha's servant, Gehazi, about the problem. In fact, she told them both that everything was fine. She wanted to speak to the one that could solve the problem. This is exactly what God wants us to do: go to Him with our problems. Why get anyone else involved? Let those around you think everything is well. They can't help you anyway. Take it to God and God alone.

God, please help me to go to You instead of others with my problems. I know You have the answer and the power to fix the problems."

Katy Ripley

29 THE PRAYERS OF THE RIGHTEOUS AVAIL MUCH

"...The effectual fervent prayer of a righteous man availeth much" (James 5:16).

One of the many assurances I felt I could always rely on from my mother was that no matter where I roamed or what I did while she was alive, she was constantly praying for me. The following story is just one of many I could share about my mother's faith and her prayers of safety and protection for her children.

My daughter and I were living in West Palm Beach, Florida, several hundred miles from my roots. Early on a Sunday morning, an intruder entered our home through the garage. He quietly made his way to my teenage daughter's room. While she lay sleeping and unaware of his presence, he locked her bedroom door and got into her bed. He was obviously strung out on drugs and alcohol. He proceeded to try to sexually molest her. She awakened in startled amazement and fear. Fortunately, she was very athletic. She played every sport you can imagine and had been training for the soccer team. With her strong legs, she kicked him off of her. She kicked so hard that she knocked the breath out of him. She clamored across the room, unlocked her bedroom door, and began running down the hallway to my bedroom. She was too scared to scream until she felt him chasing her. As he lunged forward to grab her he flicked the back of her hair. She began screaming. As she screamed, our pet cockatiel, Max, began screaming too. He was flapping his wings and ringing the bell in his cage. The ominous sound made the intruder turn around and run out of the house. The police came and an investigation ensued. The man was never identified and no arrest was made, but the most important point was that he had not accomplished his evil intention.

My daughter and I spent that morning in the police station answering questions and helping compile a composite picture for the police. When we returned home that afternoon, I felt a real need to talk with my mother. I did not want to tell her what had happened, because she worried so much about our safety. I was afraid information like that would affect her health. When I called her, she sounded relieved. She asked if we were all right. I told her yes and asked why. She said she had been awakened in the middle of the night and had been praying for my daughter and for my brother's son. She had talked with my brother earlier, and he told her that my nephew, Jimmy, had been involved in an automobile accident around 5:30 a.m. He had been thrown out of his car as the car rolled end over end down a ravine. When the car came to a stop, it landed upright on its wheels over my nephew's body. Jimmy was pretty banged up with cuts and bruises, but he was going to be all right.

I never told my mother what had happened to my daughter, but I am convinced that it was her prayers that saved my nephew's life and protected my daughter from what could have been a devastating experience. Both my nephew and my daughter learned some valuable lessons that Sunday morning, especially that there is power in the prayers of the righteous.

Dianne Stewart

30 WHO DO I CHOOSE TO BE TODAY?

"Keep thy heart with all diligence; for out of it are the issues of life" (Proverbs 4:23).

Not too long after my husband received Christ, he and I had a discussion about what our life together was like before he accepted Christ. During that conversation, I confided in him that I was having trouble with my walk with God. I told him that I knew that the things that came natural to me were not the things that God wanted for my life and that I was very disappointed in myself because of this. After hearing what my husband had to say, I began to realize that I had made some poor decisions and that I was farther away from God than I had ever been in my life.

"This is the way I look at it," he began, "today I am closer to God and farther away from the person that I was yesterday. Tomorrow I will be even farther from the person I am today and that much closer to God. As long as I can wake up each day and say that, I know that I am on the right track." After hearing him say those words, I suddenly realized my problem: I was away from Christ, and I was not becoming the person He wanted me to become. I now understood that I needed to rededicate my life to Jesus and make the decision to start being a little less like the old Tammy and a little more like the Tammy that He wants me to be. So I did just that!

Since that day, whenever I run into people that I haven't seen in a while and I hear them say, "Tammy, you sure have changed," I know that I am on the right track and am becoming the Tammy that God wants me to be.

Lord, help me today to keep my heart and mind on the things of You. I make the choice today to be better than I was yesterday. I know that it is only with Your grace and love that I will achieve these things. I ask this from You, Lord, so that when tomorrow comes and along with it the opportunity to serve You, I will be ready to do so, and bring You all the honor, glory, and praise that You are so worthy of.

Tammy Keliinoi

The Rope

There were eleven people holding to a rope suspended from a helicopter. Ten were men and one was a woman. They all decided that one person should turn loose of the rope, else it would break and all would die.

No one could decide who should let go of the rope, so finally the woman gave a real touching speech, saying how she would give up her life to save the others, because women were used to giving up things for their husbands and children, giving in to men, and not receiving anything in return.

When the woman finished her speech, all the men responded enthusiastically — by clapping.

Never underestimate the power of a woman.

1 GOD TOUCHED OUR HEARTS

"Now unto him that is able to do exceeding abundantly above all that we ask or think, according to the power that worketh in us" (Ephesians 3:20).

Each year during Decatur Baptist Church's Missions Conference, we take up an offering to help one of our missionaries with a special need. In October 2002, we took up an offering to help a missionary in Kenya start new churches. With only $1,000, we could start a church and pay the salary of the pastor for one year. We had been encouraged to pray about what God would have us to give for this offering. I prayed and thought I would give $100 to help build the churches. As I continued to pray, however, God impressed upon me to give a much greater sum. I told God that if He wanted me to give that amount, He would have to work on my husband, who at this time did not attend church with me on a regular basis. I thought there was no way he would allow me to give the amount God had told me to give.

A few days before the conference, I told my husband about the special offering and that I wanted to help with the building of churches. My husband asked me how much I wanted to give, and I asked him how much I could give. He said, "No, I want to know how much you want to give, and we'll go from there." I told him the amount God told me to give. From the look on his face, I knew there was no way he would consent to that amount. I told him to think about it for a few days. For the next few days, I prayed often, asking God to soften my husband's heart. The evening of the offering, my husband asked me if I had decided what I would give. I told him that God had already told me what to give, and I needed him to tell me it was okay. My husband said, "You know, when you told me what you wanted to give, I thought, 'That's ridiculous,' but the more I thought about it, the more it didn't seem like so much money."

I asked my husband to go to church with me that night

and listen to the presentation about the work in Kenya and then tell me what to make the check out for. After the presentation, my husband told me to make the check out for what I wanted to give. That night, our church gave a total offering of $102,000, which meant the missionary could start 102 churches in Kenya. The next night of Missions Conference, my husband went again. Just before we began the service, Brother Doug Ripley said a missionary from India needed 60 bicycles so national pastors would have transportation between villages. He said they would cost $65 each, and if we wanted to donate a bicycle or help pay for one we should raise our hand to get a special offering envelope. I wanted to raise my hand, but after the offering I had given the night before, I didn't dare. My husband looked at me and said, "Don't you want to buy a bicycle?" So we did. The offering was enough to purchase 100 bicycles for the missionary. God touched so many hearts that week to get His people what they needed to continue His work. I thank Him for touching our hearts.

Phyllis Todd

2 MY HEART'S DESIRE

"But seek ye first the kingdom of God, and his righteousness; and all these things shall be added unto you" (Matthew 6:33).

I have been saved since I was five years old. Having been raised in a pastor's home, I never remember a time when I did not know about Jesus, and it was easy to give my heart to Him at an early age. It was when I was a teenager that I took control back in the area of dating. I did not trust that God would know what or who would make me happy. I certainly did not want a "churchy" guy.

After 30 years and some bad decisions, I finally acknowledged that God could surely choose better than I could. In the Divorce Care classes here at Decatur Baptist Church, we are shown how to seek God first, just as His Word tells us in Matthew 6:33. Since I began attending these classes and joined the church, I have started to practice that principle in my life. God has poured blessings out on me, proving Who He is. He has also proved His faithfulness and His perfect knowledge of me and my desires.

Psalm 37:4 says, "Delight thyself also in the Lord; and he shall give thee the desires of thine heart." What an awesome God — a God of perfect gifts! Who knows what will please and delight us better than the Author of our being? Now I want a "churchy" guy, because I have become a "churchy" girl. I thank God for His forgiveness, and I praise Him for His mercy, which endureth forever.

Dara Smith

3 He Could Not Be Hid

"And from thence he arose, and went into the borders of Tyre and Sidon, and entered into an house, and would have no man know it: but he could not be hid" (Mark 7:24).

We have all faced deep trials and tough decisions. At times like these, we wonder, "Should we?", "Should we not?", "How can we be sure?", "What is God's will?"

A week before my family had to make a tough decision, God began to talk to me through His Word. On Sunday, He said, "...Why are ye so fearful? how is it that ye have no faith?" (Mark 4:40). I replied, "Who? Me?"

On Monday, I read in Mark 5:36: "...Be not afraid, only believe." My answer: "Okay, Lord, I'm trying."

On Tuesday, He said, "...he could there do no mighty work...because of their unbelief...And he...began to send them forth by two and two...And commanded them that they should take nothing for their journey..." (Mark 6:5-8). I said, "Lord, forgive my unbelief. Here we are: two of us, my husband and I. We lay everything on the altar before you. We have nothing!"

On Wednesday, God spoke to me through Mark 6:50 and

52: "...Be of good cheer: it is I; be not afraid...they considered not the miracle...for their heart was hardened."

By Thursday, His words struck me like a bolt of lightning: ...he could not be hid" (Mark 7:24b). I prayed, "Oh, God! Please don't be hid today! Be manifest!"

And on Friday, God scolded me as I read through Mark 8:17, 18, 21, 34, and 35: "...have ye your heart yet hardened?...do ye not remember?... How is it that ye do not understand? ...Whosoever will come after me, let him deny himself, and take up his cross, and follow me...whosoever shall lose his life for my sake and the gospel's, the same shall save it."

When God brought us to the point of decision and we successfully followed His leading, He did exceedingly above all that we could ask or think!

Linda Gilmer
Missionary to Brazil

4 MARK, MY SPECIAL SON

"And he said unto me, My grace is sufficient for thee: for my strength is made perfect in weakness. Most gladly therefore will I rather glory in my infirmities, that the power of Christ may rest upon me" (II Corinthians 12:9).

My son, Mark, is a special child who has been plagued with seizures since birth. Sometimes he would have as many as eight or nine a day. In the early years, the hospital was like our second home. At times, life was devastating, until one day back in the early 1970's, when we had the wonderful privilege of going to Johns Hopkins Hospital in Baltimore, Maryland. For the first time, we learned that Mark was mentally retarded and that he would function throughout his life as a three year old. He was given medication to control his seizures, which subsided to once every three months or so.

God's grace has always been sufficient for every new cycle

in Mark's life. About three years ago, he was anointed and prayed for at Decatur Baptist Church by Brother Doug Ripley. Mark has now been free of seizures for about three years. It is awesome, and we give all the glory and honor to our precious Lord and Savior. What a blessing Mark has been in our lives! He has taught me so much about patience and love.

Joyce Curbow

5 Sitting At His Feet

"Now it came to pass, as they went, that he entered into a certain village: and a certain woman named Martha received him into her house. And she had a sister called Mary, which also sat at Jesus' feet, and heard his word. But Martha was cumbered about much serving, and came to him, and said, Lord, dost thou not care that my sister hath left me to serve alone? bid her therefore that she help me. And Jesus answered and said unto her, Martha, Martha, thou art careful and troubled about many things: But one thing is needful: and Mary hath chosen that good part, which shall not be taken away from her" (Luke 10:38-42).

I recently visited a dear friend that has cancer. We spent about three hours together talking. She mentioned how badly her house needed cleaning, so right away, I picked up on that. As I started to leave, I told her I would be back the following week to clean it for her. She replied, "Please come back, but come to listen and to talk with me. It is much more important that you spend time with me."

Wow! Her answer reminded me of the story of Martha and Mary. Jesus wants us to spend more time with Him than for Him. Satan knows this is one of my weaknesses. I think I have to be busy doing for others, and I don't always stop for the most important thing — spending time with Him.

As I go through Psalms, I see how David knew how to listen and sit at God's feet. Psalm 18:1-2 says, "I will love thee, O Lord, my strength. The Lord is my rock, and my fortress, and my deliverer; my God, my strength, in whom I will trust; my buckler, and the horn of my salvation, and my high tower."

I want to be more like Mary. My daily prayer is to see the really important things and still be of help to others. I know that everything I do will be done much better if I have first taken time to sit at His feet.

Sally Pieper

6 It's Not In Vain

"Be ye strong therefore, and let not your hands be weak: for your work shall be rewarded" (II Chronicles 15:7).

Jeremiah was known as the weeping prophet. During the 40 years that he prophesied God's Word to the nation of Israel, the Bible does not record that even one person repented. God even told him in Jeremiah 7:27, early in his ministry, that the people would not listen to him. How discouraged the prophet must have been! Basically, God's message to Jeremiah was that looking at things with a human eye, his work for God would be a failure, totally unsuccessful.

I don't know about you, but I have felt that way before about the work of ministry God has given me to do. When you don't see any fruit-bearing going on after weeks, months or even years of dedicated service to the Lord, it makes you think, "Is it really worth it? Is all I'm doing for the kingdom of God in vain?" We like to see instant results from our labor. When we sacrifice our desires in order to obey God, we think He should immediately and visibly reward us. But that's most often not how God operates. Lots of times He does bless us with quick results, but we've so limited our vision to look for only how we want to be blessed, that we completely miss the fact that He did bless us, just in a different way than we were expecting.

Maybe you want to be the person who reaches the masses for Christ, but it could be God's plan to use that precious child you teach faithfully every Sunday in preschool to reach the masses. You may not ever see all the spiritual fruit this child will eventually produce in their life, but you will receive rewards for that fruit because you consistently poured the Word into this young servant of God. This thing of ministry for God is so much bigger than you or I. And God's definition of a successful ministry is one in which the servant is obedient and faithful to Him. The results are His job. We plant the seed of the Word, sometimes we water, but God always gives the increase (I Corinthians 3:6).

It's very human to want to move on or give up when all we see is fruitless labor. Jeremiah got to that point and said he was tired of speaking God's Word. But consider what he wrote immediately after reaching that point of frustration: "...But his word was in mine heart as a burning fire shut up in my bones, and I was weary with forbearing, and I could not stay" (Jeremiah 20:9b). This prophet could not keep God's Word hidden inside. It had to come out! God's job for Jeremiah was to preach the message of repentance to Israel. That's what he was put on this earth to do (Jeremiah 1:4-5). And he did it successfully, because he was faithful to do what God told him to do.

So whatever your ministry is, whether it's at church, on the job, or even raising your little ones, pursue it with all your heart. Philippians 2:16 says, "Holding forth the word of life; that I may rejoice in the day of Christ, that I have not run in vain, neither laboured in vain." Open your eyes to see that your labor for God is never done in vain. Be obedient. Be faithful. That's all He requires of us.

Suzanne Spiers

7 PRAYING FOR MY HUSBAND

"Wait on the Lord: be of good courage, and he shall strengthen thine heart: wait, I say, on the Lord" (Psalm 27:14).

Do you remember your teen years? The lonely weekends when it seemed like you were the only one without a date? The only one without a boyfriend? Well, I do.

It was during that lonely time that I went to one of the teen events at my church, and one lady said something that really stuck with me. She said that she had prayed for her future husband years before meeting him. Well, I took it to heart, and at the age of 13, I started praying for my future husband. I prayed that God would protect him, keep him from evil, and when the time was right, bring us together.

I married him when I was 22 years old. For nine years, I had prayed for him, and God answered all of my prayers. He not only answered me, but He also gave me so much more than I asked for. When it seems as if you have prayed and waited all you can – just hang in there – God knows exactly where you are, and He may be answering your prayers without your even knowing it. Just be patient and wait on the Lord.

Kimberly Hedden

8 GOD KNOWS WHAT YOU CAN HANDLE

"...but God is faithful, who will not suffer you to be tempted above that ye are able..." (I Corinthians 10:13).

Through all of my daughter's illness, it has seemed as if I were standing on the edge of a cliff, telling God, "Do you see me? I'm about to fall!" I've always felt that it was such a heavy burden, and I could not bear it. But now I know that He does protect me and will not put more on me than I can bear. Let me tell you how I learned this lesson.

Olivia, my daughter, had to go back on chemotherapy for her reoccurring cancer after a year and a half break. We had to have surgery to replace her port-a-cath, which the doctors used to give her chemotherapy. The doctor came out after the surgery to tell us he had trouble getting the line into her blood vessel. He was admitting her to the hospital for overnight observation. He said she had a small blood clot and wanted to watch her. That was not so bad, because we were going to be in Memphis for a week starting on a new chemotherapy treatment.

That whole week, we were back and forth at the hospital getting Olivia's chemotherapy. On Friday, she went back for a checkup with the surgeon. He ordered another x-ray and as he was looking at it, he said, "Oh, this looks much better! Her lung is almost fully inflated." I asked what he meant by that. He said, "We thought we had punctured her lung during surgery, and now we know that we did. It was more than halfway deflated." My heart sank, I got weak in the knees, and my face turned as pale as a ghost! Then the doctor said, "But she is okay now — her lung repaired itself!"

If I had known that they had punctured her lung and the severity of it, I would have lost it! Thank God He chose to protect me from hearing that information up front. God really does know what we can and cannot bear!

Pam Williams

9 My Call To Cambodia

"For whosoever shall do the will of God, the same is my brother, and my sister, and mother" (Mark 3:35).

This is my testimony of how the Lord worked in my heart when He called us to Cambodia. Honestly, I was the first person to oppose it, not because I wanted to disobey God, but because of fear for our children. I could not imagine myself leaving my country, the Philippines, the place I love so much and understand perfectly, for a less developed country like Cambodia.

My husband is a doctor, and I am a nurse. When I learned that my husband had committed himself to missions, seeds of doubt lay dormant in my heart for months. This was the time that my faith faced its greatest test. My thoughts suggested to me that if a married couple were contemplating missionary work, then the partners should be sure God had called them individually, as well as together. I thought that it could be insufficient for me to go, simply because my husband had been called to the mission field. But the Lord kept talking through our pastor's preaching and the Scriptures.

Romans 10:14 "...how shall they hear without a preacher?" and Isaiah 6:8 "...Here am I; send me" kept cropping up in my husband's mind. Many Christian friends agreed that he seemed to be the sort of person who could be a missionary. Of course, there were also those who rejected that idea and asked, "How would a doctor and a nurse fit in the mission field?" There were pastors who expressed concern, because we had not graduated from Bible College. But my husband had not found peace and contentment in most of the work he had been doing. He believes that Christian doctors should not contribute to the work through medicine only, leaving evangelism to the clergy.

Deep in my heart, I knew that God had been calling my husband to be a missionary, and little by little, He allowed me to feel that burden, too. It was then that I learned that I could never know God's will for me also until I yielded my will to Him. I began to become more supportive of my husband's calling and then I finally told him that I was ready to go with him. At that time, my husband, our four young children, and I knelt down and prayed together, thanking Him for calling our family.

Joy Castro
Filipino Missionary to Cambodia

10 BROKEN BREAD AND POURED OUT WINE

"But he giveth more grace. Wherefore he saith, God resisteth the proud, but giveth grace unto the humble. Submit yourselves therefore to God. Resist the devil, and he will flee from you. Draw nigh to God, and he will draw nigh to you. Cleanse your hands, ye sinners; and purify your hearts, ye double minded. Humble yourselves in the sight of the Lord, and he shall lift you up" (James 4:6-8, 10).

As I began my life as a new Christian, I hungered and thirsted for a daily intimacy with the One Who had saved me. I received as a gift a book written by Oswald Chambers, *MY UTMOST FOR HIS HIGHEST*. This was just what I needed to be reading at this time of my life. It was simple, easy, and quick.

The author spoke several times of becoming "broken bread and poured out wine" for Him. I began to wonder – what does this mean literally? How do you accomplish this? I could never seem to comprehend what he meant by that little statement.

After a couple of years of using the book daily, I was still searching for the meaning of that phrase. One day as I was reading the book of James in my quiet time, God stopped me. As I re-read chapter 4, it was as if a lightbulb turned on. Joyfully, I exclaimed, "I see! I see! I know what it means to become 'broken bread and poured out wine' for You. Thank You, Father!"

According to that passage, if I want to become broken bread for God, I must humble myself, because God giveth grace to the humble. Then I must submit myself to God upon receiving that grace. I must draw nigh to God, and He will draw nigh to me, if my heart has been purified. And I purify my heart by humbling myself in the Lord's presence. Then, He shall lift me up!

I must empty myself, and I must seek His face for Him to lift me up. Then I become "broken bread and poured out wine" for Him, and He can use me to serve Him.

Jane Whitt

11 NO ONE WILLING TO GO

"Go ye therefore, and teach all nations, baptizing them in the name of the Father, and of the Son, and of the Holy Ghost: Teaching them to observe all things whatsoever I have commanded you: and, lo, I am with you alway, even unto the end of the world. Amen" (Matthew 28:19-20).

Mission's Conference is here, and God's people are glad!
It's a time to recount all the blessings they've had.
Most folks are willing next year more to give.
They have plenty their lifestyle to live.
Now my husband stands to make his way.

I give a sigh for I know what he'll say.
He'll tell of China. His love for them is much!
Certainly this sermon someone's heart will touch!
But I look around, and to my surprise,
Not even one person has tears in their eyes.
How I wish someone would heed the call,
And say, "Hey folks! We'll go with y'all."
My husband speaks again of another land,
And he asks the people to raise their hand
If they know of a person who's planning to go
To the Mongolian people the Bible to show?
No one has heard of such a man-
Not even other speakers who've traveled the land.
Although China's our chosen place,
Someone must also tell them of God's love and grace.
If God is not willing that any should perish,
Then why is there no one Mongolians to cherish?
I know God is faithful to extend the call,
But somewhere, somebody is continuing to stall.
Oh, Lord! Don't they know the hour is late,
And maybe one now is entering Hell's gate?
There are so many here! Won't somebody ask
If they are the one God wants for this task?
"He doesn't want me," they say in their heart.
"I'm giving and praying. I'm doing my part!"
Now the services are over and the congregation stands
To begin the business of shaking hands.
They return to their homes – they say their hearts are aglow.
But still no one is willing to go.

Julie Monger
Missionary to China

12 A V-8 Moment

"Pray without ceasing" (I Thessalonians 5:17).

My daughter and I had been estranged for about ten years. However, when circumstances in her life spun out of control, she rededicated her life to the Lord, and then she came to me. I can't put into words the joy that filled my heart to have my beautiful daughter back in my life, and the best part was that I accepted Jesus as my Lord and Savior not long after this happened.

As we began rebuilding our relationship, my daughter starting asking my advice, and I was so afraid I'd say the wrong thing or offer poor advice. I kept telling her to pray and seek God's guidance and to stay in His Word, but anyone could tell her that and I wanted to be more specific. Then I had what I laughingly call one of those V-8 moments, a sudden revelation. I could pray about this and ask God to show me how to best advise her.

For months I prayed and searched the Scripture but kept coming up empty. Then one Sunday morning I went to Sunday School class and sat next to a woman I had never seen before. Next thing I knew our teacher introduced her as a visiting missionary, and she presented a lesson that blew my socks off! Right then and there on that beautiful Sunday morning I knew that God had put that wonderful lady next to me in that room to answer my prayer. Later that night, I typed the whole thing up in an email and sent it to my daughter. The next day she emailed me and said, "Thank you so much for sharing this with me. You were right, I needed to hear this. Thank you very much. I love you, Mom. Isn't it awesome to see and feel God answer our prayers?"

Dear Lord, all the honor and glory and love go to You. Father, I know I let You down every day, and for that I am so sorry. You deserve my very best each day. You have blessed me with so much, especially a daughter who knows, loves and serves You. I thank You for bringing us back together closer than we have ever been. I thank You for the opportunity we have to encourage each other and pray together. Lord, I pray that through our commitment to You others might accept You as their Lord and Savior.

Janet Gilliland

13 His Ways Are Perfect

"He is the Rock, his work is perfect: for all his ways are judgment: a God of truth and without iniquity, just and right is he" (Deuteronomy 32:4).

On a winter afternoon, coming home earlier than usual from work and with some daylight left, I changed into some warm "comfy" clothes to take our Labrador Retrievers for a walk. This was a treat for all of us because my schedule little recreational time. We walked across the recently rain-dampened fields behind our home and went to the far end of my family's property line. Our neighbors' swelling pond was a temporary home for wild ducks flying south. Our black Lab, Stormy, took notice and immediately wanted to give chase. I called her attention back to me for our return walk home.

I began to ponder on those wild ducks and wondered how God created them to fly south for the winter for protection from the northern winters. Then God gently spoke to my heart and reminded me that He has everything under control. It was not necessary for me to question Him on how He accomplishes His work and designs for this world, but to trust in Him as the great Almighty.

Do you ever find yourself questioning Him? Is it in a form of a demand or simple curiosity? Either way, God's ways are perfect and we are to simply trust Him as a small child does in the arms of a parent.

Dear Lord, help me today to trust in You in all Your ways, even in the times when I don't understand. Thank You for being perfect and loving me sacrificially.

Denise Phillips

14 LET GO AND LET GOD

"But verily God hath heard me; he hath attended to the voice of my prayer" (Psalm 66:19).

We had just sold our house and were packing and waiting for the closing. It was exactly one week away. We had put our house on the market a year earlier, without praying about it at first. When we finally started praying about it, the very next person who looked at it made an offer. It was too low, so we countered, and they turned it down. But it was okay, because we had put it into the Lord's hands. A few months later, the same couple came and made another offer. This time, it was good.

I worked at the front desk at my girls' school on Fridays, and this particular Friday morning was going by slowly. I was anxious about packing. It was also the middle of the month, and we were having a hard time finding a place to rent after we moved out of our house. Most places we looked at would not be available until the first of the month, or they did not allow pets, or they were too expensive. I was getting worried. My husband kept reminding me that it was in the Lord's hands, and He would take care of everything. But I just could not let it go. It was very quiet while I sat at the front desk that morning, so I decided to read my Bible and write in my prayer journal. I read a little bit and then decided to release to God all of my anxieties about the move. It was taking up all of my thoughts. I could not concentrate; nothing was taking my mind off of it. I made an entry into my prayer journal:

Dear Lord,

> I am scared. I am afraid, because we don't have anywhere to go after closing. I am releasing all of this to You. I will trust that we will find a home and that everything is going to fall into place. Right now I am giving over to You all my anxieties about closing and moving. I am relying on Your promise. I just ask You to help me find a home for us. You

know what we need. I thank You and praise You. Amen.

I finished the prayer and put the journal away. The front was still quiet, and I decided to call home to see if we had any messages on the answering machine. My friend who was helping us look for somewhere to live had left a message. She said she looked at a house that was for rent and called. The rent was more than we were considering, but she gave me the number of the rental agency so I could see if they had anything else available. I immediately called. The rental company had three houses available in our price range, and the lady said we were welcome to look at them. As I jotted down the addresses, the lady said, "Well, my son has a house he is renting, and it is available now. You can look at it today, if you would like." I told her that would be fine. We went over there that evening, and we were absolutely amazed. It was perfect. We signed the lease the next morning. God is so good. He not only provided a place for us, but He also provided more than we expected.

Since then, I have challenged myself with this question: If it is this easy to let go and let God, then why am I not doing it more often? His timing is perfect. Things may not always happen as quickly as they did with our house, but I know that if I turn things over to Him, His answer will be far better than what I ask for.

Georgeann Hept

15 OVERWHELMED

"Therefore as the church is subject unto Christ, so let the wives be to their own husbands in every thing" (Ephesians 5:24).

It may have been the day I was volunteering at school, or the day our scout troop had an activity, or the day I had a commitment at church. The house was in disarray, supper was not cooked, and the laundry was not done. I felt overwhelmed, pulled apart by commitments to my home, but also to other good organizations and causes.

I had not listened when my husband, Jamey, told me, "You need to quit." I believed if I could organize myself a bit better, I could do it all. But God showed me, "To every thing there is a season, and a time to every purpose under the heaven." (Ecclesiastes 3:1). Since that time, I am doing activities as my husband leads, and my home is happier. Obedience to my husband is obedience to God. I praise the Lord for His ways.

Lisa Watson

16 A Bouquet of Tulips

"The flowers appear on the earth; the time of the singing of birds is come..." (Song of Solomon 2:12).

A missionary in Moldova began her day with a heavy heart. The president of the United States had given the president of Iraq and his sons 48 hours to leave the country, or war would be declared. Finding herself stranded on this side of the world where the action was to take place, so far away from her homeland, the missionary suddenly felt all alone! She knew that the national pastors and team members loved her and were better children to her than many children of biological parents. She knew they were cognizant of the terrorist threats and anti-American feelings growing in Moldova. Yet she also knew that they were young and inexperienced and could enjoy the safety of their own culture and nearby families and friends. How could they truly understand?

Juleechka, the missionary's little pedigree dog, demanded to be picked up and held this morning, instead of snuggling farther down under the warm feather quilt like she usually did. In holding the warm body of her pet close to her, the missionary took comfort. Could tiny Juleechka sense there was something amiss? The missionary checked her schedule for the day. Near the bottom of the list read: Terrorism meeting at the American Embassy – 6 p.m. What plans and procedures would be disseminated this evening? Would

American citizens be urged to return to the States? Now, the missionary's heart was really torn. How in the world could she ever think of leaving the national team, her co-workers, her children?

Devotion time was a source of strength as the missionary finished reading the book of Proverbs. She also checked out Psalms 46 and 91. What a comfort! Praying to her heavenly Father under Whose wings she was attempting to abide gave a sense of security. She could picture Him embracing her safely and lovingly, as she also held Juleechka and spoke to her in soothing tones.

Team members began arriving for the day's ministry. The trauma of pending war was soon lost in the operation of a Bible Institute. The hubbub was beginning to sound normal; however, once again, the missionary experienced loneliness. "I guess I need to think about something to write about today," she thought, lifting the top of her laptop computer. Earlier she had planned to write about God's provision for a can opener when none could be found! Today, however, can openers did not seem important.

"Miss Loreen, may we come in?" asked team members waiting outside the office. "Yes, certainly, come," invited the missionary with a smile, despite a heavy heart. As they entered the office, one extended his hand with a gorgeous bouquet of red tulips! They were tearful as they assured the missionary of their love and concern. They really did understand, and — best of all — they cared!

When spring arrives in Moldova, we see tiny plant shoots attempting to push their tips out from the black soil, despite the melting snow and ice. Soon there is a profusion of fruit tree blossoms, as the sun shines once again. Sometimes, during the "harsh winter" of our lives, we face great uncertainties and possible dangers ahead. Nevertheless, we can be assured of God's presence through every trial. He will hold us close if we allow Him to do so, and if we watch closely, we will witness the "bouquet of tulips" He will bring into our lives to assure us that He truly understands. We can gain comfort and security in His unfailing promises. Let us trust Him now more than ever!

Loreen Ittermann
Missionary to Moldova

17 HAPPY

"Happy art thou, O Israel: who is like unto thee, O people saved by the Lord, the shield of thy help, and who is the sword of thy excellency! and thine enemies shall be found liars unto thee; and thou shalt tread upon their high places" (Deuteronomy 33:29).

Right before Moses died, he blessed Israel – as individual tribes and as a whole. In Deuteronomy 33:29, he blessed Israel as a whole, telling them to be happy that God had delivered them. Wow! How exciting is that! How can I not be happy when I have a God who saved me from the miry clay and set my feet upon a rock? He is my shield and my sword! I don't have to worry about the criticism that I get for my walk with God, because He will defend me. He is so good!

Anne DeKoker

18 DON'T GIVE UP

"Being confident of this very thing, that he which hath begun a good work in you will perform it until the day of Jesus Christ" (Philippians 1:6).

In June 1998, I had the opportunity to go to Zambia, Africa, on a missions trip. At the time, I had a 13-month-old son, and even though I didn't like the thought of leaving him for two weeks, I had no doubt that the Lord was asking me to go on this trip. I was very excited about the chance to see the mission field. We were going to be doing evangelism in the villages out in the bush. I had been discipled and had also gone through discipleship evangelism training, so I thought I had everything I needed to have a successful missions trip.

On our first day to go out and meet with the Zambian people, we met outdoors for a time of worship and preaching. It was a totally overwhelming experience to hear the Zambian people singing songs of praise to the same God that I worship. After the message that afternoon an invitation was given. So there I was, waiting to lead a Zambian lady to the Lord. I was so excited. I had the training that I needed. I could do this…or so I thought. As the Zambian lady approached me, I totally froze. I don't even think I could have told her my name. One of the missionary wives had to step in and share the Gospel and pray with her.

Later that night, I was so discouraged. I had come halfway around the world only to totally let the Lord down. I had depended on myself and not on Him. I had tried to do something in the flesh that can only be done in the Spirit. As I was reading that night, I read Philippians 1:6. God gave me the comfort that even though I had messed up and that I had depended on myself instead of Him, he wasn't going to toss me to the side. His Word assured me that He would finish the good work He started in me. There have been so many times since that day in the bush that I have let the Lord down, but He always brings me back to Philippians 1:6 and gives me the assurance that He is not going to give up on me. I just need to hang in there and keep trying my best to serve Him.

Amy Wright

19 SECURE IN CHRIST

"Hereby know we that we dwell in him, and he in us, because he hath given us of his Spirit" (I John 4:13).

Have you ever really thought about how secure we are in Christ? I'm sure you know the verses, but have you ever really visualized it? Awhile back in a "Mother Wise" Bible class, we were given an awesome visual on John 14:20, when Jesus says, "…I am in my Father, and ye in me, and I in you."

Now imagine a set of four baskets that fit together, nestled one inside the other. The largest basket will represent God. Now place inside it the next basket, which represents Christ; then the next one that represents you; now the last one, which represents Christ. Notice that Christ is the center of the whole set. Now put the lid on, sealing it securely. That represents the sealing of the Holy Spirit of promise (Ephesians 1:13-14).

Do you see that you are totally covered, inside and out, front and back, top and bottom? You are totally surrounded by God and Christ from every angle. There is absolutely nothing that can touch the inside without first going through the outside, and none can fall out! That set us as one unit, not four individual baskets. We are one with Christ and God (John 17:20-23).

Maybe this visual will help to remind us that we are never alone or on our own. He promised that He would never leave us or forsake us (Hebrews 13:5). He is on our inside and our outside, and that is all the sides we have! We are totally secure in Christ! Can you see it?

Dear heavenly Father, thank You for Your Word. Thank You for Your precious promises. May we live in the light of the truth You have given us.

Jennifer Barnett

20 From Earthly Jewels To Heavenly Treasures

"Lay not up for yourselves treasures upon earth, where moth and rust doth corrupt, and where thieves break through and steal: But lay up for yourselves treasures in heaven, where neither moth nor rust doth corrupt, and where thieves do not break through nor steal: For where your treasure is, there will your heart be also" (Matthew 6:19-21).

During the kickoff for a recent building fund campaign at Decatur Baptist Church, we had the opportunity to worship under a white tent and give our first commitments toward a three-year goal. As we sat under that tent, Brother Doug Ripley said God would honor sacrificial giving. During this special day, the Holy Spirit kept saying to me, "Sabrina, you can give." I said, "But what do I have, Lord?"

After the service, I told my husband, Barry, that God had spoken to me. All I could think of was a gold chain I had at home. The next day, my daughter, Isabella, and I brought the chain to church. Isabella said, "This is pretty, Mommy," but all I could see was a lost person who might hear of God's love and accept Jesus as his Savior because of the money that chain might bring. I gave the chain to our church's financial director and filled out a white slip of paper with the amount I had paid for it – $500. As we left, I felt the peace of God flood my soul.

A few days later, a receipt for the chain's value came in the mail. The reported appraisal value to the church was $2,000. I started crying when Barry showed me the receipt. He said, "Bri, God honored your obedience to Him, and He quadrupled it for His glory." Instead of hanging onto earthly jewels, I was able to invest in heavenly treasures with eternal value.

Sabrina Boshell

21 I NEED SOMEONE TO CHANGE ME

"Likewise, ye wives, be in subjection to your own husbands; that, if any obey not the word, they also may without the word be won by the conversation of the wives" (I Peter 3:1).

I received this letter from New Tribes Mission, a missions organization under which we support missionaries. I was so encouraged by this letter that I wanted everyone to have an opportunity to read it:

Last July, Gladis, a Kuna lady of Panama, trusted Jesus as her Savior. At that time, her unbelieving husband asked her to either renounce Christ and commit to the Kuna traditions or leave home. She chose to follow Jesus. The Kuna church rallied around her, providing housing and encouragement. Many people prayed.

In time, God worked a miracle in her husband's heart. One day he came to Gladis and asked her to return home. "I do not believe in the Bible," he said. "But I promise not to keep you from church or from doing the things that you believe you must do."

At a recent Kuna ladies' Bible study, Gladis told the others that a few days earlier her husband asked her why she was no longer playing the "God cassettes." (He was referring to tapes of the Kuna New Testament and songs.)

Gladis explained, "I reminded him that two months ago he was furious with me for playing them and told me to never play the tapes in his presence again. So I had obeyed him. I really wanted my testimony to be something that God can use to bring my husband to the truth. My husband said nothing for a few minutes. Then he asked, 'Is it those tapes that has made you a different woman?' I told him that the tapes didn't have any power to change a person, but that I had found the way to God through Jesus. It is Jesus who is changing me."

Gladis said her husband then put the tape player on the table and asked, "Where are those tapes?" Gladis got a tape of the Gospel of John, and her husband put it into the machine, saying, "I need someone to change me."

Gladis is living I Peter 3:1 and is able to have a profound effect on her husband. May God allow His Word to be evident in our lives to make a change in our family.

Katy Ripley

22 Never Too Old To Serve The Lord

"For we preach not ourselves, but Christ Jesus the Lord..." (II Corinthians 4:5).

In the past five years, I have given in to the belief that I am old, being 76 as I write this. Even suggesting such a thing is upsetting to my husband, who is two years older than I am. In these last years as a missionary wife, I have seen several missionary couples, even younger than we are, who have retired. They are living the typical life of retirees in the United States now. Mind you, I don't believe this is wrong, because older people have more physical problems, and medical care is unquestionably better in the States. But I have never seen this solution as proper for my husband and myself.

We are convinced that our place is right here on the field. My husband is still so very busy, teaching in our Bible seminary, making lots of visits, working on a degree from Louisiana Baptist Seminary, and preaching every week in one church or another. I am being the necessary helpmeet that my husband needs, as I edit his manuscripts and attend all of his preaching services. I love keeping up our home here — cooking and doing the laundry — and I thank the Lord each morning for the ability to get out of bed by myself. I keep busy, with some rest stops along the way.

My special joys are when the Lord gives me "reruns" of years of ministry on the field. We are now into our 50th year, and I thank the Lord daily for my children who are all very active in their churches, serving the Lord, and teaching my grandchildren about salvation. One of our daughters and her family are missionaries here with us on the field, and our ten-year-old grandson has already surrendered to be a preacher.

I must admit, my contribution to the ministry is more limited now than it used to be, and I am really seeing what prompted these missionary couples to retire. In my heart, I sometimes battle with the guilt of being on the field, wondering if my Lord is satisfied with my limited service. That's when He gives me my precious "reruns" and reminds me to keep going. I am an old woman, but I have not changed. Although I sometimes get tired of aches, pains, and the inability to make my body do what I want it to do, I never get tired of life and the work God has set before me.

Marie Strickland
Missionary to Argentina

23 SHELTERED IN HIS ARMS

"For thou hast been a shelter for me, and a strong tower from the enemy" (Psalm 61:3).

The sky had gotten very black, and the rain was coming down heavily. Michael looked scared as he sat at his desk. He looked at me, and I smiled, hugged him tight, and let him know everything would be all right. Out of the corner of my eye, I could see a figure standing out in the hall, just to the side of my classroom door. I knew it was Michael's mom. She wasn't coming in and didn't want to bother me. She wanted to be close to Michael.

You see, several weeks before, Michael had gone to spend the weekend with his aunt and uncle, and a terrible tornado came through. It was a terrifying time, and he had to watch as a fireplace fell on his aunt, killing her. Today, with bad weather so imminent, Michael's mom felt she couldn't stay away. She just had to be close to Michael, and things would be okay. She wanted to be close enough to grab him until the storm and danger passed by.

I cannot help but think of all the times storms come into our lives – small ones and life-changing ones. Where do we go? Do we take things into our own hands, or do we get closer to the One Who gave His life for us?

Dear Lord, I want to always be close to you, in a place where I know I am safe and sheltered from the storms that come my way. I know that You will not let anything come to me that You will not also give me the grace to endure. You will also give me the peace of knowing — just like Michael's mom — that being close to You means everything will be all right.

Sandra McKeehan

24 Blessings In Spite Of Ourselves

"Therefore now let it please thee to bless the house of thy servant, that it may continue for ever before thee: for thou, O Lord God, hast spoken it: and with thy blessing let the house of thy servant be blessed for ever" (II Samuel 7:29).

From II Samuel 7, we see the Word of God brought to King David through His servant Nathan. Nathan's words brought David to a place of heartfelt worship as God reminded David from whence he had come and established David's lineage as a line of blessing to the Lord. God was choosing to bless David and his line forever.

As I was caught up into worship with David, I started to understand how God had also chosen me for a blessing. I came from a non-Christian family, and yet, God reached through my desperate family life to save me as a little ten-year-old girl. His mercy was shown to me, and I, too, said with David, "...Who am I, O Lord God? and what is my house, that thou hast brought me hitherto?" (II Samuel 7:18). As I read further into chapters 8, 9, and 10, there were more accounts of how God displayed His favor toward David. Enemies were subdued, and more kingdoms were put into submission at David's feet. The name of the Lord was exalted amongst the nations. How powerful is the Lord! How wonderful was God's blessing upon the house of David! So what came next was a real surprise.

It was in the midst of God's blessing that David chose to sin with Bathsheba and have her husband, Uriah, slain. At this point, I was truly angry at David for betraying God and defaming His name. After all, it was all God's doing that David rose to his position in the first place. How could David fall so far? How could God pronounce a blessing on David even when He knew that David would sin and cause His name to be trampled?

But isn't that just like God? Didn't He choose each one of us for a blessing even though He knew that we would eventually sin against Him? For me, that became the real issue. I was no longer thinking, "How could David have sinned after such a blessing?" Instead, I was thinking, "How could I?" Our God loves us so much that He chose to call us by His name and call us heirs in His Son, even though He knows we sin. That is even more reason to rejoice.

Kathy Schaaf
Missionary to Jordan

25 A VIRTUOUS WOMAN

"Who can find a virtuous woman? for her price is far above rubies. Her children arise up, and call her blessed…Many daughters have done virtuously but thou excellest them all" (Proverbs 31:10, 28, and 29).

She was the first to rise and the last to sleep, as she cared for us, a family of six. She came home from a long, ten-hour workday, and her next job kept her busy until bedtime. She cooked our supper, washed and ironed our clothes, cleaned up our messes, bathed us, and helped us with our homework. Yet she still managed to curl up with me on the couch, and when I fell asleep, she carried me to my bed and tucked me in with my favorite doll.

God-fearing and loving, she took us children to church and prayerfully waited on the Lord to work on my dad's heart to come to know Him. After 11 years of marriage, her faithfulness in prayer and obedience to the Lord proved well as she was able to help lead my dad to the Lord, and she stepped aside and allowed him to be our spiritual leader. She cared for her own mother as her body was affected by a severe stroke. She stayed by her mother's side until the Lord took her home.

Now, as the children are grown and away from home, she still goes to work 40 hours a week and comes home to take care of my dad. Whenever a friend, family member, or church member is in need, she is quick to make a visit, cook a meal, or do whatever it takes to encourage others. Yet she still finds time to love on her grandchildren. As I watch her with my oldest son, now three years old, I am excited to see how much he enjoys visiting her. Camping out in the den floor, getting prizes, eating Push-up popsicles, and going to Chuck E. Cheese are just a few of their special treats.

Who can find a virtuous woman? I can, and I don't have to look any farther than my own family. My mother's price is far above rubies! To all us mothers, let's work toward becoming virtuous women in our homes. Wouldn't it be great if one day our children see us as a Proverbs 31 woman?

Gail Holmes

26 HOLD YOUR PEACE

"The Lord shall fight for you, and ye shall hold your peace" (Exodus 14:14).

Everyone has a tendency to talk when they're not supposed to, such as the kindergartners who interrupt the teacher's lesson and the teenagers who whisper during the pastor's sermon. Our society has come up with a variety of expressions to combat this problem, from the clever "Zip your lips!" to the crude, yet often effective, "Shut up!"

In His Word, God has His own way of telling His children that they talk too much. After He delivered the children of Israel out of slavery in Egypt, it wasn't long before they voiced complaints. With Pharoah bearing down behind them and the

Red Sea stretched out before them, they didn't see a way out. In Exodus 14:11-12, they whine to Moses that they would have rather stayed in bondage in Egypt than die in the wilderness. Moses responded with a message from God: "...Fear ye not, stand still, and see the salvation of the Lord, which he will shew to you to day: for the Egyptians whom ye have seen to day, ye shall see them again no more for ever. The Lord shall fight for you, and ye shall hold your peace" (Exodus 14:13-14). Then God proved Himself once again and parted the Red Sea so the Israelites could cross into safety.

Notice the last part of Moses' message from God – "hold your peace." It sounds as if God was telling his children to zip their lips and shut up, doesn't it? Sometimes He has to tell me that, too. Sometimes I get so anxious to fix a problem or hurry through a trial that I take matters into my own hands — or tongue. I want to talk it out to anyone who will listen so I can come up with a solution. But it's during those times that God wants me to hold my peace, so He can fight for me.

Isaiah 30:15 says strength comes "...in quietness and in confidence...." Isn't it wonderful to know that God doesn't need any commentary from us? He can fix our problems and bring us through trials all by Himself! All He desires is a "Thank You, Lord" once He has proved Himself faithful.

Dawn Kent

27 He Meets My Needs

"...for your Father knoweth what things ye have need of, before ye ask him" (Matthew 6:8).

It was the end of March 1994, and my time in Singapore would soon be drawing to a close. My husband had left me one month earlier, and instead of immediately coming back to the States, the Lord had led me to remain where I was. At the time, I didn't know why, but looking back I realize now that God used that time to teach me so much about Himself and show me in special ways how He was going to take care of me now.

On this particular evening during my prayer time, I asked the Lord what I was going to do when I got back home to Alabama. I had never had to work to support myself. My work history consisted of part-time teaching positions in Christian schools and daycares. What was I going to do? How would I make it? That night, God very clearly spoke to my heart, assuring me that He had a position waiting for me at Decatur Baptist Church. Every time I questioned Him about it, He assured my heart that it was all taken care of, and everything would be all right.

I flew home one month later during the last week of April, and a very dear friend picked me up at the airport. She asked me what I was going to do now, and I told her I was just trying to trust in the Lord. Then, she mentioned a secretarial position in the church office that had been in the bulletin since the end of March. God reminded me that He had told me He had a place for me in the church office. I thought, "There is no way. I know nothing about working in an office and even less about computers."

Two nights later, Brother Doug Ripley and his wife, Katy, picked me up for church on Wednesday night, and the Holy Spirit began to nudge me about mentioning that secretarial position. So out of obedience, and with my stomach in knots, I brought it up to Brother Doug and assured him that I had no skills whatsoever, but that I was willing to learn if they would be willing to take a chance on me. I gave the same speech to Brother Jeff Gilliam a few days later when he interviewed me. I was hired in May 1994, and God continues to meet my needs in special ways.

Sharon Collier

28 RAISING CHILDREN

"And thou shalt teach them diligently unto thy children, and shalt talk of them when thou sittest in thine house, and when thou walkest by the way, and when thou liest down, and when thou risest up" (Deuteronomy 6:7).

Perhaps the hardest part of child rearing is understanding and bridging the generation gap. Most of us try to raise our children through example. As they mature, they take on their own tastes of clothing, food, and every other decision that you have been so easily making for them all their lives. As Christians, we not only want them to love and serve God as we do, but we want them to live for Him out of their love for Him. In the process of raising girls, the proper dress is always an issue. We try to teach our children that respectable Christians would not speak or dress for this world. In doing so, we forget that our children must also be a part of today's world in order to reach the unsaved. This will not be accomplished if they do not fit in. Allowing our children to dress with some fashion sense allows them to be unique individuals. It is often at this time that I remember that I am not trying to be my child's friend, but first and foremost, her parent.

Conscientious parents continue to work toward their goals in raising well-rounded children. Parents who work alongside their children through ministries at church set a good example for them. It allows the children to witness the parents' growth. Raising well-rounded children does take time, patience, and understanding, but the rewards are endless. Nothing makes parents prouder than seeing their children succeed, whether it is spiritually, academically, or socially. The self-assurance that is reflected in a child's eyes is worth all the challenges a parent faces. It becomes evident to parents, after seeing these rewarding moments, that they are on the correct path of raising an independent, well-rounded Christian child.

Jodie Glossick

29 GOD FIRST, THEN MY FAMILY

"...Be not ye afraid of them: remember the Lord, which is great and terrible, and fight for your brethren, your sons, and your daughters, your wives, and your houses" (Nehemiah 4:14).

So many times we say we trust God, but do we really? The first time I stepped out on faith and trusted God completely changed my walk with Him forever.

I was not raised in a Christian home, but I was taught to work and study hard. I went to college with the focus of trying to find a good-paying career. I graduated and became a Certified Public Accountant with ideas of moving up the corporate ladder. When I found out I was pregnant with my first child, God began to change my heart. My focus changed from my career to my family. My boss was not impressed, and my relationship with him began to sour. He wanted someone who would be completely focused on their career, not preoccupied with wanting to spend more time with their family. I believe this was all part of God's plan for me to take the biggest leap of faith of my life.

For several months, I weighed working full time versus working part time or even quitting my job entirely. Little by little, God began to impress upon my heart to quit my job. There were several things that kept me from quitting. I was the main financial supporter for my family, and I didn't know how we could live without my income. I had health insurance through my employer, so we would have to find insurance elsewhere. Also, my boss had a reputation of completely destroying people verbally and emotionally if they quit. I was afraid. I prayed and asked the Lord to confirm to me through His Word that quitting my job was the right decision.

During Missions Conference in 2001, God gave me my answer in Nehemiah 4:14. He told me to not be afraid and to fight for my family. Within the next few weeks, I became a stay-at-home mom. The Lord has provided for us financially and has blessed us for obeying Him.

Jennifer Scheer

30 PRAYING SAINTS

"And the smoke of the incense, which came with the prayers of the saints, ascended up before God out of the angel's hand" (Revelation 8:4).

Where are the praying saints of old?
They've vanished with the wind;
There are no more within the fold
Whose prayers will ascend.

There is no one to hold the torch
And lift poor souls in prayer;
No one 'round God's throne to march
In vigil of those in despair.

The fire that once so freely fell
No longer does descend,
Because there are no praying saints
With voices to ascend.

Where are the praying saints of old?
Are you a quieted voice?
Then join the flock within the fold
And with the praying saints rejoice.

Margaret Hoskins Dellinger

31 THE ENCAMPMENT OF ANGELS

"Though an host should encamp against me, my heart shall not fear: though war should rise against me, in this will I be confident" (Psalm 27:3).

As young children, my little sister, two older brothers, and I would join Mother in a nightly prayer around her bed. As we fidgeted in our kneeling positions, Mother prayed long and fervent prayers. Mother thanked God for perfect health, a sound mind, and a compassionate heart. She asked for guidance, wisdom, protection, and peace. She prayed for the lost and gave thanks for the gift of salvation. Her prayers sought God's favor, and she would not stop until she felt she had the ear of God. Sometimes we actually fell asleep while she prayed. Mother ended each prayer with a request that God would send angels to encamp 'round about us to protect us while we slept. In my mind's eye, I could see several small cherubs floating down around us, with wings flapping and cute little smiles on their faces. Those images have always stayed with me, and I raised my daughter with that same request.

Mother died at the age of 72. A few months before she died, I had a dream that she and I were visiting in her home when a storm blew up. We could see a tornado racing toward the house as it crossed the fields of her farm. We began to pray, and as the twister approached the edge of her property, it turned into a ball of flames, rolling toward us at great speed. I begged her to seek safety inside the house, but she would not leave me. I was mesmerized by the rolling flames and watched with paralyzing fear. Just before the ball of fire reached the house, it broke into two segments that were transformed into two little cherubs. With wings fluttering, they looked at us and smiled, then flew away. That dream puzzled me for months, but when Mother became ill from pancreas cancer, I realized that the storm from my dream was the storm that was threatening Mother's life. I knew she would soon leave us to be with God, but I took comfort in knowing that the same cherubs that had protected her in life would usher her to Glory.

I still pray for angels to encamp 'round about us. I believe they do surround my home and family, and someday they will usher me into the presence of God, where I will be reunited with my mother.

Dianne Stewart

1 Wait On The Lord

"Wait on the Lord: be of good courage, and he shall strengthen thine heart: wait, I say, on the Lord" (Psalm 27:14).

A few years ago, I began to have pain in my side. Every step, and the slightest movement of my right leg, made the pain more intense. After a few days the pain was so severe I went to a doctor for help. A blood test proved my white blood count to be elevated, so he ordered more tests. A CAT scan revealed an infected place the size of a walnut on my colon. After conferring with a surgeon, the doctors agreed that surgery would be necessary. I could have no food or water, and for five days they would give me antibiotics intravenously to prepare me for the surgery.

One morning, I was reading my Bible in Psalm 27. When I came to verse 14, it read "Wait on the Lord: be of good courage, and he shall strengthen thine heart: wait, I say, on the Lord." As I was reading this verse, it seemed that the Lord was speaking directly to me!

I had an allergic reaction to the antibiotics, and the surgery was postponed for a couple of days. When they announced that surgery would be the following day, they told me they were going to do another CAT scan before the surgery. The doctor had decided they would probably need to remove the entire colon!

When he left, I called my pastor and told him what the doctor had told me, and asked him to pray for me. I knew I really needed God to help me. Again, I had the desire to read Psalm 27, and once more, I felt that the Lord was speaking to me. As I continued to read into chapter 28, I read in verses 6 and 7: "Blessed be the Lord, because he hath heard the voice of my supplications. The Lord is my strength and my shield; my heart trusted in him, and I am helped: therefore my heart greatly rejoiceth; and with my song will I praise him."

As I read these words, I felt God's power run through my

entire body. My stomach had been in pain and burning for days. Now as God touched me, it felt as if a spring of cool water ran through my stomach, the pain and burning were gone, and my heart and soul were filled with joy!

After the CAT scan, the doctor came in and said, "That spot is not there — it's gone, as if it never was there." I told him that God had healed me. He said, "It must have been God, because it certainly isn't anything we have done." Praise God for His love, mercy, goodness, and healing!

Barbara Allred

2 WHO IS MY MOTHER?

"Give her of the fruit of her hands; and let her own works praise her in the gates" (Proverbs 31:31).

It's quite easy to explain.
Sometimes she brings me tons of happiness.
At times I must admit, I've thought,
She's such a pain.
She's going to drive you crazy.
Whatever will I do?
But the older that I get
I realize more, Mama,
I hope I can be more like You!
Raise my kids to love the Lord.
To have many friends
Who adore.
To walk with God
And know His way
To hurt with others
Every single day!
I know that perfect you are not.
Neither am I.
But maybe that's why God put us together
So together we could help each other try.
I'm failing in my words

To truly express,
That when God made you my mama
He far exceeded Hallmark
And genuinely sent me the very best!

My mother is Helen Helms, and she is described in Proverbs 31 as the virtuous woman.

Bridgett Hayes

3 MY FOCUS

"Finally, brethren, whatsoever things are true, whatsoever things are honest, whatsover things are just, whatsoever things are pure, whatsoever things are lovely, whatsoever things are of good report; if there be any virtue, and if there be any praise, think on these things" (Philippians 4:8).

This is one of my favorite verses, because it teaches me where to focus my attention. The world's focus is the opposite. The world encourages us to find fault, which causes us to have a negative attitude. Our Lord wants us to understand, however, that true joy comes from having a positive outlook.

This verse doesn't give me the idea that the good, pure, just, and lovely things in life will jump out at me, but that I will need to seek them. As I think on these things, they fill my heart and come out of my mouth.

My family will see that I notice the "good report" and the "praise." This will encourage them to grow more of these things in their own lives. I believe obedience to this simple teaching unleashes incredibly positive results.

Loretta Clark

4 THE GAP

"And I sought for a man among them, that should make up the hedge, and stand in the gap before me for the land, that I should not destroy it: but I found none" (Ezekiel 22:30).

I began my Christian life alone, in a marriage of 31 years. We had always been very close within our marriage. My life (as I had known it) began to change. I would go to church, study, and read all the time. We had darkness in our home, but light began to penetrate through that darkness.

How do you serve God faithfully and obediently in a hostile world? It is only by the grace of God and with lots of prayer. Determining to be faithful in all areas of my life with Christ, it became easier with each passing day. There were dark days when I would almost give up and return to my old way of life. God would not let me go back. He would always send a blessing to encourage me and lift me up.

One such blessing came as I was praying in church during the service. God gave me a vision. That vision was a picture of my husband, coming down the aisle and sitting down beside me. Tears came into my eyes as I saw this in my mind and felt God touch my heart. This is still very much visible in my mind today. It was God's touch saying, "Stay faithful."

God began to give me hidden pearls of wisdom within His Word. As I read Ezekiel 22:30, my heart was touched by God when He could not find a man to stand in the gap for Him. When I came to Romans 12:1-2, God spoke to my heart concerning verse 2, "...that ye may prove what is that good, and acceptable, and perfect, will of God." He was saying, "I need you to stand in the gap."

After a few years went by, God reminded me of His will for me. His will is good, acceptable, and perfect. He wanted me to stand in the gap for my husband. A light bulb was turned on for me. I needed to continue praying for my husband, but most of all I needed to pray for me. I could not change him or make him come to church or receive Jesus as his Savior, but I could ask God to change me. By asking God to change me, I was allowing God to do the convicting in my husband's heart. I prayed, "Lord, change me. Transform me. Show me how I can change. Create in me a pure heart, and give me clean hands before You."

By praying this prayer and having that meek and quiet spirit that a wife must have, I was willing to die to myself — to become totally submissive to God and to my husband. As I prayed for him, my heart began to soften toward him and my love for him grew! As I stood in the gap in prayer for him, I saw his heart begin to soften. Praying for me to change released all my pent up feelings against him. When I asked God for new eyes to see my husband, God supplied those new eyes. I asked God to give him a brand new wife, and God did just that.

God really began conviction in his heart in July 2001. God allowed me to see Him move in my husband's heart weekly. His salvation came on August 12, 2001.

It is the good, acceptable, and perfect will of God for me to continually stand in the gap and build that hedge of protection around our marriage.

Jane Whitt

5 ETERNAL LIFE

"...but the gift of God is eternal life through Jesus Christ our Lord" (Romans 6:23).

Is eternal life an extension of the life you now have? Or is it a completely different type of life? Jesus spoke of a new birth. Birth is the beginning of something. Just as we all had a physical birth that gave us human life, we must also have a new, spiritual birth to receive eternal life.

If the new birth brings eternal life, how does it come about? God says, "But as many as received him, to them gave he power to become the sons of God, even to them that believe on his name" (John 1:12). We must understand that through believing, we receive God, the Holy Spirit, and in that union is the gift of eternal life. This life that is deposited in us is from God's very life that exists in Heaven. We will not go to be with God in our human bodies, but we must be born again into eternal life. This life can only be from God.

Being good or bad has nothing to do with going to Heaven or Hell. It is a matter of having "God's life" within you to inherit Heaven. Search the Scriptures to see whether these things are so.

Frances Martin
Missionary to Mexico

6 PRINCIPLE OF REAPING AND SOWING

"A man that hath friends must shew himself friendly: and there is a friend that sticketh closer than a brother" (Proverbs 18:24).

Being friendly and outgoing does not come natural for my twin daughters. Unless you are a very close friend, a greeting or question from you will generally be met with a downcast look and a mumbled, indiscernible reply, if they answer you at all! Their father and I have discussed this fact on more than one occasion. We were looking for ways to help them overcome their problem. Tossing this about in my mind one morning while cooking breakfast, I heard on the radio a story of a man who conducted a simple experiment. While walking down a busy street in Los Angeles, the man would grumble and frown. He received sneers and rude comments from fellow pedestrians that he met along the way. He then turned and came back up that same street. However, this time he cheerfully greeted those he met with a smile. Smiles and cheery greetings were his reward! The conclusion to the experiment was that the reception received from the people was in direct response to what he gave out!

The Lord brought to my mind the principle of sowing and reaping. He reminded me that we reap what we sow, and when we sow a bean, many beans are the return. Cultivate a grain of corn and God multiplies it so that we reap many ears of corn. God multiplies our investment whether it be with our money, our time, or a smile. If we sow sorrow to our companions of life, we will reap much sorrow. If we sow complaining, we will reap much complaining. On the other hand, if we sow hope, we will reap much hope. With joy and peace, we reap an abundance of joy and peace! Sow friendship and reap an abundance of friends. The choice is ours.

I began asking myself, "Am I sowing hope, joy, and peace?" I soon realized that God was not only helping me with my girls' problems, but that I also had some improvements to make in some areas of my own life. Change has not come overnight for any of us, but it is a daily choice we are making. Praise be to God for His goodness and mercy!

Melanie Cook

7 I Met the Healer

"Confess your faults one to another, and pray one for another, that ye may be healed. The effectual fervent prayer of a righteous man availeth much" (James 5:16).

In August 1997, I met Someone I had needed all of my life. It was like being released from prison. The world looked so different now. Birds sang sweeter, the grass was greener, and I loved everyone – even my enemies. I wanted them to feel what I felt and meet the Person who changed my life so much. I had not cried much in years, and now it seemed like everything made me cry. I wondered how I could be so happy and cry all the time.

In the following years, we had some serious health problems. My husband, who was saved after I was, had to have part of a lung taken out. He had a blood clot and almost died. I had known for many years that I had a heart problem. I had to sleep in a recliner to be able to breathe, and I didn't think there was anything the doctors could do about it. In

April 2000, I died in the Intensive Care Unit and was brought back to life. The next day our pastor and a friend came to see me, and I knew I was a goner, expecting to hear the angels sing at any moment. I wasn't afraid, because I knew people from church were praying for me. There was a great feeling of peace, and I knew the Lord was with me.

I was transported by ambulance to another hospital for a pacemaker implant. I was a little concerned about going through the surgery. The Lord sent a nurse who told me not to be afraid — that there were a lot of people praying for me. They prayed and came to visit. I saw the love of the Lord in them and felt their prayers. I was able to go home in two days.

This past year I had a stress test done in Birmingham, Alabama. I had another kind of test done there recently, and the doctor said my heart function was almost back to normal. He also raved to my doctor at home about the test results. My doctor at home told me, "I don't know what you are doing, but keep on doing it." I told him I would be here as long as the Lord wanted me to be, and keeping up with my two-year-old granddaughter, Zoe, is good medicine, too.

I have met the Healer, and He gave me a new heart and life twice. He gets all the praise.

Heavenly Father, Thank You for all Your many blessings, Your great love for us, and salvation through Your Son Who gave everything. Thank You for Who You are, and Your miracles we see every day because people prayed. Thank You that someday we will be with You forever.

Pat Porter

8 Filling My God Hole

"And of whom hast thou been afraid or feared, that thou hast lied, and hast not remembered me, nor laid it to thy heart? have not I held my peace even of old, and thou fearest me not?" (Isaiah 57:11).

For me, the big turning point in marriage was when God made it clear to me that my husband was not perfect. I know this sounds strange. I already knew that he was not perfect, but I did not realize the type of expectations I was placing on him. I was expecting him to be everything I needed. He was supposed to love me unconditionally, support me emotionally and financially, and be available for my every need. That is a lot for a human to bear, yet that was the yoke I had unconsciously placed on my husband.

Several years into our marriage and many disappointments later, God opened my eyes. Even though I said I had a relationship with God, I was not letting Him be God. I was filling the void of my "God Hole" (as Brother Doug Ripley says) with my husband. God revealed to me that He was to meet my every need, not just spiritually, but also emotionally and financially. He wants to be involved in every aspect of our lives. He wants to be our all, and He has designed our husbands to be our companion, friend, and lover. God is where we are to place our trust, strength, and every need.

Thank You, God, for lovingly meeting my every need.

Gayle Krohe

9 My Daddy's Hands

"Thou hast a mighty arm: strong is thy hand, and high is thy right hand" (Psalm 89:13)

As a little girl, one of my greatest and most tender memories was my daddy's hands. They were such large hands. His hands were ruddy and tanned from working outside. They were so large that they could completely envelope my small hand. They had a tender roughness but a strength that gave me a sense of security and protection. They were hands that could remove the tightest jar lids, but the were gentle and agile enough to remove the tiniest knots from the most delicate gold chains. Those hands held my hand in times of fear as I walked into a huge ocean, they held my hand when I was nervous and hurt in the emergency room, and they held my hand as I was anxiously waiting to walk down the aisle to meet my future husband. As my daddy aged and became very ill, one of the saddest and most difficult aspects of his illness was for me to watch as his hands became weaker and more emaciated.

During those times, I was led over and over to thank God for what He had given me through my daddy's hands, even though it was so temporary. I have also become very aware of how much more God has given me and shown me with His very own hand. His mighty right hand is always there to protect me, to hold me up, to be my strength, and to comfort me. He promises me that His strength is with me for all eternity. How awesome that my God wants to give me more than even my daddy ever could!

Dear Lord, thank You so much for the hands of my daddy and all they have represented to me. Thank You more for Your perfect hand, which is always there for me.

Susan Harney

10 SEEING GOD'S PROMISE IN A RAINBOW

"I do set my bow in the cloud, and it shall be for a token of a covenant between me and the earth" (Genesis 9:13).

There have been times in my life when I've been guilty of longing for something more. I wanted something visible, something solid, something more than just my faith in the unseen to hold onto when times of uncertainty would overpower me. I wanted a sign, perhaps, for the Lord to prove to me that He cared specifically for me. One such moment occurred as my husband and I celebrated our first anniversary in early August 1986. We were living in Lynchburg, Virginia, and decided to take a weekend getaway to the nearby Blue Ridge Mountains.

At this time, my world was bright and full of possibilities, when a terrible dark force pulled at my spirit, plagued me with uncertainty, and invaded my world. My parents were divorcing after 23 years of marriage. It was difficult to enjoy my own happiness knowing that my family was hurting so deeply, especially my younger brother and sister who were still living at home.

While driving home from our romantic retreat, we stopped at a yard sale and met the most precious elderly couple. They had been married for more than 50 years. We spent the afternoon with them, laughing and listening to their stories. I felt so encouraged that my husband and I would be like that one day. As soon as we left their house, it started to rain. A sadness swept over me as I realized my parents would not know the happiness that this couple had found together. I began to cry.

I was angry with God. I am the oldest sibling; therefore, I have always felt a great sense of responsibility to fix whatever problem occurred. I could not fix this. As the rain began to subside, I turned to my husband and asked him if he had ever seen a full rainbow painted across the sky. We began to ponder what Noah must have felt after going through the greatest storm known to man and finally stepping out of the ark onto firm ground. Until that moment, it had not occurred to me precisely what Noah and his family had endured. Riding out the flood was only the beginning of the journey. What comfort they must have felt while looking toward the heavens and seeing the brilliant colors of a rainbow painted across the sky! At that moment, I looked out the passenger door window. Side by side, stretching across the top of the mountain, were twin rainbows. I could see them both from end to end.

How many times as believers do we feel as though we are

in God's presence? The very hand that created the universe is revealing itself for our benefit, and it is so overwhelming that we can hardly take it in. On that day, I knew I would survive the storm of my parents' divorce, and I knew that the God I served would provide the strength I needed to face any storm in my life.

Sherry Pentecost

11 RESCUED FROM THE TRASH

"He raiseth up the poor out of the dust, and lifteth the needy out of the dunghill" (Psalm 113:7)

God has the power to take anything and anyone, regardless of the perceived value in the eyes of the world, and glorify Himself in a marvelous way. This truth is so vividly displayed in the story of two little orphan boys who lived in Moldova.

Local missionaries sponsored a drive in which thousands of dollars were raised for the purpose of erecting a building to house street kids and other children without homes. Finally, the day arrived when the children were brought to the orphanage to meet their new mama and papa.

Among the orphans arriving were two little brothers named Victor and Nicholay. They had literally been rescued from a trash pile where they had been living with an old woman who had befriended the boys when their parents had deserted them. Victor and Nicholay were thrilled to at last have a beautiful home and parents who would lovingly care for them. Their new mama and papa, Marie and John, cleaned them up and gave them warm clothes and tasty food. They had never been to school and were promptly enrolled in classes with a tutor provided to assist them with their homework. They learned quickly.

The best treasure of all was to learn that Someone loved them so much that He left His home in Heaven to come to die for them so they might be saved and spend eternity with Jesus

Christ. This was good news, and they wanted to share eternity with Jesus Christ.

One day, Nicholay rushed to the church after school with one of his classmates who wanted to find Jesus. Fortunately, the pastor was there and could explain carefully how one can be saved. Victor, the oldest, could be seen standing at the gate leading into the orphanage grounds with his Bible, stopping the children passing by, warning them that they must make a decision whether they want to spend eternity in Heaven or Hell.

How pleased God must be with Victor and Nicholay's desire to witness for Him, to share the Gospel with others! If these two orphans rescued from the trash, cleaned up inside and out, are grateful for what God has done for them, how much more grateful should we be? We have been given so much and should fulfill our responsibility to share the Good News with those whom God sends into our lives. Let us be found as faithful as Victor and Nicholay!

Loreen Ittermann

12 THE TRUE DESIRE OF MY HEART

"By faith Moses, when he was born, was hid three months of his parents, because they saw he was a proper child; and they were not afraid of the king's commandment. By faith Moses, when he was come to years, refused to be called the son of Pharaoh's daughter; Choosing rather to suffer affliction with the people of God, than to enjoy the pleasures of sin for a season" (Hebrews 11:23-25).

Moses' true desire was to live like the people of God. He was listed in the "hall of faith" of Hebrews 11 stating, "when he was come to years, refused to be called the son of Pharaoh's daughter." In Exodus 2, Moses saw an Egyptian mistreating a Hebrew and took it upon himself to be judge and jury by taking the life of the Egyptian. When he went out the next day and saw two Hebrews fighting, he tried to reason with them. In Exodus 2:14, one of them said to him, "...Who made thee a prince and a judge over us? intendest thou to kill me, as thou killedst the Egyptian?..." Moses fled the face of Pharaoh and went into the land of Midian.

When Moses arrived at Midian, he met seven daughters of a priest who came to draw water from a well. Shepherds were also at the well and were ready to drive the ladies away, and Moses stood up for them and helped them water their flock. When they returned home, their father asked them how they were able to return home so quickly. They answered him by saying in Exodus 2:19, "...An Egyptian delivered us out of the hand of the shepherds, and also drew water enough for us, and watered the flock."

Because of Moses' sin of taking matters into his own hands, he was forced to leave home, and the first people he met described him as an "Egyptian." Moses' true desire was to be known with the people of God, but he lost that because of sin.

How many times do we lose an opportunity to be the witness we desire to be, because we have allowed sin to enter our lives?

O God, keep me from sin that it might not grieve me.

Katy Ripley

13 THE ATTIC

(Dedicated to my parents: Bryce and Clara Goodman)

"And thou shalt teach them diligently unto thy children..." (Deuteronomy 6:7).

I remember as a child the fascination I had with our attic. It had a pull-down staircase and was easily accessible. Many times my mom would send me to the attic to get an item she needed that was stored there. I would end up rummaging through "treasures" of all kinds.

Our choir sings a song called "Find Us Faithful." Each time we sing it, I think of my parents' attic. One of the verses states:

"After all our hopes and dreams have come and gone,
And our children sift through all we've left behind,
May the clues that they discover, and the memories they uncover
Become the light that leads them to the road we each must find."

My dad went to Heaven in 1996, and my mom now lives alone. At one time she said, "I need to clean out that attic; you will have an awful time going through all that stuff if something happens to me."

Well, I'm sure it will be difficult, but I think I will find comfort in going through the attic once more. I will be able to see old books of mine from grade school, patterns that we used to make Barbie clothes and stuffed animals and childhood toys long forgotten. I'll see the old pressure cooker that canned quarts of green beans every summer; my job as a child was to put one teaspoon of salt in each jar. I'll see old Bibles used by grandparents to guide their lives and instill values in their families.

So, Mom, if the attic is still full when you go to Heaven, that will be okay. When I finally do sift through its contents, I know I will discover your hopes and dreams that revolved around God's Word and love for your family. That is a legacy to be proud of and to pass on to my children.

Dawn Terry

14 God Showed Me Who Was In Charge

"For he shall give his angels charge over thee, to keep thee in all thy ways" (Psalm 91:11).

At the age of 13, I was in a clown ministry when I received Christ as my Savior! For several years, as a single adult, I grew apart from Christ. God had to allow me to fall, so I would know He had control of me!

One year I earned three paychecks at one time on my job:

vacation, payroll, and a bonus. The Devil and I partied! I went to a club and left everything in my trunk. Shortly thereafter, I was drunk. When I returned to my car, I found that my purse, money, and car were gone. Although I called for help, it was too late — everything was gone. At this time, the Devil was sure having fun, but I sure was not. As a single mom with a son at home, I had nothing. Two weeks later, I finally got my car back. My job reimbursed me, and I quit drinking. I knew then that God was really the One in control and through it all He never left me! He forgave me and gave me a second chance! Sometimes we don't get that! With the help of Decatur Baptist Church and family, I grew closer to Him. My ministry grew in love for Christ, and I felt so much love from Him! It took six years for me to make the needed changes in my life. Then God brought the right man into my life, and we are now married. My love for God grew even more!

It took hitting "rock bottom" for God to show me that He was in control and that I needed to put Him first. My life with Him in it each day is so much more rewarding. I am glad Christ is always with us!

Sissy Odell

15 I WANT TO BE PERMANENT

"For I am the Lord, I change not..." (Malachi 3:6).

As I was thinking and praying about a thought to share for a devotional, I began to read in my prayer journal. I looked back to a couple of years ago at something I had written in May 2000 about preparing to leave Argentina for our first furlough. I was packing up my things, deciding on what to take home, what I could store there for when we would return, and what I had to give away. I loved my house there, because I had spent the whole first term trying to collect the furnishings we needed to make our house a home. Now, it was time to start all over again. I knew we would be in the

States for only a year, and then we would return to begin the house hunting process all over again. In my prayer journal, I wrote the following:

"During this time of transition, move, and instability, one thing that is permanent is my position with Christ and one thing I want to commit to be permanent is my service to Him — no matter where I am."

In I Peter 2:16, the word "bondservant" or "servant" comes from the Greek word "doulos." It means a slave, one who is in permanent relation of servitude to his master, his will being altogether consumed in the will of the master. In a world of disposable plates, cups, baking dishes, razors, diapers, and even marriages, the word permanent is lost. Do I see my role of a servant for the Lord as absolutely and utterly permanent? I want to be able to say without a doubt, "I don't know where I'll be in ten years, or whether I'll still have my house, health, job, kids, or even spouse, but I can promise one thing: that I will be actively serving God."

In February 2003, four moves later, never to return to my things I left in storage in Argentina, never to return to the country and to the people that we loved so dearly, and having lost the child that I then saw as a perfectly healthy and developing son to a world of autism, I once again reminded myself that one thing that is permanent and never changes is my Lord and my position with Him. He is faithful to fulfill His every promise and to work all things for our good (Romans 8:28). He also gives us the peace that passeth all understanding (Philippians 4:7), in the midst of a turbulent and unstable world. May we all once again commit ourselves to a permanent servitude to Him, no matter where we are or what our circumstances may be. We are to always find ourselves serving Him who has begun a good work in us and will perform it until the day of Jesus Christ (Philippians 1:6).

Joan Hampton
Missionary to the Hispanics in North Carolina

16 The Best Friend I Have

"But my God shall supply all your need according to his riches in glory by Christ Jesus" (Philippians 4:19).

I feel as if God has put His arm of protection around me, because of all the things that have happened in my life. My husband died ten years ago, and I knew then He would supply my needs and protect me, but I never noticed it like I do now. He is so precious and is the best friend I have.

God has always supplied my needs, and He has given me some of my wants. In my job situation, God has put me right where I need to be at the right time in my life. He has also moved me when it was the right time to be moved. I can think of so many times that I would have chosen a different way, but God would lead me through Christian people that were there. When I needed their guidance, God had already spoken to them. I was at the same job for nine years before the death of my husband. Since then, I have let God guide me in the direction He has for me, and it has been a wonderful journey. I have been able to do things and go places that I never would have gone without God's leading. I have enjoyed everything I have done and every place I have gone.

What a friend we have in Jesus!

Martha Coffey

17 72747

"But thou when thou fastest, anoint thine head, and wash thy face; That thou appear not unto men to fast, but unto thy Father which is in secret: and thy Father, which seeth in secret, shall reward thee openly" (Matthew 6:17-18).

In the spring of 1998 I was sitting at my desk talking on the phone with my daughter. She was enrolled in the Medical College of Georgia and had called for some encouragement from her mom. I talked with her a few minutes about God's love and told her that He would see her through. That was just one of the many pep talks I had given her over the past four years.

When I finished my conversation on the phone with her, I felt a small tap on my shoulder. I turned to see Miss Leila, the lady who cleaned the offices in the building where I worked. She was a small lady and worked very hard. She was an African American living in a racially-biased town. In a low tone of voice, she asked if she could talk to me. I pulled up a chair and asked her to have a seat. She was afraid she would be reported for slacking off on her duties, so she asked if she could call me at home. That was a Friday, so I gave her my business card and told her to call me on Saturday. I had no idea what she wanted, but she had always been very pleasant and believed very strongly in God.

The next morning Miss Leila called. We chatted a few minutes and she got right to the point. She said, "I don't mean to pry, but you seem awfully unhappy. I listen to you talk to your daughter on the phone, and I know you love God. I sense something in your smile and in your eyes — an emptiness or a void." Shocked, I began to confess to her that I was terribly unhappy and dismayed that someone had detected it. I thought I was hiding it better than that.

I worked for a Baptist university in a small southern town. The president and many of the executive officers were moving so far away from the Baptist doctrine that the Southern Baptist Convention was threatening to remove their support for the university. It was hard to tell I was working in what was supposed to be a Christian environment. I had been looking for another job and sent out many resumes, but to no avail.

Miss Leila asked if I ever fasted. I thought for a minute and confessed that while I had fasted many times in the past, it had been a very long time. She asked if I would go on a fast with her. Of course, I was willing since I knew she was a God-fearing woman, and I felt God had sent her to me. I asked how she thought we should proceed, and she told me she would leave that up to God and me. She gave me her telephone number and asked me to call her when I had the answer.

I hung up the phone and fell on my knees. I then sat in my recliner and fell into a deep, peaceful sleep. When I awakened the numbers 72747 were ringing in my head. I continued with my Saturday chores, chanting those numbers in my head like a jingle you can't stop humming or singing. I prayed another little prayer while mopping my kitchen floor and asked God to help me know what those numbers meant. Later that same day, I was walking across the room when the answer came.

Miss Leila needed her strength and energy during the day. She had to move furniture, run the vacuum cleaner, and empty the trash. I sat behind a computer all day and used most of my physical energy in the evenings preparing meals, running errands, and cleaning my house. I thought the Lord was telling me that I should fast from 7 a.m. to 7 p.m. and Miss Leila should fast from 7 p.m. until 7 a.m., and that we should do that for seven days, thus the 72747.

I immediately called Miss Leila. She was thrilled and thought that was an excellent plan. We started on Sunday. By Monday morning I was pretty excited. I had a new prayer partner. (God had filled the void left after my mother's death. She was quite a prayer warrior.) Each day that week Miss Leila would stop by my desk and ask how I was doing. She said, "Just keep praying; God is on His throne." The week ended, and I didn't feel much different from before. Miss Leila continued to encourage me. Another week passed, and nothing happened. Several weeks later, I received a phone call. By the time the call came, I had gone on with business as usual. How soon we fall back into complacency!

The phone call was about a job interview. The salary was attractive (double what I was making at the university), and the benefits were wonderful. The big drawback was that I would have to move to Huntsville, Alabama. My daughter and her husband were living in Mobile at the time, but moving to Huntsville would not put me any closer to them than where I was. I decided to drive to Huntsville and take a look. It was an attractive offer, and I fell in love with the Huntsville area. I returned home, called Miss Leila, and she prayed with me. She was thrilled.

I packed up and moved to Huntsville in September 1998. I knew no one and had no family anywhere close. I soon met Christian friends. Two couples seemed to take a special interest in me. They invited me to do things with them and their families.

Life seemed good, but two and a half months later, the same company that hired me filed for bankruptcy. To some it may have seemed that I was not following God's will, or He would not have allowed that to happen. Surprisingly, I handled the information quite well. I am convinced that the Lord has a purpose for me in Alabama, and I am determined to find out what it is.

In October 1999, I chose to move to Decatur. I had traveled to Decatur from Huntsville on many occasions in a sales capacity. I was forced to find other employment, and it so happened that my office was in Decatur. I thank God that I made that move, because since then I have attended Decatur Baptist Church. I stand in awe when I think of the awesome ways God works. I will always believe He brought me here for a purpose, and the numbers 72747 will always be a major significance to me — so will Miss Leila because I believed God used her to help me.

Dianne Stewart

18 DAILY BENEFITS

"Blessed be the Lord, who daily loadeth us with benefits, even the God of our salvation. Selah" (Psalm 68:19).

Last year my husband suffered with heart problems, which sent him to the hospital. It is easy at a time like this to worry, wonder why this is happening to my family, and how will this affect the future of my family. God showed me this verse during this time, and even though bad things happen, there are far more daily benefits that I was forgetting.

Many times we forget to look at the daily benefits that God "loadeth us with." Instead, we dwell on the negative: how Satan is attacking us, the job lay-offs, the financial woes, health needs, rebellious children, etc. Sometimes it seems as if there is nothing but trouble around us. We need to remember our daily benefits. Psalm 103:2-6 reminds us not to forget all of His benefits. God, Who forgives all our iniquities also heals all our diseases, redeems us from destruction, crowns us with His lovingkindness and tender mercies, satisfies our mouths with good things, renews us with His strength, and takes care of our enemies.

Have you looked at your daily benefits today? Look, see all the daily blessings that God has "loadeth" you with today. Thank Him for each one. Bless His holy name.

Dear Lord, I bless You, Lord, bless Your holy name. Help me to remember You "loadeth" me daily with Your benefits. I thank You, Lord, for each one.

Sarah Partin

19 God's Word Will Not Return Empty

"So shall my word be that goeth forth out of my mouth; it shall not return unto me void, but it shall accomplish that which I please, and it shall prosper in the thing whereto I sent it" (Isaiah 55:11).

My steps were quick, and my heart was hurting as I stepped up on the ramps to go to the office/library at the school where I was principal. I had received a call from our first-grade teacher, Mrs. Talley. She had taught at our school for more than 20 years, and she knew that I would want to take care of this problem personally. She knew that no child was ever allowed to abuse another, may it be verbally, physically, mentally, or emotionally. This would not happen at Roper schools!

She told me how the sixth-grade boys had taken a wig from a fellow girl student's head and tossed it around the playground while the girls watched. My first thought was, "Where was the teacher?" My next thought was how quickly could I get to school to spank the living daylights out of every child involved. I also knew the punishment needed to be one that all the children would remember.

Mrs. Talley told me that this girl and her fourth-grade brother were adopted. Because of a nervous condition, she had pulled every hair out of her head, including her eyebrows and her eyelashes. As the founder of the school, I had promised God I would make every effort to see that no child would ever be abused. I wanted to make every child proud of who they were.

Immediately, I cried out to God, "This is too important for me to handle, Lord. I don't know what I am going to say or do when I get to the office. You, O Lord, will need to be me, live within me, talk for me, and think for me. You will need to be me! I know that You know how to handle this, so I am Yours, Lord. I am what You have to work with today!"

I took the Lord's hand and went into the office and waited for His guidance. Once I gave it to Him, I trusted Him to do a good job! I called the sixth-grade girls first. I smiled and greeted them as usual, because they are wonderful children. I told them I wanted to share some stories and thoughts with them. I had used stories many times before, but I reminded God that this time was very important. I started out by telling them how healthy, beautiful, and pretty their hair and eyes were, and how beautifully their bodies were shaped. I explained how lucky they were to have all of this. I asked them to raise their hands if they knew that God had done this for them, and they did. Then I began telling stories about what could happen before they returned to school the next day. They could be in a car accident that would leave them scarred or disabled. I asked them to raise their hands if they would want their friends to be kind and helpful to them, and, of course, they all raised their hands. I smiled and thanked the girls for coming to the office. Next I sent for the sixth-grade boys. I told them the same stories, but I was more forceful. The little girl's name was never mentioned. When I left the office, I took the Lord's hand and said, "You did a good job. You gave me Your thoughts, not mine."

About two months later, I saw Mrs. Talley, and she asked me if I had seen the little girl's cute little pixie haircut. She had grown hair, eyebrows, and eyelashes. God had touched the hearts of those sixth-graders. They showed her so much love and treated her so special that her nervous condition vanished. I smiled and thanked God that I could give my problems to Him, especially a big and important one like this!

Neita Roper

20 DON'T FORGET TO PRAY

"Evening, and morning, and at noon, will I pray, and cry aloud: and he shall hear my voice" (Psalm 55:17)

So many times rising up in the morning, starting off my day and getting the kids ready for school, the day goes by with nothing going right. Sometimes I find myself feeling bad. I wonder what's going on as the day is creeping by. I find myself asking, "Why?"

Finally, it comes to me, did I pray? Did I stop and thank God for waking me up? Did I thank Him for another day? You know, the word "why" is a big word. I have always heard from older people to never ask God "Why?" Then I asked myself, "What if God asked us, 'Why?'" Living in the world as it is today, sometimes I wonder does God ask, "Why? Why did I give my Son? Why didn't you pray?" Then I have to confess, and confession is good for the soul. I tell the Lord, "I know I haven't been good some days, and I don't do what I should, yet Your mercy somehow endures."

So as you start off your day, start it off with a little prayer. Just remember, don't forget to pray!

Dear Lord, thank You for forgiving me for my sins. As I start the day off, lead and guide me on the way You would have me to go. I love You, God.

Tammy Staten

21 SHARING OUR THANKSGIVING HOLIDAY

"Let us come before his presence with thanksgiving, and make a joyful noise unto him with psalms" (Psalm 95:2)

For the past few years, my family and I have invited the national leaders and their families in our church to come to our house and share the Thanksgiving holiday with us. Even though the country of Mexico doesn't celebrate the holiday, our people think it is a lovely time to set aside things and participate with us on this special day. They bring a covered dish, we share our food with them, and we give thanks to our heavenly Father for each other, the food, and for all of our many wonderful blessings. After our meal we have a great time giving testimonies and glorifying our Almighty God with songs of praise.

Each year our group grows in number. Last year we had 50 present. One of the leaders of our church, as he gets a new calendar of the year, always circles the date we celebrate Thanksgiving. He eagerly looks forward to being with us and can hardly wait until this day arrives.

I am so very glad that God called us to Mexico to labor in His vineyard as missionaries and gave us workers to help carry the load. We are so very thankful for them, and for this reason, we joyfully share our Thanksgiving Day.

Heavenly Father, I thank You for sharing Your love to all people. Please help me to always have the same attitude to want to share with others my love for them.

Betsy Gates
Missionary in Mexico

22 Make Me A Better Christian

"To every thing there is a season, and a time to every purpose under the heaven" (Ecclesiastes 3:1).

My most memorable experience with God is when I asked Him, "Do whatever it takes to make me a better Christian." On one Sunday night my pastor preached on "Getting Self Out of the Way." I prayed for God to get me where I needed to be, to be able to let Him use me. Little did I know, He had already begun to use me and to prepare me.

I work in our church's daycare. I had my materials prepared for a bulletin board. I had prayed for days for the right inscription for the board. On a Monday morning after I had prayed that prayer, I went to put the materials on the board. As I began, the Bible verse, "...the fields; for they are white already to harvest," came to my mind. I had no idea where to find the reference. I had half of the daycare looking for the verse. Someone found it: John 4:35. I put it on the board, but it still needed something else. I began my daily Bible reading. For some reason, I began reading the verses at the middle of the chapter, working myself up to the beginning of the chapter. I came to Ecclesiastes 3:1-8. These verses speak of, "to every thing there is a season...A time to be born, and a time to die...." I had no idea why, but I had to put the verses on the board. I knew it was right.

A few days later, my mother-in-law went to meet Jesus. Both John 4:35 and Ecclesiastes 3:1-8 were given to me as a comfort to my husband, family, friends, and me. These verses helped me to comfort those who were not living right, and to soften their hearts. The greatest thing was when I looked upon my mother-in-law's face of death — I knew why I had placed those verses on the bulletin board.

I know that God will speak to us if we will only listen. He is always there to lead, guide, and comfort us, if we will only let Him. My prayer is that this will be a comfort to you.

Janice Vinson

23 GRACE TO FLY

"And he said unto me, My grace is sufficient for thee: for my strength is made perfect in weakness. Most gladly therefore will I rather glory in my infirmities, that the power of Christ may rest upon me" (II Corinthians 12:9)

I will admit it. I am terribly afraid of flying. It is not a lack of faith, I can assure you. I don't mind being in an airplane when it is my time to go. I just don't want to be in there when it is the pilot's time to go. I also can't breathe in enclosed places. This has been a plague on our life and ministry. It has always been a struggle to get to the mission field and back. God's grace has always been sufficient, but there was one trip that the Lord was especially gracious. I had to return the States alone to deal with a family matter. My husband, Mickey, knew that I was struggling. He had been led of the Lord to preach, teach, and talk about II Corinthians 12:9. Someone even mailed us the song, "New Grace," which he promptly sang for me.

On the day of the flight, I was really hurting with fear, and I was honestly not experiencing that sufficient grace. After much effort and several nerve pills, I was finally helped through the gate, saying goodbye to Mickey as he told me repeatedly, "I know God's grace will be sufficient for you." While waiting to board, it was announced that the plane had broken down, but they would do their best to repair it. That was not what I needed to hear at that moment.

When we finally boarded, I was helped to my seat. There was an older lady in the aisle seat, and my seat was next to her. I sat down and began to buckle up amidst my tears and sobs. The old lady asked if I was fearful of flying, to which I emphatically affirmed. She then reached over and patted my knee and said kindly, "Now, don't be afraid. My name is Grace, and I'm going to take care of you." When she touched me and spoke to me, it seemed that all the fear and anxiety flooded out of me, and a perfect calm settled on me. From here you must make your own judgment, but I am telling you exactly what happened.

Grace introduced me to her son-in-law across the aisle. She told me they both had bad knees and would not be getting up during the flight, and they didn't. Calmness reigned supreme. After we landed in Atlanta, Grace let me into the aisle and said that she and her son-in-law would have to wait for wheelchairs because of their knees. After I retrieved my bag from the overhead compartment, I was moved forward by those anxious to get off. I really wanted to say thanks again, so I made my way back to our seats. They were empty. I then had to get off the airplane, but I waited at the door for them to bring out the wheelchair passengers. When none came out, I asked the stewardess about them. She told me that they had no one on this flight that needed a wheelchair. What?!? I believe that whatever the explanation, God was being especially gracious to me at that very difficult moment in my life. Thank You, Lord.

Christine Schrimshire
Missionary to Great Britain

24 PATIENCE AND ANSWERED PRAYERS

"Rest in the Lord, and wait patiently for him..." (Psalm 37:7).

Waiting and having patience have never been my strong points. *WEBSTER'S DICTIONARY* offers this definition of these words: wait — to remain stationary in readiness or expectation; patience — bearing pains or trials calmly or without complaints.

Having been the wife of a military man, I had become used to the moves and leaving loved ones behind. This particular move was going to be different for two reasons. First, we had been stationed at one location for over seven years, and I had made friendships that I knew were going to be hard to give up. Secondly, I knew this was going to be the last move for us, and like it or not, this would be our home from now on.

Good friendships have always been important to me, and I was already praying for God to either let us stay where we were, or if and when we moved, to bring new friendships into my life. One day, about a year after our move, I was reading in the book of Psalms and the minute I read Psalm 37:7, I knew that God wanted me to read that particular passage for that day. He was talking to me and I knew that day if I would believe in His Word and wait patiently, He would answer my prayers. You know what? He did!

It has been three years now, and God's Word is still true in this area of my life. He has sent friends that love me, friends that pray for me and for my family, and friends that, if need be, are just a phone call away. Now, I have friendships with women that are not even my own age.

I am a true believer that God's work comes at just the right time. I know that God was all the while getting a larger supply of friends ready for me and all the while getting me ready for that supply.

Thank You, Lord, for patience and answered prayers.

Tammy R. McCarthy

25 God Has a Plan

"And Joseph said unto them, Fear not: for am I in the place of God?" (Genesis 50:19).

I am so thankful that God has a plan for my life! I am His child, and He wants to use me in His kingdom! God also had a plan for Joseph, but He put him through a lot of tough times before showing him the plan. Joseph was sold into slavery and imprisoned before being made governor of the land in Egypt. In that position, Joseph saved his father and brothers during a famine. God knew exactly what was going to happen the whole time.

Esther gained her position as the queen of Persia, seemingly by chance, but her Uncle Mordecai thought differently.

He believed God gave Esther her position, so that she could save the Jews from certain death. God placed her in a position of influence in order to use her.

In the same way, I know God wants to use me. He has a plan for my life, and all I have to do is give Him control. If I seek Him with my whole heart, He'll honor my desire to serve Him and reveal His plan to me!

Julie Keenum

26 THE UNIQUE CURE

"...pray one for another, that ye may be healed..." (James 5:16).

One frightening aspect of living in a Third World country, where medical care is very limited, is the dread of becoming sick, having an accident, or experiencing any other health-related malady. The medical personnel may have much knowledge, but without adequate equipment and supplies, they find themselves restricted in providing the proper remedies.

Such was the case when a missionary in Moldova awoke one morning only to discover that it was difficult to function because of serious back pain. This was of grave concern to her, because she was not only responsible for the 50 national full-time Christian workers, but a team of Americans were soon to arrive to assist in the ministry for a week. There were many preparations to be made and much responsibility to shoulder.

Knowing that prayer can change things, the missionary corresponded with American friends and also asked the nationals to pray. The pain persisted, but the people of God kept praying

The American team arrived full of enthusiasm and energy to begin their ministry. They had brought with them a back brace and heating pads to alleviate some of the missionary's back pain. These supplies, although they did not eliminate the pain completely, did provide some relief.

On Sunday morning, the team and nationals attended the morning worship service in the beautiful national church, which the Americans had helped build and furnish. It was a good service, but the back pain continued its course. That afternoon, the missionary, along with some of the Americans, attended a little village church where the interior of the humble building resembles a stable. The Christians there were godly and eager to hear God's Word. The missionary continued to nurse the sore back with the heating pad and back brace.

Then something unusual occurred when the visiting pastor, sitting on the other end of the wooden bench from the seated missionary, arose to go to the platform to speak. The weight of the bench shifted, causing the bench to fly up. The missionary toppled off the other end onto the concrete floor. The Americans sitting behind the missionary saw what was about to happen. One American grabbed the missionary and broke her fall, while another American snatched the bench on the other end and brought it back to its original position. In the course of the confusion, something happened. When all the excitement subsided, the missionary discovered the back pain was gone. The back was definitely healed!

God appreciates our sharing our requests with Him, but He also delights in answering our prayers in His way and in His timing. He loves us and will take good care of us, but He demands that He receive the glory for what He alone can accomplish in our lives. Let us give Him that freedom.

Loreen Ittermann
Missionary to Moldova

27 MY HELP

"I will lift up mine eyes unto the hills, from whence cometh my help. My help cometh from the Lord, which made heaven and earth. The Lord is thy keeper: the Lord is thy shade upon thy right hand. The Lord shall preserve thee from all evil: he shall preserve thy soul. The Lord shall preserve thy going out and thy coming in from this time forth, and even for evermore" (Psalm 121:1-2 and 5-7).

Whenever you feel sad and alone, remember God is always watching over you. If you let Him, He will keep His hand on you and guide you through life. He will give you strength, and He won't let you stumble and fall. No matter what, and no matter where you are, God will always be by your side protecting you from all harm. All you have to do is ask Him!

Lisa McGregor

28 GOD DOES ANSWER PRAYER

"But seek ye first the kingdom of God, and his righteousness; and all these things shall be added unto you" (Matthew 6:33)

Ever since high school my chosen life verse has been Matthew 6:33 and I believe with all my heart that if you seek to put the Lord in first place in your life, He will take care of putting into order all the rest of the details.

Of course, in order to strengthen my faith, there have been times of great testing. Several years ago our youngest daughter went through some struggles that took her away from us for 16 months. There was a time when we had no idea where she was, and my heart was just simply broken. Our family has always been so close that I could not believe that this was happening to us. I thought that surely if I could just see her and talk to her, she would come to her senses and realize how very much we loved her. However, my husband kept explaining to me that she needed time to realize that she wanted that love more than her freedom to choose, and I knew I must wait! Oh, what agony that was for me! There were moments when I felt that it would be easier for me to know that she was in Heaven than to think of the possibility that she was out there someplace living in sin and serving the Devil. Oh, what pain!

Since my laundry room was on the roof of my house, I spent hours up there both day and night. Looking into the heavens and crying out to my Lord in brokenness and in faith, realizing that He could see me and also see her, even though I did not know where she was. As I prayed for her day by day during those seemingly endless months, I knew with all my heart that God was the only One Who could actually reach her heart. I finally realized that even if I could see her, we would only be able to have a surface-based conversation. As I prayed for her to an omnipotent, omnipresent God, I began to understand that He could talk inside her heart and bring her to Him without my help at all. I am thrilled to say He did!

He further emphasized that lesson to me when she finally called to say that she was coming home on Thanksgiving! The call came completely out of the blue. It was God-sent! After she came home, we talked for many hours. But her struggles were not over. It took her leaving again before she got her heart right with God.

What mixed emotions I felt! My human heart wanted to believe that as her mother, our love and relationship could be won over this evil world in her life. God told me that only my faith in Him could overcome this world. As He says in I John 5:4-5, "For whatsoever is born of God overcometh the world: and this is the victory that overcometh the world, even our faith. Who is he that overcometh the world, but he that believeth that Jesus is the Son of God?"

That faith is not only for our salvation from sin, death, and Hell, but it also is for every day of our lives to believe His Word and to live by it. In I John 5:14-15, He says, "And this is the confidence that we have in him, that, if we ask any thing according to his will, he heareth us: And if we know that he hear us, whatsoever we ask, we know that we have the petitions that we desired of him."

I knew then, and know now, that it is God's will that my daughter should love Him and serve Him. So, I could pray for that with all confidence. My growth came in actually seeing Him work in her heart and live hundreds of miles away without my presence or influence. You see, He is faithful to keep His Word. We just have to believe it enough to practice it with all our hearts! Then we will begin to see prayers answered!

Lori Brown
Missionary to Mexico

29 SUSIE ANN MCGREENE

"And the lord said unto the servants, Go out into the highways and hedges and compel them to come in, that my house may be filled" (Luke 14:23)

This is a story of "ifs" and "what woulds"
A story of a time machine
This is a story of a little girl
Named Susie Ann McGreene.

Susie Ann's parents did not go to church
And neither did she.
So one day I wondered if
She'd like to accompany me.

I called Susie Ann's house
And her daddy picked up the phone.
"No." he said. "Don't call again
And leave us alone."

So I didn't bother Susie Ann
Or her daddy anymore.
We grew apart
And the world Susie Ann began to adore.

One night in the gleaming headlines
Of our six o'clock news,
Susie Ann's name flashed beside
The type of drug she did abuse.

And as the reporter signed off,
He questioned the "ifs" and "what woulds."
As I began questioning my past
And wondering about the "coulds."

So I took some plans of a time machine.
In full pursuit of correcting the wrong
I went back to my telephone call
To do what I should have done all along.

The day after my conversation with Mr. McGreene
I talked to Susie Ann.
"You could spend the night," I told her.
"Okay," she said. "I'll see if I can."

On my trip back in time
Susie Ann came to church with me.
And the six o'clock news had no broadcast
For Susie Ann got saved, you see.

When Susie Ann went home,
She and her daddy had a long talk.
As she told him of her plans with God,
Susie Ann's daddy prayed and began his own walk.

Now, we all can't correct our mistakes
By going back with a time machine.
So never give up on those people
Like the daddy of Susie Ann McGreene.

Dear Lord, help me to not get discouraged and lose hope when I witness. Help me keep my faith strong and true.

Sandy Smith

30 I Was Not Alone

"The Lord is my light and my salvation; whom shall I fear? the Lord is the strength of my life; of whom shall I be afraid?" (Psalm 27:1).

One afternoon I was home alone. A television show came on that scared me so badly that I turned it off, but that was not enough. I had not been a Christian very long, but I knew God would help me. I had no idea where to turn in my Bible for comfort. I prayed holding my Bible tightly and asked God to show me where to read. I opened my Bible to Psalm 27. As I began to read, "The Lord is my light and my salvation; whom shall I fear? the Lord is the strength hold of my life; of whom shall I be afraid?"

I felt the peace of God surround me. My fear was gone and was replaced with love, comfort, and joy. Psalm 27:1 was my very first memory verse. It still comforts me each time I say it.

Anita Blunier

1 God Provides

"Give, and it shall be given unto you; good measure, pressed down, and shaken together, and running over, shall men give into your bosom. For with the same measure that ye mete withal it shall be measured unto you again" (Luke 6:38).

God provides in mysterious ways. This is something that my husband and I experienced personally while on a trip to visit relatives for Christmas. With another 200 miles to go, our car broke down. My husband realized the problem, but needed to purchase a part to fix it. Being in pre-cell phone days, we had to wait for providential help. After a short wait, along came three men who had already begun their holiday "celebrating." My husband accepted, with some apprehension, a ride with them to the nearest exit with a promise from them to return him with the much-needed car part.

When they reached the next exit, they found a garage with just the part we needed. Before returning my husband to our car on the side of the highway, the "celebrating" men decided to stop at a store and buy their wives presents with their Christmas bonuses. They asked my husband if he had already purchased a Christmas gift for his wife. My husband explained that our gift to each other was to visit family for Christmas. Money was tight for us at the time.

They returned him nearly two hours later to a waiting wife who wondered if her husband was dead or alive! The men waited in the warmth of their car while my husband repaired our car. They would not leave us until our car was running and on the road again. After my husband completed the repairs, he went to their car to thank them and offered them what little money he had for helping us out. The men refused to accept his money and gave my husband a $20 bill with the orders to buy his wife a Christmas present!

This is one of my husband's favorite stories, which he calls "The Drunk Samaritans," to share with others how God provides for our needs. Many times, God has answered our prayers in uncomprehending ways. This could be one of His ways to show us that He is the One who meets our needs and not by mere chance!

Dear Lord, help me to be thankful for all the needs You have provided for me and my family. Forgive me when I lack the faith in times of need and when I don't acknowledge all the times You have intervened and provided.

Denise Phillips

2 MOMMA, YOU CAN HAVE DADDY

"The heart of her husband doth safely trust in her, so that he shall have no need of spoil" (Proverbs 31:11).

My daddy built houses; that was his occupation. Many times when he was working on a large subdivision, he would have to work on Saturdays. Because the weather was so unbearably hot, he would get up in the wee hours of the morning, and it might be a few days in a row when I would barely see him.

I was always a daddy's girl, and I had dreams of growing up and marrying him. But on one particular Saturday, I gave up that dream. My momma asked me if I would like to go with her to take daddy his lunch. I jumped at the chance to go see my daddy at work. It was a great trip, just Momma and I going to see our man! As we arrived at the job site, Daddy came up to the car with a big smile on his face, so happy to see us. I remember just watching them talk as Momma handed Daddy his lunch. I will never forget the look on both of their faces as they talked.

We sat in the car as Daddy walked back to the job site. My momma just sat there looking at him. In a few moments, she said, "Isn't that the best looking man you have ever seen?" I just smiled and nodded my head. I decided then and there that I was not going to marry Daddy. I was going to let momma have him, because she loved him so much.

My parents celebrated 50 years of marriage September 18, 1999, and I praise the Lord for their example of the joy of being in love with each other. Dear God, may I be an example of Your love in all that I do as a wife, mother, grandmother, and member of Decatur Baptist Church.

Katy Ripley

3 HARD QUESTIONS

"...she came to prove him with hard questions" (I Kings 10:1).

I Kings 10:1-13 has been such a blessing to me and must be of utmost importance to the Lord, because it is repeated in II Chronicles 9:1-12. In this passage, the queen of Sheba is speaking to King Solomon, and I have personalized the story by placing my name in the place of the queen, while Solomon is a type of the Lord Jesus Christ (Matthew 12:42).

In I Kings 10:1, the queen's difficult questions are not spelled out for us, but we do know that she was not seeking material things, as she came with a very great train of spices, gold, and precious stones. The passage tells us that she first "communed with him of all that was in her heart." She didn't hide anything from King Solomon, just as we can't hide anything from Jesus, the King of kings. He knows everything about us, as is so beautifully expressed in Psalm 139:1-3 "O, Lord, thou hast searched me and known me. Thou knowest my downsitting and mine uprising, thou understandest my thought afar off. Thou compassest my path and my lying down, and art acquainted with all my ways." God knows my heart's attitude, my doubts, my questions, my discontentment, and my pain.

When the queen honestly poured out her heart before King Solomon, in verse 3 "...Solomon told her all her questions: there was not any thing hid from the king..." That means she had no more doubts, self-will, rebellion, bad attitude, and bitterness, and then she proclaimed, "Howbeit I believed not?" Because she honestly communed with the king all that was in her heart, her "hard questions" were answered, she was emptied of her self-spirit, and filled with God's Spirit of truth. And then she begins to bless the Lord and give out of a selfless heart.

The end result of her time with the king is found in verse 13, "And king Solomon gave unto the queen of Sheba all her desire, whatsoever she asked, beside that which Solomon gave her of his royal bounty..." God promises us that if we delight ourselves in the Lord, He will give us the desires of our heart (Psalm 37:4). They will be godly desires, because we have come honestly before the Lord, proved Him with our hard questions, communed with Him all that is in our hearts, and listened as He told us the truth.

What hard question do you need to prove the Lord with today? A difficult marriage? A rebellious child? Single motherhood? Widowhood? Loneliness? Rejection? Unforgiveness? Sickness? Depression? Fear? Whatever it is, all You need to say is "Lord, I've come to You with a hard question. Help Thou my unbelief!"

Elaine Rogers
Missionary to Mexico

4 WINGS OF HEAVEN

"Thou wilt shew me the path of life: in thy presence is fulness of joy; at thy right hand there are pleasures for evermore" (Psalm 16:11).

No one can understand the pain of a miscarriage except a woman who has had one, especially a woman who has no children other than the one she has just lost. My miscarriage came at a time when my culture stress was at its height. I couldn't seem to learn the language, and our country was in a civil war consumed with gunfire and exploding bombs. Then a little baby was conceived, and the several months of joyful expectancy turned to grief when my baby inside me died. The doctors chided my pain. My treasured friend, Carrie Marshall, gave me a gift of song called "Wings of Heaven." Here is the text:

"Little one so dearly loved, yet known from just our hearts
Our wounded souls we offer Him alone
To the Giver of all life and breath, Father of light and love,
The Sovereign Lord sees fit to take you home.

Now you can sing with the angels, walk with the Lord
Soar upon the wings of Heaven — praising evermore
Now you will know more deeply the love and endless grace
You are basking in the presence of our Jesus face to face.

From where we stand our vision's blurred
In vain we try to seek the purpose of our God on this cruel earth
But in our weakness He is strong, our faith is not undone.
Through our tears He shines a hope rebirthed.

Because you sing with the angels, walk with the Lord
Soar upon the wings of Heaven — praising evermore
Now you will know more deeply the love and endless grace
You are basking in the presence of our Jesus face to face.

And though we long to hold you and love you in this world
We know that you are resting in His arms.
Soon we'll join the chorus of heavenly anthems raised
Side by side with you our Lord we'll praise!

And we will sing with the angels, walk with our Lord
Soar upon the wings of Heaven — praising evermore
And we will know more deeply the love and endless grace
We will bask in the presence of our Jesus face to face."

Kristi Hosaflook
Missionary to Albania

5 MEMORIES

"Finally, brethren...whatsoever things are pure, whatsoever things are lovely, whatsoever things are of good report...think on these things" (Philippians 4:8).

All of us have vivid memories, good and bad, that have become a part of who we really are. Some bring a smile and a warm feeling to our very being, while others may be so painful that we can hardly bear the sharp ache in our hearts. While none of us can totally shut out from our memories the sting of harsh treatment, the death of a loved one, the pain of a wayward child, or any other past hurt, God's Word gives us the clue to overcoming the overwhelming hurts that such memories can evoke.

The Apostle Paul tells us in Philippians 4:8, "Finally, brethren...whatsoever things are pure, whatsoever things are lovely, whatsoever things are of good report...think on these things." He goes on to tell us in verse 13 of the same chapter, "I can do all things through Christ which strengtheneth me." Can any of us deny that Paul could have taken the self-defeating role by becoming bitter and harboring resentment for the injustices done to him? He had learned how to have victory in Jesus.

Since we know that no two things can occupy the same spot at the same time, we must think on the "pure," the "lovely," and things of "good report" in order to have victory over the unpleasant memories that eat away at the foundation of our trust and faith in the Lord. We must not succumb to the devices of Satan that would rob us of joy in our Christian walk.

While it may seem an impossible task – making the decision to take that first step of filling our hearts with good memories and giving the unpleasant, hurtful ones to the only One Who can heal – we are freed to take a second step, then a third with the same tenacity of a baby just learning to walk. It is a conscious decision that our Lord leaves up to us. We can do it, because just as a baby has a parent hovering close by ready to help, so our heavenly Father hovers over us gathering us under His wings of love. Give Him your hurts and replace those with pure and lovely memories.

Memories

There is a tiny secret room
With treasures all in store,
And I alone possess the key
That opens up its door.

Sometimes in quiet moments
I slip away to see
And open up its passage with
My solitary key.

A happy child is laughing,
A tiny one has tears.
And lovingly a soothing voice
Calms hearts with unknown fears.

Two lovers share a sunset
That turns from red to gold,
And leaves are drifting slowly
In winter's icy cold.

A drop of dew is sparkling
In early morning light.
A ruby-throat is sipping
Before he takes his flight.

A symphony is playing,
The notes are long and low.
A rainbow arches upward
And paints the sky just so.

The boughs of trees are sighing
Beneath their weight of snow.
A waterfall is dashing
Upon the rocks below.

How could so many treasures

Be stored where no one sees?
My heart's the tiny secret room
The treasures, memories.

Anita Williams

6 Wait On The Lord

"Wait on the Lord: be of good courage, and he shall strengthen thine heart: wait, I say, on the Lord" (Psalm 27:14).

For many years on the mission field, the Lord has shown me that His time is not our time. I do remember thinking as I prayed for days and weeks that He would never answer my prayers. But our Lord has always shown me that by grace and mercy, I will never have a battle that He cannot see me through.

My mind goes back to when my children were small and growing up on the field. They didn't understand why they had so much persecution. What do you do when your child has his arm broken because his father is a preacher? What do you do when no school wants to admit them because they are Baptist and not Catholic? I remember praying to our Lord for strength and courage to be able to answer my children's questions. Some of the most difficult times for them were around Christmas, when they would ask if Santa would remember that they were in Argentina and fly their presents to them. As a parent, I would get desperate and worried, but as a Christian, the words of King David in Psalm 27:14 came to my mind: "Wait on the Lord: be of good courage, and he shall strengthen thine heart: wait, I say, on the Lord."

At that time the Lord used this verse to comfort my heart and give peace to my soul. Then one week before Christmas, we received a package from one of our supporting churches. It was as if they had read the Christmas list that my children had made. There was a toy car, a ball, and clothes for little Rocky. For Patricia, there was a baby doll with a bottle, crayons, and coloring books, as well as clothes. But the item that they enjoyed the most was Kool-Aid. My children really missed Kool-Aid, and they didn't want to drink all of it at once. We took a packet each day and set it on the table to make for dinner. They were so happy just looking at the colorful packages, and eventually they drank it all.

One of the precious memories I will always remember is how the Lord used people so far away to be my family's Santa Claus. Remember that I said our time is not the Lord's time? The secret is to wait upon the Lord and have faith. Like the old preacher used to say, "He is never a day late or a dollar short." By the way, do you want to know what church it was? Yes, it was Decatur Baptist Church that played Santa for that Christmas, but not only that one, as there were many more to come. May the Lord richly bless you for it.

Marta Bustos
Missionary to Argentina

7 Hurt Feelings Vs. Offenses

"Great peace have they which love thy law: and nothing shall offend them" (Psalm 119:165).

When I was a little girl, I wore my feelings on my sleeve, as my mother would say. Consequently, they were always getting hurt. You could look at me wrong, and I would be wounded. Of course, as I grew into adulthood, it did not get any better and it seemed I was continually nursing hurt feelings or an offense of some kind. Once I passed 40 years old, however, I realized that it was time to get a grip.

God's Word says in Matthew 5:45 that it rains on the just and the unjust. We will not go through life without hurts, whether they be physical or emotional ones. But we choose whether to let the hurts become an offense or not.

When I allow hurt feelings to become an offense, I have made it a stumblingblock in my life that will keep me from being all I can be for the Lord. People change ministries, Bible study care groups, or even churches, because they allow their hurts to become offenses. Instead of allowing these to become stepping stones that make us stronger and draw us closer to God, we use them as excuses to quit. We can be at peace during these hurtful times and keep them in the right perspective if we love God's Word.

Sharon Collier

8 BITTERNESS: ROADBLOCK TO JOY

"Finally, be ye all of one mind, having compassion one of another, love as brethren, be pitiful, be courteous: Not rendering evil for evil, or railing for railing: but contrariwise blessing; knowing that ye are thereunto called, that ye should inherit a blessing" (I Peter 3:8-9).

You don't have to go very far in life to experience the sting of betrayal from someone you thought was your friend. To experience such things in childhood, perhaps on the playground at school, amounts to valuable lessons to be learned about relationships. The sting soon goes away, and children are better for the lessons they have learned.

When we are betrayed as adults, the wounds are much deeper, and healing tends to be more complicated. We may blame ourselves for being gullible, or perhaps we may even blame God for not protecting us from the betrayal that He must have seen coming. We know a physical wound can heal on the surface and yet be festering underneath with infection. Bitterness over betrayal and disloyalty can be much like that hidden infection.

Bitterness is more devastating than betrayal. Betrayal is external, while bitterness is internal. While betrayal is something that others do to you, bitterness is something you do to yourself. Thousands survive betrayal easily. Very few can survive the currents of bitterness. Hebrews 12:15 says, "Looking diligently lest any man fail of the grace of God; lest any root of bitterness springing up trouble you, and thereby many be defiled."

Disloyalty is a product of an unthankful heart. Betrayal is usually the child of jealousy. Everybody has experienced tragic situations in their lives: a co-worker or an employee slanders you behind your back, a boss fires you without explanation, someone you confided in reveals your secrets. These things hurt deeply.

Jesus knew who would betray Him. Mark 14:18 says, "And as they sat and did eat, Jesus said, Verily I say unto you, one of you which eateth with me shall betray me." Jesus knew He would be betrayed, yet he saw something more important than the hurt and wounds of betrayal. Someone once said, "Injustice is only as powerful as the memory of it." Read Mark 14:43-50, and you will see the most demoralizing experience. Although Judas betrayed Jesus with a kiss, Jesus refused to be bitter. He did not penalize Judas, but Judas destroyed himself. Jesus did not disconnect from Peter who denied Him. When Peter cried out for mercy and forgiveness, he was restored and became the greatest preacher on the Day of Pentecost.

"Let all bitterness, and wrath, and anger and clamour, and evil speaking, be put away from you, with all malice: And be ye kind one to another, tenderhearted, forgiving one another, even as God for Christ's sake hath forgiven you" (Ephesians 4:31-32).

Eliminate any words of bitterness in every conversation. Do not remind others of your experience unless it is to teach and encourage them to rise above their own hurts. Jesus saw the chapter beyond betrayal. He refused to be bitter.

We must pray that the Lord would remove bitterness from our heart, and must guard against bitterrness in the future. Finally, we should remember that when we are betrayed or judged unjustly, we should look past the hurt and see that bitterness is only a roadblock to our relationship with the Lord and to a happy life.

Sharon Butts

9 Chosen By God

"Thy word have I hid in my heart, that I might not sin against thee" (Psalm 119:11).

While I was teaching a fourth-grade girls Sunday School class, we studied the birth of Jesus. In Luke 1, the angel Gabriel appeared to Mary, a young Jewish virgin. He said, "Hail, thou that art highly favoured, the Lord is with thee: blessed art thou among women" (Luke 1:28). God had chosen her to give birth to His Son. Imagine that! Chosen by God!

During the lesson, I asked the class, "Which of you girls would God choose to do something so great?" They all spoke up in a chorus: "Courtney!" I asked, "Why Courtney?" They answered, "She's polite and respectful. She comes to class prepared, with her lesson studied and her Bible verses memorized." It seems they all knew the qualities that please God.

Dear Lord, help me to hide your Word in my heart, so I will be prepared when You choose me for Your work.

Jalena Holmes

10 The Good Part

"And Jesus answered and said unto her, Martha, Martha, thou art careful and troubled about many things: But one thing is needful: and Mary hath chosen that good part, which shall not be taken away from her" (Luke 10:41-42).

My mother, a widow with great faith in God, was diagnosed with advanced lung cancer, even though she was a non-smoker. On top of that, she had moderate Alzheimer's disease. She really needed me. I found myself having to make medical decisions, run two households, and maintain a lot of responsibilities. It seemed every situation was always urgent. Like Martha, I felt as if I was doing everything. I began to grow impatient and resentful and even began neglecting my prayer and Bible study time.

One night, while caring for my mother, I cried out to my heavenly Father for help. Gently and wisely, He showed me I needed to choose "the good part" with the time I had left with my precious mother. From then on, I read God's Word to my mother every day, we prayed together, and I sang her favorite hymns. Other family members joined in as her final days came.

When the time came for my mother to go home to Heaven, we both had been sitting at Jesus' feet together. She breathed her last breath, and my mother was in Glory! Remember to choose and do "the good part" in your life. Focus on the things that really matter the most — the things that count for eternity.

Julia Hill, wife of Jim Hill
Pastor of Pinson Baptist Church
Pinson, Alabama

11 A BIRTHDAY MESSAGE

"He that dwelleth in the secret place of the most High shall abide under the shadow of the Almighty" (Psalm 91:1).

Weeks before my birthday, I always make it a point to ask for a birthday gift from God. His answers are spiritual or material. One year on my birthday, I had my early-morning devotion, and the Lord gave me Psalm 91, which talks about His protection. I had been working full time in a church-school, and the pastor allowed me to stay in the rented house that served as the church and the school. Since I am single, it was easy for me to stay.

About a month later, I experienced the verses that God gave me on my birthday. As I was sleeping about 3 a.m., I was awakened by a light outside my door. I was concerned, because I knew I had turned out the lights when I went to bed. My first reaction was to get out of bed right away, but I could not lift my hands or my feet. I felt as if I was being held.

A few minutes later, I saw a human hand trying to get inside through the small window over the door to my room. At that moment, I felt released, and I jumped out of bed and shouted and stomped my feet. Outside the room I heard a thump and feet running down the stairs. When I opened the door to my room, I saw the outside door to the building open, and the classrooms were trashed. All of the electric fans were gone, along with money that was kept inside the tables.

What if the thieves had been able to get inside my room and harm me or kill me? God's hand of protection was there with His angels.

Thelma A. Obid
Missionary to Cambodia

12 WHOSE ROBE ARE YOU WEARING?

"But put ye on the Lord Jesus Christ, and make no provision for the flesh, to fulfil the lusts thereof" (Romans 13:14).

In one of my precepts Bible study classes, we did a wonderful study on "covenant." One of our homework assignments was to write a prayer or poem about what we had learned that day. We had just read about the covenant between Jonathan and David. When Jonathan gave David his robe, David was symbolically "putting on Jonathan," so the two exchanged identities.

When we receive Christ, we enter into the New Covenant of Grace, merging ourselves into Him and Him into us. We are to put on Christ, taking on His identity and characteristics (Galations 3:26-29, Ephesians 4:17-32). A Pharisee looks good on the outside but is dead on the inside. A hypocrite says one thing but does another. My robe is still in my fleshly ways so as you read this poem, consider whose robe you are wearing.

Each night before I go to sleep, I give myself this test,
It will help me to evaluate just Who I love the best.
Today, when others looked at me, Oh Lord, who did they

really see?
A Pharisee, a hypocrite, You, or only me?
On what and where did I spend my time? Who occupied my thoughts?
Did I seek to do as You would, in the decisions that were brought?
Oh may the answers always be, You, Your work, Your Word, and yes,
So then I may know true joy and peace as I lay my head to rest.

O Father, I fall short so many times. So often I find myself hanging onto that old, nasty, stained robe of mine instead of wearing Your glorious robe of righteousness. Help me to take off the old robe of my life and wear only Yours.

Jennifer Barnett

13 SIMONA PRAYED FOR A DOLL

"And all things, whatsoever ye shall ask in prayer, believing, ye shall receive" (Matthew 21:22).

Little Simona, a three-year-old girl, was brought to a new orphanage in a village in Moldova. The money had been provided, the labor had been spent, and the final government papers had been processed, permitting orphan children to live in this beautiful new facility.

The mama and papa of this orphanage, Marie and John, were so pleased that God had answered their many prayers. They had been praying for children for years and were unable to have them. God had other plans for them. After prayerful consideration, the couple joyfully accepted the challenge of making a home for ten orphans who would live in the facility.

The children were thrilled to have a warm house, tasty food, nice clothes to wear, and best of all, a mama and papa who really cared about them! The rooms soon resounded with boundless energy and laughter from all the orphans except little Simona.

"What's wrong?" asked Mama Marie. "Why are you so sad?" Simona replied, "I want a baby doll to love." Mama Marie said, "Well, we have no such doll, but I know Who can help us. Let's pray to Jesus and ask Him to give you a doll."

Simona did not know who Jesus was, so Mama Marie and Papa John explained to her carefully what they thought she could understand. It did not take long for Simona to be assured that Jesus loved her and wanted to take good care of her. Believing He was able to grant her request for a doll, Simona prayed, "Dear Jesus, please send me a doll. I want to take care of a baby doll. Please, Jesus."

Two days later, a group of nationals who were ministering in Moldova came by the orphanage to visit the children, bringing clothes, candy, and toys. Among the gifts was a beautiful, big baby doll. The nationals did not know about Simona's prayer request. All they knew was that just before they left for the orphanage, a lady said, "Here, take this doll to the orphans."

When the nationals handed out the gifts, one young adult held up the baby doll, spied Simona's face alit with anticipation, and happily declared, "And here's a doll for Simona!" Little Simona grabbed that doll, hugged it close to her, and looked with joy at Mama Marie. Both of them knew immediately that Jesus had heard Simona's prayer! It was the first prayer of many prayers that Simona will pray over a lifetime, and yet she knows this is one prayer she will never forget!

Loreen Ittermann
Missionary to Moldova

14 GIVING UP CONTROL

"He that is of a proud heart stirreth up strife: but he that putteth his trust in the Lord shall be made fat. He that trusted in his own heart is a fool: but whoso walketh wisely, he shall be delivered" (Proverbs 28:25-26).

When Ron and I were married, he had a son that came to live with us. For many, many years, I tried my very best to make everyone happy. I tried to control everything my own way, and in doing so, I made myself miserable, because it was beyond my abilities to do what I was trying to do. Then one day, it dawned on me that only God could do what I had been trying for years to do on my own. So I simply prayed to God to take this burden from me and told him that I truly trusted Him to do a much better job in trying to make everyone happy than I had done. When I turned control of the situation over to God, I felt a tremendous burden had been removed from my shoulders.

It was almost Christmas, and I was hoping that we could spend some time with Ron's son and his family during the holiday season. For various reasons, we had not been able to spend time with Ron's son for the past three Christmases, as we had done in years past. When I got out of the way, God took control and within a week or so, Ron's son called and asked if they could spend Christmas with us. He explained that he and his entire family had really missed the joy we had experienced in previous years. Of course, our answer was yes, and Ron and I began to prepare for their visit. We were so excited that we acted like two little kids getting ready for Santa Claus to come. Ron's son and his family came, and we all had the very best holiday season that we have ever had. When I finally let go and turned it all over to God, He provided abundantly as He always does.

Darleen Hill

15 STAND STILL

"Be still, and know that I am God" (Psalm 46:10).

I was saved when I was 12 years old, and over the past 52 years, Psalm 46:10 has always spoken to my heart. Whether I am confessing my sins, fighting a spiritual battle, or seeking guidance, I know that it is important to be still so I can hear God's voice.

When I fail God as I have so many times, I go to I John 1:9, which says, "If we confess our sins, he is faithful and just to forgive us our sins, and to cleanse us from all unrighteousness." I have encouraged so many people over the years to confess their sin as soon as they sin and not wait for Satan to do a work in their life. I am not saying that I have followed this plan every time I have sinned, but I can tell you when I have failed to do that, I have suffered.

I have faced many battles over the years, and in those time I draw strength from II Chronicles 20:17, "Ye shall not need to fight in this battle: set yourselves, stand ye still, and see the salvation of the Lord with you, O Judah and Jerusalem: fear not, nor be dismayed; tomorrow go out against them: for the Lord will be with you." The Lord has proven Himself faithful in every battle I have faced in my life.

I pray that I can be silent and listen to God speak to me in every area of my life, whether there is sorrow or happiness surrounding me. I want to continue to believe that nothing can touch me unless God has put His approval on it. My desire is to be used of God and to be fruitful in all that I do.

Shirley White Teal

16 STARS AND BLESSINGS

"A faithful man shall abound with blessings..." (Proverbs 28:20).

I was standing outside looking for a star
When all the clouds were blocking all the light from afar.
Then I noticed a single light trying its best to shine
Through all the clouds, serving as a sign.

But as my eyes accustomed to that one light,
All the other stars that were there were not extremely bright.
Yet as my sight wandered from that one source,
The other stars grew in strength, and my eyes followed that course.

I was standing outside looking for hope
When all the obstacles in life were causing me to mope.
Then I noticed a single blessing trying its best to shine
Through all of life's tribulations, serving as a sign.

But as I concentrated on just that one,
I could not see the other miracles that God had done.
Yet as my sight widened from little to large,
I began to realize just how really blessed we actually are.

Sandy Smith

17 LOVE

"For God so loved the world, that he gave his only begotten Son, that whosoever believeth in him should not perish, but have everlasting life" (John 3:16).

This was the first Bible verse I memorized as a child, and it has always been my favorite. To think of that kind of love is mind-boggling. We think we know what it is to love someone or something, but do we really? God does!

He knew what we were going to be and do before we ever were, but still He loved us enough to let us be. Think about it, if we knew what our sons and daughters were going to be and do, would we have the kind of love necessary to have them in the first place? Knowing the future might make it a hard decision for us, but not for our heavenly Father.

Could I love enough to give my only son to die for someone else? I'm sure I could not. That kind of love does not exist on earth. We would like to think we could do it, but we could not. Could we give our own lives to die for someone else? Maybe for our spouses, children, or other close family members and friends, but could we do it for strangers? Only God knows the true answer to that question. We would like to think we could, but when it comes right down to it, could we?

God shows his love for me every day. He started showing me when Jesus was born, when He died at Calvary, when He rose from the grave, and when He ascended to Heaven. God never stops showing it, even when I fail Him.

Do I love Him as much as He loves me? I don't know how. I love Him as much as I can within the bounds of this earthly life, but my love is not measureless, like His. All I can do is love Him with my whole heart and serve Him with my whole life.

Next time you read or recite John 3:16, stop and consider what the words really mean. We think we know what it is to love, but we don't. Only God did and does and always will. Maybe when I am ruling with Him in Heaven I will finally know and understand that kind of love.

Cathy Johnson

18 WHY? SO GOD CAN BE GLORIFIED!

"Jesus answered, Neither hath this man sinned, nor his parents; but that the works of God should be made manifest in him" (John 9:3).

When my daughter, Olivia, was first diagnosed with a rare disease, we were very confused, scared, and could not help but ask, "Why?" We got home from a week long stay in Memphis, Tennessee, where we had tried to get a correct diagnosis. We were exhausted but glad to be home.

Within the next few weeks, everything seemed to go wrong. Our air conditioning unit went out at home, costing us more than $3,000 in repair bills. A spring broke in our garage door, and it also had to be repaired, along with two tires on one of our vehicles. It got to where we just laughed, which was better than crying all the time.

We could not understand why this was happening to us. We were in church faithfully serving in ministry, and we were tithing. We were doing what God wanted us to do to the best of our knowledge. We searched our hearts and knew of no sin in our lives, so we knew these things were not happening as a form of chastisement. So why were they happening? Why would God allow this?

When Brother Lowell Holmes came to repair our air conditioner, I shared our situation. He said, "You know, this reminds me of a story in Bible about a boy who was born blind. Everyone wanted to know who sinned – him or his parents. Jesus said neither. The boy was blind so that He would be glorified."

I really didn't know how our situation would glorify God, but I clung to that story. I have been able to help others who are hurting and who have to deal with a sick child. I have been able to share my testimony and what God has taught me through the past seven years. Now I know how God is being glorified and I pray I will have the heart to continue glorifying Him. He has seen us through thus far, and I know He will continue to watch over our family.

Pam Williams

19 EACH DAY

"But the fruit of the Spirit is love, joy, peace, longsuffering, gentleness, goodness, faith, meekness, temperance: against such there is no law" (Galations 5:22-23).

I use a devotion from Max Lucado's book, *WHEN GOD WHISPERS YOUR NAME*, as a prayer for each day. The devotion talks about choosing to live the fruit of the Spirit: love, joy, peace, patience, kindness, faithfulness, gentleness, humility, and self-control.

I pray that each day, I will reject bitterness, refuse the temptation to be cynical, forgive others, overlook the world's inconveniences, keep my promises, put demands only on myself, and be influenced only by God.

I succeed in some areas, but I have never succeeded in all areas. I seek God's grace continually throughout each and every day.

Linda Collins

20 THE OVERFLOWING JAR

"And the things that thou hast heard of me among many witnesses, the same commit thou to faithful men, who shall be able to teach others also" (II Timothy 2:2).

On December 20, 1992, God touched my heart and gave me a saving knowledge of Jesus Christ. As I gave my life over to Him, my heart began to thaw, like Ezekiel 11:19 says, "...and I will put a new spirit within you; and I will take the stony heart out of their flesh, and will give them an heart of flesh."

Immediately, I received a thirst and hunger for righteousness that could only be satisfied within the Word of God. On January 1, 1993, I began to read the Bible in Genesis and continued to Revelation, finishing in September.

As I grew in Bible study, my love and devotion to the Lord did, too. I began dating everything that I was reading.

This has provided an excellent historical record. The next year, I started in Genesis with the goal of reading through the Bible again. The Lord pressed upon my heart to look at the dates recorded in my Bible. Joy and excitement came over my soul as I realized that I had read God's Word through every year since my salvation. God has enabled me to completely read His Word through each year for the past ten years.

With the study and insights that God has given through the Holy Spirit, His Word has been revealed in many areas. He has shown me that I am to give to others what He has given to me. As a pint jar is filled to the brim, there is no room for more. But I've discovered that in pouring out my jar — or heart — to others, it leaves room for God to give me more.

Dear Lord, pour out through me what You will not give to me.

Jane Whitt

21 LIFE IN ZAMBIA

"I thank my God always on your behalf, for the grace of God which is given you by Jesus Christ; That in every thing ye are enriched by him, in all utterance, and in all knowledge" (I Corinthians 1:4-5).

I have often wished I could adequately explain the interesting experiences we have had while serving God in Africa. I have longed to be able to share with our supporters the fruits of their many prayers and help them to glimpse life here.

Here are a few memories from our seventh Christmas season in Zambia:

"You are the first people to give me this book of life," said a chief in the Eastern Province upon receiving his first Bible. This was music to our ears, of course.

My new Bible study in the village reaped great results in Bible memorization and interest in learning. The new converts were eager to learn and loved the bar of soap and small bag of sugar that I offered as incentives. Some of them brought their children and had them quote the verses as well. More stuff for the family, that way!

Food distribution was a regular part of my husband's work. It was a blessing for Bob and me to be able to give each of our churches plenty of food for a large Christmas service. Many reported visitors were saved and filled their hungry stomachs.

We saw a youth choir perform for the first time in one of our bush churches. It was a blessing to see such a cultural change. Most children are not welcome in churches, so our emphasis on giving priority to the next generation is finally starting to take hold. We were all thrilled to hear them sing under the pastor's wife's leadership.

I wish I could share more about our life in Zambia, but I hope I have offered enough of a glimpse so our supporters will know how to pray for us. You dear folks have been so faithful to this ministry — how we thank God for each of you!

Jody Hayton
Missionary to Zambia

22 THE GIFT OF JESUS

"For by grace are ye saved through faith and that not of yourselves: it is the gift of God. Not of works, lest any man should boast" (Ephesians 2:8-9).

One year on the Sunday before Christmas, we were rushing around trying to get dressed for church. The candy canes on the table caught my eye. I had recently heard the story about the candy cane — how its maker wanted to share Jesus with the world. He made a stick of candy in the shape of a "J" to represent Jesus. He then added the red stripes to represent the blood Jesus shed for us.

As I stared at the candy canes, I noticed some were laying

as the candy maker intended – simple "Js" with red stripes. Others were multi-colored, offering an appealing look and taste. I then began to feel extremely heavy-hearted. The world has done to salvation what the candy cane companies have done to the candy maker's "J." The world has added things God never intended to add to His simple salvation message, such as baptism, giving money, and church attendance.

The only way to Heaven is God's way. Anything the world adds taints God's way. God's salvation requires forgiveness by grace through faith. We just need to ask for that forgiveness in order to receive the gift of Jesus.

Bridgett Hayes

23 TEACHING CHILDREN ABOUT CHRISTMAS

"...Suffer the little children to come unto me, and forbid them not: for of such is the kingdom of God" (Mark 10:14).

When we had grandchildren, we started the tradition of having a birthday cake on Christmas Eve and singing "Happy Birthday, Jesus." This put the emphasis of the holiday on Jesus.

Since Christmas has become such a commercial holiday, it is easy for people, especially children, to get caught up in the joy of gifts and decorations. Many times, we overlook the true meaning of the holiday, which is when God sent His Son to save the world.

So when you are planning your Christmas celebration this year, don't forget Jesus, and be sure that your children don't forget Him either. God wants the adoration of all of His children, especially the littlest ones, and there is no better time to thank Him than during this special season.

Ruth Beatty

24 MARY

"And the angel said unto her, Fear not, Mary: for thou hast found favour with God" (Luke 1:30).

Have you ever thought of Mary,
The mother of the perfect child?
He, a child who did no wrong,
Whose heart was always filled with song;
He was that sinless being
And she, a mortal one,
With only flaws within her life
To guide the son of God.
She must have been some puzzled
To why God would send a child —
The Christ child — in her home to live.
He knew all. He needed no one
To show Him the way,
Or scold Him when He failed
For fail He never did.
Then God bent down from Heaven above,
And whispered in her ear,
"Mary, He needs not one to show
Him the way, neither one to scold or nag
'Till His heart has no more song.
I gave you my Son for I knew you were the one
Who would love Him to the depths of your soul
For that is what mothers are for.

Margaret Hoskins Dellinger

25 I CHOOSE YOU

"And the angel came in unto her, and said, Hail, thou that art highly favoured, the Lord is with thee: blessed art thou among women" (Luke 1:28).

Christian singer Rachael Lampa recently recorded a song about Mary, the mother of Jesus, called "I Choose You." The chorus of this song says, "I choose you to bring the world a Savior..." Can you imagine how overwhelmed Mary must have been as the angel Gabriel delivered this awesome message from God of how He would save the world? We all know this account from Luke 1:26-56 very well. But why would God choose Mary to play such an integral part in His plan of redemption for mankind?

What an honoring yet humbling experience it would be to hear God's angel say to you that you have found favor with God! Wow! At first, we might think God would never say that to us. But in reflecting upon some of the attributes that God's Word tells us Mary possessed, I believe a nod of approval from our Lord awaits us if we seek to have those same attributes.

The very first thing the Bible says about Mary is that she was a virgin (Isaiah 7:14), symbolizing not only the purity Jesus brought to our lives when He washed our sins away, but also the purity brought by living a clean, holy life before God and man. The next quality mentioned about this young woman was that she was completely surrendered to her Lord. In Luke 1:38 Mary refers to herself as the handmaid of the Lord, which simply means servant. Mary was God's willing servant. Luke 1:45 tells us that faith was another of Mary's attributes. She believed that God would bring to pass something that was humanly impossible. And finally, verses 46-55 reveal that Mary lived a life of worship. She gave God what He wanted: praise from a pure, adoring heart.

What an exciting yet life-changing event this would be for Mary! I'm sure she was thrilled to hear the news that God had chosen her, but she must have been tempted to fear what this could have cost her. How would others respond when they saw that she was pregnant out of wedlock? In her culture, even the world's standards considered that disgraceful. But Mary proved she didn't place value on what the world thought about her. She only sought God's approval. And let's not forget Joseph. There was no indication by the angel that Joseph would be made aware of this. Mary was willing to risk losing the man she loved, knowing that he had every right to call off their espousal when he discovered she was pregnant. Now that's reckless abandon to God!

Do you have that same abandon? Do you want to be a modern-day Mary? Do you long to be "highly favoured" in God's eyes? If you know Jesus as your Savior, you've already found God's favor. But I want to be more than just a casual Christian. I don't want complacency to plague my walk with God. I want to be "highly favored." I know that physically I can't bring the world a Savior, but I am given the privilege of bringing the Savior to a hopeless world that is desperately searching for spiritual healing. Let's relinquish the fear of condemnation from the world or even from those closest to us. God has chosen you, so step out and make a difference for the kingdom of God. You hold the "Light of the world" in your hands – Jesus! Wrap Him up and give Him to someone today!

Suzanne Spiers

26 Being Out Of Love With God

"Go and cry in the ears of Jerusalem, saying, Thus saith the Lord; I remember thee, the kindness of thy youth, the love of thine espousals, when thou wentest after me in the wilderness, in a land that was not sown" (Jeremiah 2:2).

This Scripture touched my heart and helped me in a difficult time. After deserting God and then rededicating my life to Him, my relationship with Jesus did not seem to be the same as before. Every aspect of my walk was different, and

I did not understand why. I had confessed, repented, and received forgiveness for my sins, but my relationship was still different.

In Jeremiah 2:2, the Lord told me that he remembered a time when I was in love with Him and that being away from Him made my love die. This was difficult for me to accept, because I thought I would always love the Lord. But, if I loved Him, I would do the things He asked of me. Over a period of time, the love that I once had became greater and stronger. Thank the Lord for His mercy.

DeShanna Metz

27 MAMA'S MANSION

"In my Father's house are many mansions: if it were not so, I would have told you. I go to prepare a place for you. (John 14:2).

As a child, I always wanted nice things for my mama. Once I talked my stepfather into buying her a fancy robe for Christmas. Mama promptly returned it for something more practical. Life was hard, my stepfather was disabled, and Mama was the main provider for her three children. At one time, she held three jobs. I carried my desires for Mama into adulthood. Once while visiting a nice home, I cried out to God, "It's not fair, God, if Mama had a house like this, everything would shine." Even after my stepfather's death, no prosperous Prince Charming entered Mama's life as I had dreamed. The years passed and Mama even had to work during her retirement years. Her last two years of life were spent in a nursing home, dying of Alzheimer's. What I wished for my mama was not going to happen in this life. But oh how great to know that my hopes and dreams will be a reality once my mama reached heaven. Yes, then golden streets, pearly gates, and a big mansion awaited my Mama!

I heard a story that made me think of my mama and her reception into heaven. There was a missionary who was returning to the United States after serving God for 25 years in Africa. On the same ship was the president of the United States, returning from a three-week hunting expedition. When the ship docked, there was a hullabaloo for the president that included balloons, confetti, choirs, and bands. Meanwhile, there was no one to greet the missionary. He began to complain to God, "Lord, I have served you for 25 years, and there is no one here to even greet me." The Lord spoke to his heart, "But my dear son, you are not home yet."

I believe this was the way it was for Mama. Yet one night the harshness of her life overwhelmed me with sadness. I called a prayer line for encouragement, and my prayer counselor listened to me pour out my heart and then said, "I want to tell you a story." She began telling me the same story about the missionary. God had blessed me with a second witness, giving me the encouragement I needed that my mama was receiving all the grand things in Heaven that God had prepared for her.

Vivecia Coomer, wife of Harold Coomer
Pastor of Austinville Church of God
Decatur, Alabama

28 ESCAPING FROM PAIN

"Give ear to my prayer, O God; and hide not thyself from my supplication" (Psalm 55:1).

If there were moments of deep pain that have touched my life, it was not in the death of brothers and sisters in Christ, but rather in their betrayal. This happened with one of our closest friends, who we had in our home and had discipled. He was like a son to us, but when we found out about his rebellion against the Lord, it caused a disaster for his family and ministry. For years, he had been fooling us. At one time when my husband was traveling in the Ukraine, I was alone to receive this man's wife and three small sons, who were overwhelmed by the situation. Even though I didn't want to, I was compelled to confront the situation.

I was broken, and as I looked to God's Word for strength, He gave me Psalm 55. I was able to understand things from God's point of view and discovered the solution through His Word. I learned that:

Betrayal produces pain.
"My heart is sore pained within me..." (Psalm 55:4).

Betrayal produces fear.
"Fearfulness and trembling are come upon me..." (Psalm 55:5).

Betrayal produces a desire to escape.
"...Oh that I had wings like a dove! for then I would fly away, and be at rest" (Psalm 55:6).

Facing the pain of betrayal requires total dependence upon God.
"Cast thy burden upon the Lord, and he shall sustain thee: he shall never suffer the righteous to be moved" (Psalm 55:22).

Through His Word, God showed me how to help our friend's wife and sons deal with his betrayal. He also showed me how they were feeling, so I could understand their pain. The just do fall due to the weight or burden of sin, but a most common malady is to forget that we have an all-powerful God who can take away that burden. How marvelous it is to have a merciful God who walks with us, lifts us up, takes our burdens, and helps us as we carry the burdens of others.

Griselda Gimenez
Missionary to Argentina

29 FROM GOD TO WOMEN

"And the rib, which the Lord had taken from man, made he a woman, and brought her unto the man" (Genesis 2:22).

I recently read a story entitled "A Letter From God To Women." It talks about how God spoke the heavens and earth into being and created man by forming him and breathing life into his nostrils. But when God created woman, He fashioned from one of man's rib bones, the one that protects his heart and lungs and supports his body. Recall how Adam said, "This is now bone of my bones, and flesh of my flesh." Adam recognized how significant and important Eve was to him.

What a wonderful picture of how we, as women, are to protect and support our husbands! While man represents God's image, we represent His emotions. Together, we represent the totality of God. As the family is a picture of Christ and the church, we want to be consistent to show the world that unique and special unity between husband and bride.

Sharon Kirby

30 PRECIOUS IN HIS SIGHT

"Since thou wast precious in my sight, thou hast been honourable, and I have loved thee..." (Isaiah 43:4).

I've been in church all my life, and have never questioned that God loves me. But the past few years, God has been revealing to me how "precious" I really am to Him. Please know that there is absolutely nothing that I have done to make me worthy, neither do I deserve his affection for me. I'm no different than anyone else. I'm a sinner that's been saved by the grace of God. But it was beyond my understanding that I could be "precious" to Him. I knew the verses about:

God thinking I am more important than the sparrows.

God clothing the lilies of the field so He would certainly take care of my needs.

God creating man and woman in His own image, with a living soul (His greatest creation.)

God giving His only begotten Son to die in my place so that I can spend eternity with Him.

But somehow I always perceived God as my judge. I knew in my head that He loved me, but somehow I felt that He was more concerned about my following all the rules than about being my loving Father.

Finally, one day, it all began to fit together. I knew a holy and perfect God sent His precious and beloved Son, Jesus, to pay for my sin. Why would He do that if I were not also "precious" and beloved? Why He feels this way is beyond my comprehension, but I can honestly tell you that I had never in my life felt the kind of emotions that welled up in me that day. Immediately, I began to better understand how He feels about me. I felt that I was God's little princess, dressed in a beautiful pink gown complete with a pointed hat that has a flowing veil on the tip.

He isn't just my judge. He isn't just my heavenly Father. He is my loving daddy who holds me in His lap, wraps His loving arms around me, and spends time with me. Oh, yes, He loves me, and I'm precious to Him.

I pray that it will not take you years, as it did me, to realize the depth of His love for you. How precious you are to Him! You are dear to His heart. He desires such great things for your life.

Daphana DeKoker

31 The Task That Lasts

"Her children arise up, and call her blessed; her husband also, and he praiseth her" (Proverbs 31:28).

There are many times in the morn, as a mother, I think
I must spend the whole day standing here at the sink;
But somehow, I move on for I've beds I must make
And the floors I must sweep and the rugs I must shake.
You ask, have I a schedule? Oh, yes, there's no doubt
But I've never been able to make it work out.
There are things I'd not planned, but they, oddly, bring joy
Like the kiss of a bruise, the repair of a toy.
In the midst of these duties, the little ones plead
"May I go outside?" So, time out for this deed.

As I put on their garments, I know I won't win
For not ten minutes later, "May I come back in?"
There was also some sewing I wanted to do
Which reminds me how quickly the little ones grew.
And there's washing and ironing and so much to mend
Every week after week – oh, it never will end!
For the truth about all of these everyday tasks
I have found is – not one single one of them lasts!
Then I suddenly think, Ah, but yes, there is one
Of the tasks that I'm doing that can't be redone.
It's the teaching and training of these little lives
You've entrusted to me, Oh, dear Lord, make me wise.
Help me to know how to use these brief years to do best
The one job most important – the task that will last!

Reba Cofield
Missionary to Canada

Index

Kim Abernethy 81
Cheryl Adams 87
Deborah Allen 82
Barbara Allred 32, 144, 234, 281, 337
Tammy Allred 8
Pam Anderson 167
Louise Anglin 127
Nerissa Appleton 96
Patricia Arce 171
Lorrie Austin 85, 284
Peggy Baker 78
Jennifer Barnett 43, 156, 223, 253, 292, 324, 388
Amanda Barnette 124
Erla Bartell 151
Becky Baxter 293
Myra Bazzel 285
Ruth Beatty 399
Cassie Belbey 45, 188
Beth Bennett 297
LaVone Benton 133
Pat Bishop 56
Calista Blankenship 180
Janice Blankenship 145
Anita Blunier 129, 185, 374
Becky Bonner 72
Frances Bonner 35
Sabrina Boshell 122, 258, 325
Sherrie Britton 238
Gloria Brown 271
Lori Brown 111, 237, 370
Marta Bustos 382
Sharon Butts 384
Nora Byrd 44
Xochitl Canada 255
Joy Castro 313
Loretta Clark 22, 341
Jo Clifton 17
Martha Coffey 356

Reba Cofield 233, 407
Sharon Collier 13, 172, 333, 383
Linda Collins 396
Melanie Cook 146, 344
Vivcia Coomer 403
Cyndi Copeland 59
Vickie Copeland 11, 168
Janice Cross 200
Joyce Curbow 308
Cherrio Cyphers 88
Sandi Davenport 288
Anne DeKoker 24, 136, 207, 323
Daphana DeKoker 406
Stacy DeKoker 70
Margaret Hoskins Dellinger 67, 121, 203, 337, 400
Theresa Dickens 105
Tonya Dotson 249
Colleeon Dozier 294
Tricia Dubbe 243
Reba Dutton 42, 177
Mildred Eldridge 267
Debbie Frank 298
Cheryl Freeman 215
Katherine Fretwell 110
Betsy Gates 363
Cheryl Gibson 265
Stephanie Gilliam 224
Terri Gilliam 71, 189, 245
Janet Gilliland 93, 195, 263, 317
Linda Gilmer 307
Griselda Gimenez 276, 404
Jodie Glossick 219, 335
Tammy Gordon 69, 141, 240
Shelley Graham 95
Barb Grenon 100
Cecilia Hagood 126
Tamara Haden 208
Karen Hainline 211
Kellie Halbrooks 147

Alli Hale 247
Joan Hampton 354
Jessica Hancey 180
Sylvia Hancock 103
Donna Haraway 175
Danna Harbin 28, 163
Susan Harney 9, 347
Geri Frances Harris 120
Bridgett Hayes 340, 398
Barbara Hays 186
Jody Hayton 20, 397
Darlene Heath 213
Kimberly Hedden 221, 311
Helen Helms 72, 269
Georgeann Hept 37, 178, 319
Melissa Herring 18
Darleen Hill 245, 391
Julia Hill 386
Tina Hill 109
Annita Hoagland 22, 134
Carolyn Hogan 104, 170
Susan Hogan 118
Susan Holladay 275
Gail Holmes 331
Jalena Holmes 386
Srichand Horn 261
Kristi Hosaflook 196, 378
Regina Hudson 33
Jo Ann Huggins 97
Laurie Hurt 34
Loreen Ittermann 10, 48, 108, 161, 198, 228, 248
279, 321, 350, 368, 389
Elsie James 31
Cathy Johnson 393
Jenny Jones 79
Kelly Jones 57
Julie Keenum 367
Mary Ann Keeton 132
Tammy Keliinoi 302

Shannon Kelley 90
Dawn Kent 64, 183, 260, 332
Wanda Kimbrough 208
Rebecca Kirby 231
Sharon Kirby 405
Judy Knight 252
Martha H. Knight 39
Gayle Krohe 41, 174, 347
Martha Kunberger 125
Denny Lane 190, 286
Sue Laparra 65
Charlotte Lowery 149
Tammy Loyd 23, 210
Stephanie Lunday 287
Valerie Lunsford 158
Teresa Mabe 206
Christine Maddox 91
Margaret Bond Marble 143, 271
Frances Martin 343
Provi Martin 214
Joanna McAbee 63, 142, 235
Sherry McAdams 194
Tammy McCarthy 366
Ruby McCulloch 114
Sharon McCulloch 222
Cheryl McCurley 66
Lisa McGregor 370
Debbie McKaig 159
Amanda McKay 61
Amanda McKee 155
Amanda McKeehan 192
Sandra McKeehan 47, 295, 329
Peggy McKleroy 140
DeShanna Metz 402
Sandy Micklow 129
Sylvia Miller 176
Cindy Mills 282
Rebecca Miyashita 85
Julie Moline 257

Julie Monger 315
Mindy Monroe 86
Elena Moore 80, 259
Pam Morgenthaler 227
Vanessa Nicholson 26
Mitzi Sims Oaks 27, 235, 290
Thelma A. Obid 165, 241, 387
Sissy Odell 353
Carolyn Olive 162
Cadie Palmer 113
Sarah Partin 50, 359
Lisa Pensworth 107, 169
Sherry Pentecost 348
Denise Phillips 60, 117, 252, 290, 318, 375
Sally Pieper 197, 309
Pat Porter 53, 284, 345
Tracey Prince 99
Mary Raths 256
Jan Reid 296
Katrina Reid 92
Rachel Ribeiro 135
Ginger Richey 12
Katy Ripley 7, 51, 106, 137, 216, 239, 299, 326, 351, 376
Claire Roberson 281
Elaine Rogers 377
Melissa Roe 130
Neita Roper 360
Kathy Schaaf 15, 330
Jennifer Scheer 336
Christine Schrimshire 268, 365
Alison Schug 40
Jennifer Screws 75
Beth Ann Severt 139
Marcia Sheffield 200
Peggy Sheffield 115
Jo Ann Shelton 94
Ruth Shelton 19
Alisha Sherman 228
Dara Smith 166, 306

Juanita Smith 278
Marvaline Smith 52
Sandy Smith 49, 264, 372, 393
Irene Sommerville 39
Suzanne Spiers 83, 152, 212, 250, 310, 401
Sheila St. John 25
Kathy Stark 119
Tammy Staten 362
Dianne Stewart 21, 150, 203, 300, 338, 356
Marie Strickland 328
Suzanne Taglialatela 269
Marilza Tavares 187
Shirley White Teal 131, 392
Dawn Terry 36, 352
Donna Terry 154
Marisol Adanari Tippett 138
Phyllis Todd 98, 305
Amy Tumlin 218
Katie Tumlin 116
Mary Turner 262
Joan Tyson 225
Aloha Vance 54
Peggy Vaughn 277
Rina Venter 148
Laura Vest 76
Janice Vinson 364
Anita Voss 274
Lisa Watson 153, 230, 320
Anne White 89
Lisa White 14
Patty White 232
Jane Whitt 30, 182, 273, 314, 342, 396
Melissa Whitt 62, 191
Anita Williams 55, 380
Pam Williams 77, 164, 242, 312, 395
Eve Williamson 29
Debbie Woodard 58
Karen Woodward 13
Amy Wright 160, 323